Environmentalism
and the Future
of Progressive Politics

Environmentalism
and the Future
of Progressive Politics

Robert C.
Paehlke

Yale University Press

New Haven and London

Designed by Jo Aerne, and set in Palatino type with
Gill Sans for display by Rainsford Type, Danbury,
Connecticut. Printed in the United States of
America by Murray Printing Company, Westford,
Massachusetts.

Library of Congress Cataloging-in-Publication Data
Paehlke, Robert.
Environmentalism and the future of progressive
politics / Robert C. Paehlke.
    p.   cm.
Bibliography: p.
Includes index.
ISBN 0-300-04021-0
    1. Environmental policy—United States.
2. Environmental policy—Canada.
3. Environmentalists—United States.
4. Environmentalists—Canada.   5. Progressivism
(United States politics).   6. Progressivism
(Canadian politics).   I. Title.
HC110.E5P34   1989   88-27529
363.'056'0973—dc19   CIP

The paper in this book meets the guidelines for
permanence and durability of the Committee on
Production Guidelines for Book Longevity of the
Council on Library Resources.

10 9 8 7 6 5 4 3 2

For my parents
and my children

Contents

one   Environmentalism without Apocalypse   1

part one   **The Evolution of Environmentalism**

two   Conservation, Ecology, and Pollution   13
three   The Malthusian Dilemma Updated:
Population and Resources   41
four   The Energy Crisis: Limit and Hope   76

part two   **Science, Values, and Ideology:
Environmentalism in Overview**

five   Environmental Science and Environmental
Realism   113
six   Environmentalism as a System of Values   143
seven   Environmentalism and the Ideological
Spectrum   177

part three   **An Environmental Perspective
in Contemporary Politics**

eight   Neoconservatism, Environmentalism,
and Contemporary Political Realities   217
nine   Environmentalism and the Restoration
of Progressive Politics   243

ten   Environmentalism and the Politics of the
Future   273
Notes   285
Index   321

chapter 1

Environmentalism without
Apocalypse

Things fall apart; the center cannot hold;
Mere anarchy is loosed upon the world,
The blood-dimmed tide is loosed, and everywhere
The ceremony of innocence is drowned;
The best lack all conviction, while the worst
Are full of passionate intensity.
W. B. Yeats
"The Second Coming"

Some environmentalists in the 1960s and 1970s saw the future as an inevitable hell, others as a likely paradise. The pessimists feared that the future promised nothing but a return to the world envisioned by Thomas Hobbes (1588–1679) in which society was "a war of all against all" and life was "solitary, poor, nasty, brutish and short." The near-paradise of the optimists was envisaged as decentralized, bucolic, and organic, built on a wholesome communalism based somehow on solar energy, Jeffersonian democracy, and crunchy granola. The reality of the now waning millennium is, of course, proving less straightforward than either vision suggested.

A notable characteristic of environmentalism in the 1960s and 1970s was that it was often apolitical. Some environmentalists, labeled cosmetologists by Allan Schnaiberg, equated environmental protection with litter cleanup and scenic plantings. The problem for them was wholly aesthetic, the solution offensive to no one. Another group saw environmental problems as multidimensional and serious but consciously rejected politics in favor of voluntaristic, individualistic solutions—a simpler life-style, a back-to-the-land rejection of the material glut of contemporary society. However, most who sought such autonomy discovered, as did the native peoples of the Black Hills, James Bay, and the Mackenzie Delta, that the consumer society eventually came calling, even if one had not left a forwarding address.

Many of the most apolitical environmentalists found themselves swept into a reluctant politicization when they encountered, for example, a hazardous waste dump upstream from their bucolic retreat. But the environmental politics most often and most effectively practiced in the 1970s and early 1980s was largely a politics of single-issue negativism. People had not abandoned the freeway life-style only to stand by while a nuclear waste dump or multi-lane highway was built next to their organic vegetable patch. But lacking still for many who have a sympathy for environmental protection is an overview that is at once political and yet disinclined to either easy paradise or, if you will, easy apocalypse.

I describe in this book a view of the future that is both more and less than that offered by the environmentalists of the 1970s. It is less because neither ecological doom nor the straightforward recovery of a preindustrial sense of community and comfort with economic limits seems as likely now as during the initial moments of environmental awareness. The world of the 1980s, while somewhat more restrained in its use of resources, entails a less precipitous and consistent decline than was anticipated by early commentators. The energy conservation necessary to avoid an economic tumble has proven easier than most imagined in the early 1970s. Indeed, one might argue that energy conservation may now be a threat to its own parent, the Organization of Petroleum Exporting Countries (OPEC). In the rich countries almost all of the economic costs of rising energy prices have been borne, thanks to the rise of neoconservatism, by the young, the poor, and those industrial workers trapped in declining industries. These same people have also borne most of the costs of both disinvestment and advancing automation. On balance, however, the future promises to be less dramatic and draconian than the pessimistic environmentalists had anticipated.

An environmentalism without a millennial dimension, however, may turn out to be a much more important movement than was anticipated in the early years. Environmentalism, I attempt to show, has been underestimated, even by its adherents. It provides a very useful base from which to make individual life choices, from which to take collective political action, and from which to decide a surprisingly broad range of public policy issues. Environmentalism even has the potential to become the first original ideological perspective to develop since the middle of the nineteenth century.

This book treats analytically both environmentalism as it is today and its potential as an effective set of ideas. I attempt herein to develop a political theory with ideological potential. The word *environmentalism*, as I use it, is a construct drawn from the ideas of many individuals, only a few of whom might accept the whole perspective I create. Few political actors now march under this banner; whether more will in the future is difficult to foresee. Indeed, I assume that few, if any, will follow these ideas exactly as I have developed them.

This book, then, is about environmentalism as politics. It is not about the Green Party but about "green" ideas—their evolution, meaning, and importance. Environmentalism has already played an important part in the political life of Europe and North America for several decades. In practice the movement has not usually been more than a loose coalition of interest groups. But if we look deeper than day-to-day practice, environmentalism can be understood as an evolving set of political ideas. It can be developed into an ideology able to see the developed economies through the difficult transition from an industrial to a post-industrial society, much as liberalism, conservatism, and socialism saw us through the formation of a new society during the Industrial Revolution.

Yet environmentalism as an ideology still lacks the mass following that conservatism, liberalism, and socialism in their time attracted; and it is by no means certain to attract such a following. In order to do so, environmentalists must develop clear and consistent positions on the full range of political and social issues. Environmentalism thus far has been a truncated ideology, with both intense and mass support in many countries, but only addressing a very narrow set of issues. A full development of environmental ideas—an environmentalist ideology—becomes possible only when environmentalism is seen as neither "left" nor "right." I try to show that such an assertion is more than a mere slogan. By clarifying the meaning of the notions of "left" and "right" in this context, I seek to develop a consistent and clear environmental position on a full range of important political and social issues. In doing so I direct my discussion at several audiences, bearing in mind the views both of scholars in several subfields (environmental policy, political theory and ideology, and social and political movements) and of the more general public, including environmentalists and moderate (or even not so moderate) political progressives.

If we extend the logic of environmentalism into the contemporary political setting, we find an important and distinctive point of view with regard to such issues as employment and unemployment, feminism, social welfare expenditures, government deficits, inflation, and economic development in the so-called third world. Obviously there will not be a single position on each of these issues that everyone concerned about the environment will automatically embrace. But there is a limited range of consistent possibilities and, potentially, a dominant set of themes that might well appeal to broad sections of the public as a whole. Thus environmentalism can be developed into an ideology as coherent as any of the three classical ideologies of liberalism, conservatism, and socialism. And it may be more effective than either of the contemporary Western ideologies, which I call neoconservatism and progressivism.

Before I develop further the links between environmentalism and these two contemporary ideologies, let me briefly discuss the central term *ideology*. *Ideology* is defined in the *Oxford English Dictionary* as "ideal or abstract speculation," "unpractical or visionary theorizing or speculation." The OED *Supplement* adds, "A systematic scheme of ideas, usually relating to politics or society, or to the conduct of a class or group, and regarded as just actions, especially one that is held implicitly regardless of the course of events." *Webster's Collegiate Dictionary* identifies ideology as "idle theorizing," "an extremist sociopolitical program . . . with a factitious or hypothetical basis." Finally, D. D. Raphael, in his now standard *Problems in Political Philosophy*, defines it as "a prescriptive doctrine that is not supported by rational argument."

Ideology as generally understood, then, is not something to which a decent, humane, and honest set of ideas ought to aspire. Orthodox Marxists, for example, see all ideologies as lies (conscious or not so conscious) of the ruling class, explaining all non-Marxist worldviews with reference to the class position of their holders. Pluralists and other orthodox capitalists, on the other hand, are much like Marxists in their anti-ideological ideology. To them, ideologies are appropriate only to some other age, one not so scientific and pragmatic as our own. Those in the "free West" are taken to be beyond ideology, something communists use to create "dupes," the capitalist equivalent of false consciousness. Neither side, therefore, defines ideology simply as a widely held and comprehensive point of view on political issues.

Against these views, one might suggest that no ideology is widely accepted for long unless it contains some truth. To think otherwise is to assume that all those to whom ideologies are directed are fools. However suspect the concept may seem to those with democratic proclivities, it surely has some usefulness.

In this book I use the word *ideology* in a more neutral way than it is usually used. I take an ideology as a set of political ideals, a worldview both value laden and comprehensive. Perhaps using the word *ideology* in this sense will serve as a reminder that any set of ideas, environmental ones included, can become a closed system, hostile to other or newer ideas, or even to the evidence presented by science. In fact a tendency to closure is probably inevitable, since one cannot come to a coherent political overview without shutting out, at least for a time, something of other intelligent versions of reality. But environmentalism, if it is to be worth the effort of further intellectual development, must remain more open than the ideologies that preceded it and more willing to appreciate the strengths of competing sets of ideas.

I hope this understanding of environmentalism will place front and center a consciousness of the forces of extermination built in the name of earlier ideologies. Seeking to establish environmentalism as an ideology may help to develop a "third way" able to defuse the ideological duality of the contemporary world. Plainly, any third way must reject the bureaucratic and exterminist character of both the contemporary superpowers, capitalist and socialist. It should also help to slow or halt the expansionism inherent in both capitalist and socialist systems, which tend to seek ever-larger economies well past the point where greater economic activity is either sustainable or desirable.

Environmentalism conceived as an ideology thus moves a very long way from its modest and apparently apolitical origins. Since 1980 many have come to see that, in effect if not in intent, environmentalism has been political all along. Opponents of environmentalism apparently saw its ideological potential before its advocates did, judging by the considerable political reaction provoked by the environmental efforts of the 1970s, especially in the United States. Even Lady Bird Johnson's effort to remove highway billboards was skillfully defeated in the long run. (There are probably as many billboards today in the United States as there were in 1970.) There has also developed, in state after state, province after province, a fierce and very expensive political opposition to efforts so seemingly bland as container-deposit legislation. Even litter has had strong political allies: millions upon millions of dollars were spent to defeat the California "bottle bill" in a public referendum, and as recently as the autumn of 1987 such an initiative was turned back in Washington, D.C.[1] Thus we can see that the environmental successes of the 1970s led to a clear, strong political reaction—a powerful ideological opposition to environmentalism that was scarcely visible prior to 1980. This opposition is concentrated in the neoconservatism that currently prevails in America, Britain, and Canada, an ideology that has shown itself to be consistently and vigorously anti-environmental.

The opposition to environmental protection from the political right thrusts environmentalists toward an alliance with the "progressive" forces of the moderate left. Many, though not all those who articulate environmentalism in North America and Western Europe place themselves in sympathy with the moderate political left. A neoconservative environmentalism is by no means impossible to conceive of, but the more important question is, What would an alliance of environmentalism and the moderate left look like? Neither has fared very well alone in recent years. That said, I want to make it very clear from the outset that environmentalism has dimensions that place it altogether apart from the traditional left–right ideological spectrum.

The most obvious point of similarity between environmentalism and the moderate left is their shared willingness to intervene in a market economy on behalf of values that are not economic in the usual sense—that do not promote further economic expansion. The left, however, has traditionally sought to improve the distribution of ever-expanding economic benefits. Indeed, like the right it has argued that its policies result in greater economic growth. Environmentalism questions whether expansion beyond a reasonable level is a net benefit at all, regardless of how those benefits are distributed. Finally, the economic techniques of the left may carry a greater threat to environmental goals than those of the right. Governmental economic activity historically has forced economic growth where otherwise it might not have occurred,—market forces appear at times less effective than government as sources of economic expansion, however unwilling neoconservative economists might be to acknowledge this.

Environmentalism is an ideology distinctive first in its unwillingness to maximize economic advantages for its own adherents, or for any contemporary group. Environmentalists do of course on occasion defend their own and others' property against intrusions such as highways, airports, dumpsites, or pipelines, and this can be described as self-interested. But environmentalism requires accepting limits to certain forms of economic development, and those limits apply as much to environmentalists as to anyone against whom environmentalists might be politically engaged. Environmentalists too must accept the unavoidable inconveniences of public transport, the extra effort involved in recycling, and the tax shortfalls associated with deferring the use of scarce resources. Environmentalism has minimal appeal by way of personal economic gain; it may be the least economically self-interested of all ideologies.

Because it is not an ideology of self-interest, and because self-interest is deeply ingrained in our society, economy, and polity, environmentalism does not easily attract an intensely committed mass following. It appeals most to those with a reasonable degree of economic security (as distinct from much wealth), and only rarely does it appeal to the economically insecure.

The first principle of environmentalism is that the earth-as-a-whole, for all time, must be seen as a "commons." Environmentalism grants both other species and future human generations consideration in economic and resource decisions. One might say that this perspective extends the generosity of the liberal grant of economic, political, and religious freedom. Environmentalism thus also stretches beyond Marx's lucid case against liberalism (he noted that it was meaningless to declare both the poor and the rich equally free to sleep under bridges). Just as socialism forced the progressive liberal mind to expand its embrace, so too does environmentalism seek yet a further expansion.

Liberal and socialist intellectuals were speaking on behalf of others more often than for themselves. The early socialists felt that they themselves were poor so long as the majority of their fellow citizens were poor. For them the common good required that they gain relatively less than the peasants and workers in the coming transformations they so fervently advocated. Advocates of liberalism, too, sought not gain for themselves so much as the education and political development, the political and intellectual freedom, of those less well situated than they. The same breadth of mind and spirit motivates environmentalists, who seek principally to ensure that the gains in political and economic equity thus far achieved will be extended to future generations. Therefore, although there are profound differences between environmentalism and the ideologies that preceded it, the generosity of spirit that has propelled progressivism may be carried forward in environmentalism.

Liberalism, socialism, and environmentalism also share the intellectual trap of masochistic self-denial. Socialist revolution has never been principally a project of the working class: socialism was developed on behalf of, and in the name of, the proletariat. Likewise, environmentalism advocates for generations not yet born, seeking nothing less than the perpetuation and future comfort of all species. This is empathy at its logical terrestrial bounds. But, just as the "proletarians" of most developed nations have seen that the gains of socialism are worth little if they come at the expense of those established earlier by liberalism, the future success of environmentalism depends on a reasonable level of security and comfort for the majority in society. Environmentalists must heed the wisdom of Edmund Burke and build on the past rather than seek to destroy or escape it.

Ideology itself—a complex of ideas seeking a widespread following—presumes the technical ability to communicate such ideas to large numbers of people: the notion only entered our vocabulary with the Industrial Revolution. Only in a society well beyond industrialism can we imagine that a large proportion of the population might apprehend something of the needs of the world-as-a-whole over the long-term future. And only in a truly post-industrial era can we imagine a majority with sufficient time to experience the seemingly impractical world of ideas and ideals.

It has never before been more important that vast numbers of people understand the logic of progressive ideas. Environmentalism might also be seen as a third wave of progressivism, developing in response to the atrophication of liberalism in the West and socialism in the East. The ideologies are armed to the teeth and face each other with only one obvious way out. A widespread acceptance of an environmental perspective seems even more necessary when conceived of as embracing antimilitarism. So conceived of, environmentalism, perhaps in defiance of all historical experience, is an ideology whose time has come.

This book cannot suggest with any precision how wide acceptance of the perspectives of environmentalism might ultimately lead to military disarmament. It might be best simply to invite faith in the assumption that the will to peace with nature and to peace among nations are linked together—and together might make a difference. Perhaps a future sustainable and healthy in terms of environment, ecology, and resources is one that would less likely succumb to nuclear armageddon. Finally—and here is something a bit more practical as a project—if any nation were to develop a nonoffensive, nontechnological defense, other nations might eventually follow that example. Some of the links between "exterminism" and "expansionism" are discussed more extensively here, but this is not the book's principal theme.[2] I simply do not have an answer to this most important of questions.

But international security is not unrelated to domestic economic and political stability and progress. The restoration of moderate progressivism and the achievement of political and economic stability are the consistent themes of this book. I hope that the environmentalist-progressive platform I develop can help to sustain, echoing Yeats, *a center that holds*.

part one

The Evolution of

Environmentalism

two

Conservation, Ecology,
and Pollution

The basic building blocks of an environmentalist ideology are the twin issues of conservation and pollution. Both rest on an understanding and appreciation of nature and ecology, and both require that one see human society as intertwined with the ecological web of life. Environmentalists accept that nearly every economic benefit has a measurable environmental cost and that often the sum total of such costs, in an already comfortable society, exceeds the value of the benefit. And some environmental costs are not worth bearing regardless of the benefits they might bring. Present and future human societies are bound in significant ways by the physical and biological realities of our world. We should seek not to overcome these natural limitations but to understand how best to live within them. Environmentalists see enormous possibilities for continued human development without the continually expanding use of materials and energy.

Human society must embrace more completely a perspective that has come to be called ecology. As John Wadland put it:

> From the ecologist's perspective, there is no dichotomy between man and nature. In ecological terms, each organism constitutes part of the environment of all other organisms. The complex, cyclical set of interdependencies thus established depends for its complete survival upon the continued existence of its own weakest link. There is, therefore, an immutable set of

biological laws—ordered, organized and efficient—demanding
the concurrence of all the species that live under them. . . .
 . . . Defenders of ecology are defenders of limitation. . . . ecol-
ogists maintain that man is not only in nature, but of it.[1]

Wadland and others have made very clear the philosophical distinction between an ecological perspective and those that preceded
it. I hope in this chapter to elaborate the importance of this distinction, which has evolved, sometimes more and sometimes less consciously, over a century, and to clarify how it became the foundation
for an environmentalist concern with pollution.

The Conservation Movement

Environmentalism has its historic roots in the conservation movement, which in North America began in the mid-nineteenth century.
The importance of nature, the appreciation of nature, and the need
to preserve nature and wilderness were articulated by Henry David
Thoreau, who in 1851 asserted, "in Wildness is the preservation of
the World." John James Audubon's *Birds of America* contained a less
directly philosophical expression of the same hope and concern,
inherent in such statements as his poignant "the greedy mills told
the sad tale, that in a century the noble forests . . . should exist no
more."[2] Many others expressed similar concerns through the nineteenth century and into the early part of the twentieth century.

The rapid expansion of outdoor and nature education followed
from the conservation perspective. It also led to the creation of the
two national park systems in North America and later the national
forest system in the United States and, in Canada, the effort to
conserve and protect the forest of the Crown Lands. Regulation of
the forest industry has never been a thorough success; nonetheless
the effort has been an important and underappreciated part of the
history of North America.[3]

The early conservation movement was largely anthropocentric in
character and chiefly concerned with the efficient use of natural
resources, particularly renewable resources. Most of its supporters

did not achieve what might be identified as an ecological perspective. They were concerned less with the preservation of nature and wilderness than with scientific management practices; they wished to avoid wasting resources, but above all they emphasized maximum, long-term yields. The natural world and its products were there to be used; the goal was wise management and, thereby, more effective use. The question of whether it was appropriate to view the natural world as merely a collection of resources to be used was rarely asked. Forests were there to be cut and replanted; rivers should be dammed to yield power and to prevent the waste associated with flooding. The measures taken were important, but more fundamental questions about industry itself and its products—including pollution— were rarely raised by conservationists.

Three conservationists saw past the anthropocentric notions of the "gospel of efficiency": George Perkins Marsh (1801–82), John Muir (1838–1914), and Aldo Leopold (1886–1948).[4] Their writings took conservation a step further, applying an ecological perspective to the activities of men and women. Their thought laid the groundwork for the writings of Rachel Carson and others in the 1960s and 1970s who helped develop a deep and widespread public concern with pollution along with a sense of the extent to which human beings are inextricably a part of nature. These writers showed us that our prosperity, our health, and even our lives depend on our understanding of and respect for nature and its processes.

George Perkins Marsh has been credited with creating the modern concept of ecology, the "study of the interrelationships between organisms and environment."[5] His most important work, *Man and Nature: Physical Geography as Modified by Human Action* addressed the unintended negative effects of human economic activities on the environment. *Man and Nature*, published in 1864, contained many insights that were still astonishingly relevant a hundred years later. It is almost eerie to realize that Marsh wrote before the automobile, before the significant use of oil, before the mechanized clearing of forests, and before the development of most modern methods of mining and factory production. His introduction to the book, written in 1863, claimed that "the importance of human life as a transforming power is, perhaps, more clearly demonstrable in the influence man has exerted upon superficial geography than in any other result of his material effort."[6]

By "superficial" Marsh did not imply that the changes wrought were unimportant. Indeed, he argued that no effect upon the natural surroundings could be assumed in the long term to be minor. Marsh concluded by observing that "our inability to assign definite values to these causes of the disturbance of natural arrangements is not a reason for ignoring the existence of such causes in any general view of the relations between man and nature, and we are never justified in assuming a force to be insignificant because its measure is unknown, or even because no physical effect can be traced to it as to its origin."[7]

Marsh's work attempted to establish such links—between the cutting of forests and the erosion of soil, between the draining of marshes and lakes and the decline of animal life, between the forced decline of one species and alterations in the population of others, even between human activity and climate. His exploration of these matters was truly global; his sensibility informs contemporary arguments regarding pollution and its impact on ecological systems and human health. The above quote could easily be part of an attack on governmental dawdling over acid rain or toxic chemicals—issues about which it is commonly argued that remedial action cannot be taken until all the evidence is in. Marsh's conclusion reflects the distinction now drawn between a conservationist sensibility and an ecological one: he noted that all his concerns were relevant to "the great question, whether man is of nature or above her."[8]

John Muir had little doubt about the answer to this question: nature, for him, was an entity to be revered. Muir was even more a transcendentalist than Ralph Waldo Emerson, who turned down Muir's invitation to join him "in a month's worship with Nature in the high temples of the great Sierra Crown."[9] Nature and wilderness were for Muir a spiritual experience, and he saw people, at their best, as part of that spiritual whole. Both politically and intellectually Muir went further than Marsh. He campaigned tirelessly to save wilderness from the effects of human activities, seeking to preserve it for itself and for quiet observation. Muir believed people could learn more by living in nature than by any other means. As Roderick

Nash put it, "in contrast to the original proponents of Yellowstone National Park and the Adirondack reservation, Muir made it clear that wilderness was the object to be protected. He declared the Sierra around Yosemite Valley to be 'a noble mark for the . . . lover of wilderness pure and simple.' Drawing on the idea of George Perkins Marsh, Muir emphasized the importance of safeguarding the Sierra's soil and forests as watershed cover. But . . . his primary concern was to prevent 'the destruction of the fineness of wilderness.' "[10]

Prior to the development of such massively destructive pollutants as acid rain, toxic wastes, and radioactive fallout, Muir's efforts on behalf of wilderness were all that the world might ask of one of its human offspring. Muir's campaigns were prototypical of the amateur tradition in the politics of conservation and environment that has been in force throughout the twentieth century.[11] Muir wished not merely to conserve natural resources for later economic use; he strove to preserve wilderness for its own sake, and perhaps for what humans might learn from it. Muir's perspective set him in opposition to the unfettered growth of the American economy, as the "wise use" conservationists were not. In this sense Muir was a more direct ancestor of modern environmentalism than they.

The best human economic activity, for Muir, was nearly invisible to nature. He wrote admiringly of the native peoples of North America who "walk softly and hurt the landscape hardly more than the birds or squirrels, and their brush and bark huts last hardly longer than those of woodrats."[12] In contrast stood the ravages of the gold rush, the scars of which, made in a few short years, would last for a very long time: "roads blasted in the solid rock, wild streams dammed and tamed and turned out of their channels and led along the sides of canons and valleys to work in the mines like slaves. . . . imprisoned in iron pipes to strike and wash away hills and miles of the skin of the mountain's face, riddling, stripping every gold gully and flat." Muir believed humans had no right to alter the natural surroundings in ways nature could not restore within a short period of time. The world was not made for humanity to subdue—in this the Bible was wrong. The natural world was sacred, meant to be lived in and enjoyed, but by no means did it exist merely to be "used" for human purposes.[13]

Aldo Leopold saw wilderness as that which gave "definition and meaning to the human enterprise." According to Roderick Nash, Leopold saw that "protecting wild country was a matter of scientific necessity as well as sentiment."[14] For Muir the necessity to protect did not derive solely from "sentiment," but one senses that for Leopold science and sentiment were more evenly balanced than for Muir. Leopold was indeed an ecologist; a true descendant of G. P. Marsh, he grasped the complex importance of the relationship between organisms and the whole of their environment. In his willingness to make a political effort for preservation, he followed Muir as well.

Leopold's most singular achievement was his intelligent blending of ecology and ethics. He saw the land itself an organism, a living reality. From Darwin and his own detailed scientific observations he learned the extent to which humanity was a part of nature. Humans had evolved from the land, the earth, in the same way that other species had evolved. Muir wrote, "the opinion 'that the world was made especially for the uses of man' was an 'enormous conceit.' "[15] Leopold concurred thoroughly, and he went on to develop a rich ethical basis for the preservation of nature. People, he pointed out, are the only species that can threaten nature-as-a-whole. If we do so we will, of course, destroy ourselves. (Survival and self-destruction later became a central theme in the twentieth-century environmental movement.) Most modern humans imagine that they are sustained by economy and industry. Leopold noted that these in turn are sustained, as are all living things, by the land. We are but one part of an interactive global ecosystem, and we injure the land in any way at our own peril. Only by studying reserved wilderness regions can we possibly understand scientifically the interactive system on which we ultimately depend.

Popular interest in conservation has been far from negligible. Although the golden era of achievement in both "wise use" conservation and wilderness preservation can be dated from the U.S. Civil War until World War I, in 1955 there remained at least 78 national and 256 state-based conservation organizations in the United States. Membership in the many U.S. conservation organizations totals millions; some individual organizations count their members in the hundreds of thousands. The largest Canadian organization, the Canadian Wildlife Federation, numbers over two hundred thousand members and others claim tens of thousands. Though there is a long history, conservation organizations today remain strong both in membership numbers and, particularly in the United States, in their ability to raise money. The conservation movement is both a historical antecedent and a contemporary companion of the environmental movement. Organizationally environmentalism has neither supplanted nor superseded conservationism.

The history of the Canadian and U.S. conservation movements sheds light on the differences in political methods between the two countries. The U.S. movement began earlier and both the establishment of the national parks and the protection of forests were achieved earlier there. Yellowstone Park, the first U.S. national park, predated Banff by some fourteen years as settlement of the American West preceded that of the Canadian. The American parks were established following a period of widespread public concern and pressure. The Canadian parks, by contrast, were initiated by apparently unprovoked federal government fiat and developed by skillful federal civil servants, most notably J. B. Harkin. J. I. Nicol began an article curiously entitled "The National Parks Movement in Canada," with the claim, "In the broader meaning of the term, it is doubtful if one could say that there has been a national parks movement in Canada."[16] The initiative came primarily from within the government, was of a fundamentally entrepreneurial character, and had as a not incidental cobeneficiary the Canadian Pacific Railroad.[17]

The preservation of forests (as opposed to the creation of recreational opportunities in the wilderness) also came later to Canada than to the United States. It was as much in opposition to government initiatives on Crown lands as to the rapacity of private enterprise. H. V. Nelles' view is instructive here: "The problem with the forests was not that the public drew too little revenue from their exploitation, but rather too much. Various governments, it began to appear, had sold timber to pay their bills." Nelles contrasted the U.S. and Canadian movements: "At the root of the American crusade for public ownership lay the assumption that ownership necessarily implied rational management, but the Canadian conservationists learned from experience that it was not so."[18] One must conclude here that it is a distinctively North American naiveté which accepts the premise that government regulation and/or ownership necessarily curbs the power of economic elites. Here we glimpse for the first time an important argument of this book: environmental protection does not naturally follow from either a capitalist or a socialist political economy.

Many of the founders of the U.S. conservation movement came from prosperous and leading families, and throughout its history its membership has been drawn almost exclusively from the educated middle class. This is the norm for voluntary associations other than trade unions and groups based on ethnic or racial interests. In Canada the constituency of conservation has been far more likely to come from within the professions and civil service hierarchies—those already occupationally concerned with conservation. In the United States conservationists constitute a more genuine "movement." The U.S. conservation movement fought hard in innumerable political battles and its single-issue efforts rested on a sophisticated philosophical perspective. This perspective, however, rarely took on either a partisan or an ideological character until the development of environmentalism in the 1960s and 1970s. Few, if any, of the conservation movement's most articulate spokespersons, American or Canadian, questioned the system of political authority, the structure of political institutions, or the character of the economic system.

We should recall here the distinction between the conservation goals of the progressive era and contemporary ecological goals. It is the latter set of goals for which Marsh, Muir, and Leopold first laid the groundwork. The age of conservation was concerned with efficiency, which in turn implied "a large measure of rational, human control over nature." The conservation movement accordingly sought rational and efficient use of nature's riches. Conservationists on the whole retained a high order of technological optimism. Environmentalism, which seeks ecological goals, speaks of technological limitation and claims "that man can neither control nor dictate to nature."[19] Biological rules, again to use the words of John Wadland, render powerless all human ideologies—except, perhaps, for environmentalism itself as an ideological force.

If its origins could be linked to any one event, environmentalism might be said to have begun in 1960 with the publication of Rachel Carson's profoundly important book, *Silent Spring.*[20] In the decade that followed, hundreds of antipollution organizations sprang up around a wide range of issues concerning the unintended alteration of the chemistry of air, water, land, and food. The principal concern of this new movement was not with the preservation of wilderness or distant forests. Rather, it was with the destruction of the environment within or near agricultural and industrial centers and with the biological underpinnings of human health. The new concern about pollution was immediate, basic, urban; it even crossed class boundaries. Not everyone has the time and money necessary to appreciate wilderness, nature-at-a-distance. But everyone eats, drinks, and breathes. Antipollution environmentalism thus potentially has a broad political appeal.

The new ecologically informed interest in pollution was quickly joined by concern with the related issues of overpopulation, food production and distribution, and in the early 1970s the depletion of resources, especially energy resources. All these new concerns reinforced the view that humanity must learn to live within the limits of its world, if it is to live well—indeed if the species is to survive. Some aspects of these concerns can be linked back to the conservation movement. That said, however, I wish to conclude this section by describing four important ways in which the contemporary environmental movement differs from the earlier conservation movement.

First, the environmental movement, from the mid–1960s to the present, from antipollution proponents to those who oppose nuclear power and toxic wastes, is largely political and ideological in its perspective. Unlike conservation and most other modern ideologies, environmentalism has an antitechnological dimension. Second, environmentalism is not concerned only with forest and wilderness far from population centers, as was the conservation movement. Environmentalists are oriented to the protection of wilderness principally in the sense that it is part of the viability of the global biosphere.

Third, as Allan Schnaiberg put it: "New environmental groups questioned the logic of private investment decisions and the conventional treadmill model of production expansion to generate economic growth."[21] Fourth, the environmental movement harbors a strong asceticism embedded in doubts about the North American consumer lifestyle. Asceticism was, of course, much a part of Thoreau's, Muir's, and some other early conservationists' messages. But in mid-twentieth-century North America such moral or aesthetic predilections seem in themselves to challenge directly both the ethos and the socioeconomic structures of the day.

Pollution and Politics

Pollution is an unintended by-product of (usually economic) human activities, released into the water, air, or land. To say that air, water, or land is polluted is to assert that its quality has been diminished. The extent of the damage is determined by assessing the effect of the altered water, air, and land on the web of life it once sustained. Pollution, then, is not simply a matter of using resources inefficiently; it entails damage to life or health. Pollution existed before the concept was developed and preceded public concern about its effects on the natural environment or on human health.

Detailed scientific knowledge of the interaction of living systems and the cycling of organic and inorganic materials has only recently become available. Prior to its development, many of the worst effects of pollution were unknown; others were ignored; and often visible pollution was interpreted in ways that now seem absurd. Belching smokestacks were seen as beautiful—evidence of virtuous labor and confirmation of humanity's progress. Some may still view pollution so, but never again can we deny scientific understanding of its ecological impact—however desperately political leaders unwilling to act might try to ignore the facts.

A nonscientific understanding that air and water pollution have serious undesirable consequences has been with us for some time.

This is apparent, for example, in Frederick Engels' *The Conditions of the Working Class in England* (1845), based on the reports of factory inspectors:

> The air of London is neither so pure nor so rich in oxygen as that of the countryside; two and a half million pairs of lungs and two hundred and fifty thousand coal fires concentrated in an area of three to four geographical square miles use up an immense amount of oxygen, which can only be replaced with difficulty. . . .
> . . . River water is so dirty as to be useless for cleansing purposes. . . . Not satisfied with permitting the pollution of the air in the streets, society crams as many as a dozen workers in to a single room.[22]

Engels' scientific understanding was limited by his time, but his humanity and ideology led him to see the by-products of industrial society as unhealthy pollution. In this view he was by no means alone. The novels of Disraeli (later Tory Prime Minister) and of Elizabeth Gaskell portray a similar quasi-scientific concern.[23] And the Reverend Benjamin Armstrong entered these words in his diary in 1855: "July 10th, 1855. Took the children by boat from Vauxhall Bridge to show them the great buildings. Fortunately the Queen and Royal Princes drove by. The ride on the water was refreshing except for the stench. What a pity that this noble river should be made a common sewer."[24] The Thames of which Armstrong wrote is in considerably better condition today.

In the nineteenth century both England and the United States took considerable notice of pollution and enacted limited legislative action against it. In Britain, parliamentary committees to study the problem were established in 1819 and 1843; some laws were passed between 1845 and 1875, but they were not enforced.[25] The first legal actions on air pollution in the United States were taken in 1876 in St. Louis and in 1881 in Chicago. These limited efforts called for, respectively, a minimum twenty-foot height for industrial smokestacks and a fine for the release of "dense smoke."

In the early nineteenth century the British managed sewage by transferring "the filth from the streets to the rivers and so created the modern problem of river pollution."[26] In London, accordingly, cholera broke out in 1866 and 1872—undaunted by the Royal Commissions on Rivers Pollution established in 1865 and 1868. Finally, in response to public concern the Disraeli government passed the Public Health Act of 1875 and, in 1876, the Rivers Pollution Prevention Act.

Consciousness of pollution has existed throughout history. The ancient Romans, for example, were aware of air pollution. In 1273 coal burning was prohibited in London. The first tract against air pollution was probably that of one John Evelyn, who submitted his *Fumifugium: or, The Inconvenience of the AER, AND SMOAKE OF LONDON* to Charles II in 1661.[27] Evelyn proposed planting "sweet-smelling" trees to remedy London's pollution problems. Little came of his proposal, however, which would not have been an effective remedy in any case. Evelyn also campaigned against the deforestation of England in a work entitled *Silva*.

Concern about water pollution from human sewage is found in the Bible (Deut. 23:12–13). In addition, Louis Klein discovered that "long before even the days of Moses, Zoroastrianism, the religion of the ancient Persians, laid great stress on purity and . . . definitely forbade the discharge of organic refuse or indeed any filth into the rivers."[28]

Another body of knowledge, developed even earlier than interest in air and water pollution, was that concerning workers' health. The ancient Romans knew, for example, that slaves who worked with asbestos were adversely affected. In Ellenburg and Agricola in the fifteenth and sixteenth centuries respectively some associations were noted between certain occupations and illnesses. The Italian physician Bernardino Ramazzini published in 1713 a pioneering compendium of a wide variety of occupationally induced illnesses. In 1775 the British physician Percivall Pott made an epic discovery when he linked scrotal cancer to the exposure of young chimney sweeps to coal tar. But it was still too early for this knowledge to be extended to the possible health effects of environmental pollution.

Indeed, the knowledge that the health and lives of workers were endangered has often had precious little effect on industrial practices. Only rarely has such knowledge led to preventive medical efforts or changes in the workplace. Indeed, as Joseph K. Wagoner wrote in 1975, the two-hundredth anniversary of Percivall Pott's discovery: "Today is indeed an occasion for sober reflection. For on this bicentennial, thousands of coke-oven workers in the steel industry of the United States alone are inhaling the very same class of substances that caused scrotal cancer in the chimney sweeps, and, as a result, are dying of lung cancer at a rate ten times that of other steel workers."[29]

For another example of this sort, consider that in 1907 a British government report publicized the effects of asbestos on health. In 1918 asbestos workers in North America were denied life insurance—but it was not until 1975 that serious steps were taken to protect the health of asbestos workers in Ontario. This sluggishness was all the more inexcusable in light of the fact that Canada has been the world's largest producer of asbestos, and major epidemiological studies of Canadian asbestos workers were completed as early as 1935.

It is all too common that the early findings of toxicologists and epidemiologists fail to provoke timely efforts to protect workers' health. Likewise, their data rarely finds its way into the public eye, and it is rarer still that their findings are considered in light of the effects of the substances they study upon the air, water, and population outside the factory.

This point cannot be made too strongly. It is central to understanding the links—or absence of links—between science and public policy today. There are hundreds of cases, not confined to any one political system, in which scientific and medical knowledge has failed to reach either the general public or the political process.[30] Exposure to radon daughters, common among uranium miners, was known to be hazardous in the nineteenth century; yet the danger had to be rediscovered with the rapid growth of the uranium industry in the 1940s and 1950s. The association between inorganic arsenic and cancer was made before 1850, but in the 1920s and 1930s arsenic-based insecticides were the chemical of choice in North American agriculture, and as late as 1975 more than 1.5 million workers in the United States were inhaling the substance on the job.[31] The costs of these failures to translate scientific knowledge into public policy were driven home to the public only in the 1960s and 1970s, well after the rapid expansion of chemical use in industry and agriculture that took place in the 1940s and 1950s.

Government action against pesticide pollutants since the popularization of their dangers by Carson's *Silent Spring* stands in sharp contrast to its previous ostrich-like behavior with regard to such highly hazardous compounds as arsenic, the principal component of pesticides from the 1890s until the advent of dichloro-diphenyl-trichloro-ethane (DDT) in the 1940s. As early as the 1890s, in New York and elsewhere, public concern was developing regarding the use of arsenic-based insecticide sprays on grapes and other crops. This isolated public interest did not, however, lead to political action. As James Whorton noted, "The necessities of insect control seemed to demand arsenicals; there was little legal machinery available to keep oversprayed produce off the market."[32] Just after the turn of the century the use of arsenicals expanded considerably. The limited concern with this growth that arose in North America focused on the health of the fruit trees or on the unlikely possibility of acute poisoning from eating recently sprayed strawberries—there was no wide understanding of the potential dangers of bioaccumulation or of the effects on human health of cumulative exposures to hazardous substances. In the early 1920s in Europe, especially in England, public attention to the matter again focused on the alleged danger of acute poisoning. The only result was that Canadian and Australian apple growers attempted to move into the market opened by concern in England with U.S. growers' use of pesticides.[33]

Only in the late 1920s was public attention in North America drawn to the dangers of arsenical pesticides. Much of the research on lead arsenate had by then been completed and communicated to the public by Dr. Karl Vogel. James Whorton explained, "Although few wallpapers still contained arsenic, Vogel did find the poison generally present in smelter exhaust gases, in the local smoke which befouled American cities, in fruits and other foods bleached with contaminated sulfur. . . . The American food supply, he pointed out, was largely poisoned by lead arsenate and other arsenical insecticides."[34]

In the 1930s widespread scientific and medical concern with the impact of both lead and arsenic were finally coming to the public consciousness. Two 1930s bestsellers, Kallett and Schlink's *One Hundred Million Guinea Pigs* and Lamb's *American Chamber of Horrors*, castigated the use of lead arsenate sprays.[35] Spray residue regulations for arsenical insecticides were established in 1932, but leaded gasoline was not regulated until the 1970s—and, of course, it remains available today. And in the United States, once the public stir had declined, the standards of protection were reduced between 1938 and 1940. The reduced standards became easier and easier to meet as DDT replaced lead arsenate as the leading pesticide.

World War II slowed the development of public consciousness regarding pollution as the wartime sense of emergency forced aside other concerns. The war also boosted the chemical industry, which has rarely paused in its expansion from that day to this. But, on a more positive note, concern with protection of workers' health in North America advanced considerably in the interwar period. Dr. Alice Hamilton, North America's leading pioneer in the field of occupational health, described in her autobiography the horrors of the World War I munitions and chemical plants: "engineering problems . . . were being solved, not in advance of the actual production, but while it was going on. If anything went wrong it was not a laboratory accident, it involved the workmen on the job, men who knew little or nothing about what they were working with or how to protect themselves."[36] By the second war, though the dangers had increased, a medical community with some knowledge of the nature of occupational health hazards had developed—largely through the efforts of Hamilton herself.[37] "Industrial medicine had at last become respectable . . . where earlier there was a great dearth of experts now there are hundreds of physicians who know what to do and are doing it," she wrote.[38]

Perhaps Hamilton herself was swept up in the war effort as she wrote. The war multiplied the chemical problems that workers and, later, the wider environment had to endure, and the war and post-war years were characterized by rapid expansion, especially of the chemical and automobile industries, and of oil, the industry on which both were based. The urgency born of the Cold War spurred the development of the uranium mines and mills of Canada with total disregard of occupational health and environmental protection. This development was shrouded in the secrecy associated with nuclear weapons production.[39] Thus from the beginning of the Second World War until well into the 1950s public awareness of pollution and related issues was very limited.

With the publication of Rachel Carson's *Silent Spring*, however, concern with pollution returned and broadened. *Silent Spring*, published in *The New Yorker* in 1960 and in book form in 1962, was written to inform the public about the unrestricted proliferation of chemical pesticides in the environment.[40] The considerable popularity of this book followed closely on the heels of public concern that had resulted in the first U.S. federal air pollution legislation in 1955 and the Delaney Clause in 1958, which excluded carcinogenic additives from foods. *Silent Spring* dispelled once and for all the lack of environmental awareness associated with the war effort, the consumer boom, and the Cold War hysteria that had for twenty years submerged all else in their wake.

Silent Spring made two critical additions to the developing public concern with chemical pollution. First, Carson brought together the findings of toxicology and ecology and opened the way for a deeper public appreciation of epidemiology. These three sciences together describe the modern understanding of pollution's effects on ecosystems and on human health. Carson's second contribution was her articulation of these vital sciences in language accessible to the educated public. Her style, a blend of scientific, political, and moral arguments, built upon the work of Aldo Leopold and became the hallmark of popular environmentalism. It put into motion a process that may yet lead to wide public understanding of the necessity of linking scientific knowledge and political action. Carson's intent was described by Frank Graham: "Science must be the foundation for her work . . . but it must be given another dimension by the sympathy and compassion without which the finest scientists in the world are dehumanized. She knew that her book must *persuade* as well as inform; it must synthesize scientific fact with the most profound sort of propaganda."[41] *Silent Spring* documented in impeccable detail the scientific evidence against the unrestricted use of DDT, methoxyclor, dieldrin, and other pesticides, introducing many of its readers to the term *the web of life*. Finally concern with pesticides no longer focused only on direct human ingestion—now the public had an ecological understanding of the impact of this form of pollution. Considerable controversy and a series of public decisions—including bans on such pesticides as DDT—followed directly from Carson's work.

In December, 1952, four thousand people died in the killer smog that besieged London. This tragedy, following the acute air pollution incident in Donora, Pennsylvania, in 1948, marked pollution's return to public consciousness. The Donora incident saw six thousand people (40 percent of the population) taken ill in a three-day period, but fatalities were fewer than in London. A decade later, Rachel Carson galvanized public interest in pollution by popularizing an understanding informed by toxicology, ecology, and epidemiology—the three sciences of pollution.

Although ecology was influential in the development of the conservation movement, an ecological awareness was missing from the public consciousness during the nineteenth century and through the 1940s. But the concept of ecology can be traced to the ancient Greeks, especially Hippocrates and Aristotle. Antonie van Leeuwenhoek, an eighteenth-century Dutch scientist, pioneered the study of food chains. The word *ecology* was in use in 1869; its first use has been credited to the German biologist Ernst Haeckel. The earliest North American pioneer of the field was perhaps G. P. Marsh, and a significant early contribution was made by Ellen Swallow who, in 1871, was the first woman to enter the Massachusetts Institute of Technology. By the beginning of the twentieth century, ecology was recognized as a subfield of biology, but the science of ecology rarely came before the wider public; conservationists' arguments more often appealed to economic opportunities or aesthetics. Only with Aldo Leopold, and then in the 1960s, did the word *ecology* and the perspective and concepts associated with it reach the public eye. Late in that decade, in fact, environmental groups in North America were using billboards to put the term before the public. They realized that only a widespread ecological perspective would bring people to the understanding that pollution ultimately reaches us all: something "out there" *can* make its way into our own guts.

Only with an integrated understanding of the three vital sciences of pollution can one see its full dangers. That integration can, of course, take place at a basic level: it helps even to know only that some substances are extremely hazardous to the health of both animals and humans. With that knowledge one can begin to understand why it is so important that more and more fish in the Great Lakes are developing cancers as a result of environmental exposure to chemicals known to be hazardous to human health. In spite of what ecology tells us, however, chemicals are still released to the environment. Their advocates argue that they are harmless because releases are ordinarily small and the chemicals are rapidly diluted in the air and water to minute levels. Some few chemicals, such as dioxin, are recognized to be dangerous even at barely detectable levels—but in general industry continues to argue that low-level exposure to carcinogens is either safe or a tolerable "price of progress." This argument collapses, however, in the face of four key natural processes that exist within living ecosystems.[42]

The first process is bioaccumulation, the buildup of toxic substances in food chains. In *Silent Spring* Carson explained bioaccumulation by recounting the story of Clear Lake, California. In an anti-mosquito campaign, the lake was treated in 1949, 1954, and 1957 with dichloro-diphenyl-dichloro-ethene (DDD), an organochlorine insecticide, at .02 parts per million (ppm). After a time DDD residue in the water was undetectable. In the plankton, however, the DDD concentration mounted to 5 ppm. The insecticide DDD is fat-soluble (as are polychlorinated biphenyls, or PCBs, and many other carcinogens) and accumulates in the fatty tissues of fish. In small plankton-eating fish, therefore, concentrations reached 40–300 ppm, and larger (fish-eating) fish accumulated 2,500 ppm. At the top of the food chain at Clear Lake were the grebes, water birds that accumulated an average of 1,600 ppm of DDD and at that level died out in the Clear Lake region.

It is not necessary to look far to find other examples. Cows graze up to fifty square meters of field in a day and many of the contaminants thereby gathered collect in their milk. Mollusks, which filter enormous quantities of water, can concentrate heavy metals by a factor of 300,000 times their concentration in the water, organochlorine insecticides by 70,000 times. The class of chemicals known as PCBs is highly susceptible to such bioamplification. Concentrated 10- to 100-fold at each step in the food chain, by the time PCBs reach carnivorous sea mammals, they may be concentrated 10-million-fold over levels in the surrounding water. Human diets that concentrate heavily on the lower end of food chains are clearly prudent given this reality.

The second process, natural resistance, is related to the first. Quickly multiplying lower-order species eventually shrug off concentrations of toxins to which higher-order, slower-breeding, longer-lived species, such as humans, cannot adapt. At Clear Lake, for example, the plankton and fish remained healthy while the grebes disappeared. More important when considering insecticides is the fact that, although one can eliminate 99 percent of a given insect population with an insecticide, those remaining and their millions of descendants are sometimes resistant to the toxin which killed their siblings. The mosquitoes of the Mississippi Delta thrive in the face of doses of poisons 120 times stronger than those that used to kill them. The human beings who constantly increase the dosage of deliberately spread toxins are among the more vulnerable species at the top of the food chain.

The third process is natural dispersion. High concentrations of DDT have been found in penguins and polar bears living great distances from direct sources of the substance. Toxins are dispersed in the environment in a wide variety of ways: they travel in the wind and are washed out in the rain; those buried on land are leached out by water. All ultimately travel the watercourses and ocean currents. Many species carrying toxins migrate thousands of kilometers before being eaten by a member of another species. A persistent carcinogen thus will soon find its way to the ends of the earth. Once in the environment such substances cannot be retrieved, a fact overlooked by those who believe there is nothing to worry about because we can always clean up a polluted environment. With regard to persistent chemicals, we can only stop polluting, wait and hope and, at least for a time, live with what was done.

The fourth process is the biochemical interaction of toxic substances. These chemical reactions occur without human permission, plan, or even awareness. Metallic mercury, for example, has been converted to harmful methyl (organic) mercury in the mud of Canadian rivers and Japanese bays. Synergistic and catalytic chemical and biological effects also occur within the human body. Asbestos and cigarette smoke are more than additively carcinogenic, for example. Some chemicals are carcinogenic primarily in combination with other chemicals: the pesticide kepone and alcohol are suspected of acting in this manner. We have hardly begun to investigate such interactive effects, either in the workplace or in the wider environment. We may well never understand them fully.

Together these four processes distinguish persistent carcinogens and other toxins from other forms of pollution and require that these substances be treated differently, legislatively and administratively. Persistent chemicals are dangerous even if highly diluted in air or water. As at Love Canal, they can create extreme health hazards even decades after being buried carefully in the ground. Locally released chemicals can spread throughout the globe, interacting with other substances in unknown ways. In the end the burden of evidence regarding persistent substances must be reversed. Any hint of danger must certify guilt; with hazardous chemicals, for all the above reasons, it is innocence that must be proven.

Given these conclusions it is not surprising that the study of the health impacts of chemicals is often seen as a branch of science even more dismal than economics, sometimes compared to paranoia and often presumed to appeal only to the morose. On the contrary one might argue that only epidemiology can hope to surpass the achievements of modern medicine—through it we can learn to prevent disease, not just cure it. Epidemiology and toxicology, the disciplines underlying the study of both occupational and environmental health, can suggest societal and behavioral changes that might reduce disease without medical intervention. What could be more profoundly hopeful?

Epidemiology measures the distribution and describes the determinants of disease in human populations. In the 1920s one of the field's most illustrious figures, Jacques May, adapted the ecological model of disease to the study of certain illnesses in humans. Thus ecology and an understanding of the health impacts of science and technology have common roots. May studied the relation of schistosomiasis, a parasitical infection, with Chinese wet-rice agriculture, and he found that the disease was transmitted by waterborne parasites and was common among those who worked in the rice paddies. Obviously wet-rice cultivation is not a technology likely to be abandoned. The point is that we must look closely at the negative aspects of technological benefits in order to learn how to ameliorate or avoid their costs. May's findings also remind us that humans are inevitably no less than the other animals a part of the global ecosystem. Only when we see ourselves in this way will we begin effectively and efficiently to maintain our collective and individual health.

Occupational and environmental health problems, especially in the developed world, have in recent years been associated in the public mind with artificial chemicals, or chemicals like asbestos introduced into the airborne and waterborne environment by human technological activities. It is undeniable that we have introduced thousands upon thousands of new artificial chemicals into our work and living environments and that some of these chemicals pose serious hazards to human health. However, one should take care not to envision a division between an "evil" world of artificial chemicals and a pristine and innocent nature. The natural world is not benevolent; many artificial chemicals have indeed been created to help protect us from it or to allow us to survive better within it. Even DDT produced considerable benefits as well as unanticipated negative ecological impacts.

Bruce Ames has catalogued an array of carcinogens to which we are exposed in a normal, even "natural" diet. Carcinogenic foods include celery, pepper, mustard, and some peanuts. Of course, legions of healthy human bodies have survived the effects of these chemicals through the centuries. We do not know why some bodies withstand these carcinogens and others do not. Similarly, we do not understand why some bodies are affected by artificial carcinogens and some not. Science warns us of potential dangers in each case, and only science can aid us in finding the mechanisms of response. We must make our own assessments of what is prudent, in both our personal lives and our policy decisions.

Environmentalists have sought to generate public demand for policies that are suggested by scientific findings. This can be achieved only by educating the public about science. If scientific knowledge is predominantly controlled by those who will profit through inaction, inaction will be the likely result. If bureaucracy limits public access to scientific information, inaction will again be the result. As Wagoner put it so succinctly, "The scientific community must, in my opinion, not only investigate but inform, not only advise but dissent when appropriate, and, most importantly, provide firm, prudent leadership in the formulation of public health policies."[43]

Wagoner was referring to society's failure to prevent vast numbers of occupationally and environmentally induced cancers that could have been avoided. But his assertion can be applied to other issues as well—indeed, to virtually all those we have come to call environmental. Scientific findings that point to a need for political decisions must be communicated widely outside the specialized scientific world. Such findings must be publicized as soon as possible, in everyday language, along with their policy implications. Many scientists have followed this course in the tradition of Rachel Carson. One of the most successful has been Barry Commoner. Although not all scientists see his policy advice as prudent, environmentalism would scarcely exist were it not for scientists like Commoner. Like Leopold and Carson, he has integrated science with ethics and has communicated his conclusions to the widest possible public.

Barry Commoner has been active since the early 1960s in bringing the concerns of biologists together with the world of politics and economics. Such attempts to communicate environmental science to the general public lie at the very heart of environmentalism. Commoner's first book, *Science and Survival* (1963), in its tenth printing by 1971, described modern science as a sorcerer's apprentice. "We hear of masterful schemes for using nuclear explosions to extract pure water from the moon; but in some American cities the water that flows from the tap is undrinkable and the householder must buy drinking water in bottles," Commoner noted. He also discussed the greenhouse effect, pointing out that "between 1860 and 1960 the combustion of fuels added nearly 14 per cent to the carbon-dioxide content of the air, which had remained constant for many centuries."[44] (Since 1960, carbon dioxide in the air has increased by another 15 percent.) Regarding the lead added to automobile fuel Commoner wrote, "Since tetraethyl lead was introduced in 1923 as an automobile fuel additive, lead has contaminated most of the earth's surface. Increasing amounts of the metal are found in surface ocean waters, in crops, and in human blood, in which in some areas the amount may be approaching toxic levels."[45]

The sluggish progress from scientific finding to public awareness to political action is apparent in Canada, which only in 1987 moved to legislate significant reductions in the lead content of leaded gas-oline. Leaded gas still held 55 percent of the Canadian market in 1985; because it is still less expensive, many consumers still add it to the newer automobiles that require unleaded gas. But Common-er's book had some more immediate effects. He sparked the public discussion of detergent pollution and broadened concern regarding radioactive fallout and DDT. In some cases significant legislative action was undertaken as a direct result of his book.

Commoner's most important contribution has been his ability, while writing in a lucid popular style, to bring together a wide range of issues into an integrated whole. Throughout his works he has stressed the importance of publicizing all potential dangers to human health. He has discussed the importance of freedom of choice in research, decrying the shift of funds from the U.S. National Science Foundation to the National Aeronautics and Space Administration (NASA), a mission-oriented agency. Finally, and this will be sur-prising to some, he discussed the currently popular topic of nuclear winter as early as 1963.

Science and Survival concluded:

If science is to perform its duty to society, which is to guide, by objective knowledge, human interactions with the rest of na-ture, its integrity must be defended. Scientists must find ways to remove the restraints of secrecy, to insist on open discussion of the possible consequences of large-scale experiments *before* they are undertaken, to resist the hasty and unconditional support of conclusions that conform to the demands of current political or economic policy. . . .

. . . The obligation which our technological society forces upon all of us, scientist and citizen alike, is to discover how humanity can survive the new power which science has given it. . . . Solutions to our pollution problems will drastically affect the economic structure of the automobile industry, the power industry, and agriculture and will require basic changes in urban organization.[46]

Statements like these were crucial to the development of the North American environmental movement of the late 1960s to mid–1970s. Commoner argued that broad changes—social, economic, and political—flow from economic and technological activities. Economic activities affect the ecological systems of whole nations, indeed the entire globe—not just through the use of distant forest resources, but through urban pollution as well. At stake was not merely the "wise use" of resources or the setting aside of ecological reserves. The new environmentalism claimed that problems lie at the very heart of the modern political economy, even in our basic philosophical and cultural outlook. Everything fits together—the physical, chemical, biological, social, political, economic, and philosophical worlds—and must be understood as a whole. The symptoms of environmental problems may be measured biologically, but the disease itself lies in our socioeconomic organizations, and the solutions are ultimately political.

And political these issues have proven to be in the years since Commoner first wrote. In an important article entitled "Workplace Burden," Commoner made clear the great environmental costs of decades of ignoring the health of industrial workers.[47] Chemical PCBs, for example, were known before 1930 to be hazardous to workers' health, and in the early 1940s they were associated with serious human diseases. But not until the late 1960s, following widespread production and distribution of PCBs, did scientists point out the problems they caused for many fish and bird species and how widely they had been dispersed. Only when PCBs had been irretrievably launched into the wider environment was notice of them taken by more than a few scientists, citizens, or decision-makers. Effective government and industry action did not come until the mid–1970s. In 1985 PCBs remained in newspaper headlines, helping, for example, to end more than forty consecutive years of Conservative government in Ontario.[48] Barry Commoner's concern with the chemicals was again more than a decade ahead of its time.

There are many reasons for the slow pace at which scientific information regarding the effects of toxic substances is translated into political action. Scientists' reluctance to communicate with the public is an important cause, but not in itself decisive. Six other reasons are worth mentioning here.

1. Our society has tended to prefer wealth to health. Many corporations do everything in their power to avoid regulation of their production and use of toxic and carcinogenic substances. Even after *Silent Spring* ministries of agriculture have continued openly to encourage the extensive use of chemical biocides, claiming them necessary and on balance safe. Medical agencies and the medical profession have been reluctant at times to add to their efforts at curing cancer a greater emphasis on prevention. Workers and unions have hesitated to push occupational and community health concerns to the forefront of their bargaining demands, preferring to emphasize wages and benefits.

2. Environmentalists have not taken occupational health issues to be a central concern. They have been slow to realize that today's occupational health problems are tomorrow's environmental problems. Preventive, as opposed to reactive, environmental protection requires us to orient our environmental concern toward the workplace.

3. The considerable delay—usually from fifteen to thirty years—between exposure to a carcinogen and onset of visible health effects makes pinning down the causes of disease extraordinarily difficult. It took decades to establish conclusively, for example, the extent to which asbestos is hazardous.

4. Only very recently have we been able to measure the presence of some carcinogens that have toxic effects even in minute amounts. Although fewer cases of cancer occur when dilution is greater, many carcinogens can affect human health at very low levels. This knowl-

edge has led some scientists to dismiss the myth that there are safe thresholds for toxic substances in the workplace and in the environment.[49]

5. Cancer strikes on a statistical basis that allows us to distance ourselves from the possibility of its affecting our own lives. Some individuals, for reasons we do not understand, smoke heavily and live and work in the most hazardous of environments and remain unaffected. All we know is that it is statistically safer to avoid exposure to certain substances. Many people imagine they are immune or if they are young, remain unconcerned about what might happen later.

6. The final reason has to do with prejudice. Those who work in hazardous occupations often have few economic options and little political power. Their needs are often forgotten by research scientists, medical professionals, middle-class environmentalists, and political and economic decision-makers. Since the work of Ramazzini, Hamilton, Doll, Hammond, Hueper, Maltoni, Saffioti, Selikoff, Wagoner, and so many others, however, we have begun to see that the health of those in the "hazardous trades" has been undervalued to the peril of all. Since Irving Selikoff's 1964 study of asbestos insulation workers in the World War II shipbuilding industry there has been precious little reason for underestimating the danger of industrial workers' exposure to carcinogens.[50]

Less advantaged members of industrial societies have been at disproportionate risk in other ways as well. Industrial workers and the poor are more often subject to air pollution than members of higher-income communities.[51] The political importance of this fact is not widely enough appreciated. Pollution reduction would benefit these less advantaged groups, both on the job and in their communities, more than it would help higher-income people—yet these groups have often been convinced that they will bear the costs of environmentalist's demands, while the benefits go to others.[52] This misunderstanding can be alleviated through alliances between environmental groups and trade unions, which have traditionally defended the interests of industrial workers and their communities.[53]

Wider public understanding of the dangers of occupational exposure to pollutants followed from the work of Selikoff and others in the 1960s, and this understanding was quickly conveyed to environmentalists. Commoner's "Workplace Burden" was an important part of that communication, as were the efforts of Franklin Wallick and many others at the United Auto Workers Union (UAW) and the Oil, Chemical, and Atomic Workers Union (OCAW). (Wallick, the author of an early popular work on occupational health, *The American Worker: An Endangered Species*, also wrote for environmental publications.)[54] A campaign was developed to educate workers about occupational health problems. Such information had previously been available only within the medical and scientific communities; both the victims and the public had remained largely innocent of the dangers. In the 1960s and 1970s, however, understanding of the problems became sufficiently widespread outside the medical community that workers, communities, and environmental groups began to form common cause.[55] One of the most important of the educational works was the 1973 *Work Is Dangerous to Your Health* by Jeanne Stellman and Susan Daum.[56] In some ways reminiscent of Hamilton and Hardy's *Industrial Toxicology*, published some forty years earlier, this book, by contrast, aimed directly at the victims and the lay public, not medical practitioners. Its publication represented a very important step in the amelioration of the class bias that has exacerbated the problem of workplace pollution since its beginnings.

Love Canal further linked in the public mind the once seemingly separate worlds of pollution and occupational health. The pollution danger there was clearly part of the life of a working-class community, not an abstract problem of "nature" or "wilderness." And the chemicals involved were the very ones that had posed problems for industrial workers.[57] The Love Canal issue followed a political pattern reminiscent of the occupational health controversies of the 1960s and early 1970s. Local public concern led to industry's and government's official denial of danger; citizens, environmentalists, and journalists then combined to force public attention on the issue.[58] This incident brought to public awareness a whole new world of environmental health dangers posed by hazardous waste disposal, whose past due bill for North Americans runs well into the tens of billions of dollars.[59]

Two books together marked the development of new relationships among a wide range of environmental issues and groups. *The Politics of Cancer* by Samuel Epstein and *Hazardous Waste in America* by Epstein, Lester O. Brown, and Carl Pope, both published by the Sierra Club, are perhaps the best popular books available on their subjects.[60] This organization, which counts John Muir among its founders, has come a long way from its nineteenth-century conservationist origins. The Sierra Club now places strong emphasis on the concerns of the urban working class. *The Politics of Cancer* tied together occupational health hazards such as asbestos, vinyl chloride monomer, and benzene with the consumer issues of the safety of such substances as estrogen, saccharin, and tobacco, as well as with environmental dangers such as pesticides. Branching out in this way apparently has not altered the organization's effectiveness on conservation issues. Much of the credit for the Sierra Club's evolution must go to Michael McCloskey, who has led the group to take many initiatives in areas of concern to a broad segment of American society.[61] Without forgetting its origins, the movement as a whole has traveled from a perspective rooted in wilderness, mountains, and forests to a point far nearer to the immediate concerns of urban North Americans.

three

The Malthusian Dilemma Updated:
Population and Resources

The transition from conservationism to environmentalism began with a renewed emphasis on the pollution of air, water, and land. In the late 1960s and early 1970s another concern was added: that of resource depletion. Its roots lay in the conservation movement. The focus of this movement, especially that of the wise-use conservationists, was on sustaining and developing the inputs into the production process, rather than on the unintended outputs of that process. Both conservationists and environmentalists saw that resource depletion and pollution are two sides of the same coin, but the latter movement broadened the former's emphasis on forest, water, and soil resources to include the whole resource base of industrial society. In this broad focus environmentalism went well beyond the single-issue, single-cause outlook of Thomas Robert Malthus (1766–1834), the principal forebear of those concerned with resource scarcity.

Malthus, a deeply conservative man in a vigorously, sometimes hysterically progressive age, produced his *Essay on the Principle of Population* (1798) largely as a rebuttal to the liberal ideology of the Marquis de Condorcet, William Godwin, and his own father, Daniel Malthus. The younger Malthus rejected the utopianism so dominant in his day that Condorcet could write the buoyantly optimistic *Sketch for a Historical Picture of the Progress of the Human Mind* while in hiding from the Terror of the French Revolution. Malthus, however, concluded that humankind would never achieve perfect justice and perfect equality for the simple reason that population growth inevitably tended to exceed growth in humanity's ability to produce food.

Modern-day followers of Malthus sometimes add to "food" the wider range of resources essential to an industrial economy. An important work of contemporary environmentalism, the 1972 publication *The Limits to Growth*, did just that.[1] *Limits* was essentially a computerized Malthusian perspective applied to an industrial rather than an agrarian society. Even more indebted to Malthus was Paul Ehrlich's sensational *Population Bomb*, published in 1968.[2]

Malthus' *Essay* was a speculative inquiry into the political and ethical implications of the inevitable tendency toward overpopulation and resource scarcity. The dream of progress and perfectibility that launched, and was in turn propelled by, the scientific and industrial revolution Malthus saw as a grave illusion. To others, Malthus seemed a stern and dour man, but he viewed himself as a realist in an age of foolish dreamers—whose dream was the essence of the industrial world soon to be born. Political philosophers of the time argued that humans were innately good, corruption and failure were products of social institutions, and both human beings and their societies were perfectible. Progress was virtually inevitable—all that was needed was economic and political freedom, education, democracy, and the economic advances that would naturally follow from them. But a few thinkers—including Hobbes, Burke, and especially Malthus—saw humans not as naturally perfectible but as inherently greedy and violent (Hobbes) or at least lazy (Malthus).

Malthus concluded from his assumption regarding population and resources (for which he offered "mathematical proof") that England must abolish the Poor Laws that minimally sustained those with no means through parish communities. "Man," he wrote, is "inert, sluggish, and averse from labour, unless compelled by necessity."[3] In Malthus' view, there must be no means of survival save hard work and moral restraint—otherwise more and more people would become unable to sustain themselves and society would collapse under the burden. Shortage, for Malthus, was inevitable and permanent. Even allowing that "the produce of the earth" might "be absolutely unlimited, scarcely removes the weight of a hair from the argument, which depends entirely on the differentially increasing ratios of population and food." The Poor Laws removed misery, one of the three natural "checks to population."[4] The other two checks were moral restraint, which Malthus felt was virtually absent among the poor, and vice, which must be avoided because it was sin. Only the third, misery for the poor, could prevent greater future misery for all. Without maximum effort in food production, without the check of misery to restrain population growth, food prices would rise inexorably and more and more people would become dependent upon those who remained productive.

Malthus' dismal view contrasted startlingly with the liberals' praise of the glories to be found on the path of progress. His perspective was rejected, even reviled, by thinkers from Godwin to Coleridge to Marx and Mill. The 150 years that have followed Malthus' *Essay* have, of course, suggested again and again that his argument was both unsound and unduly negative. But on reflection from the end of the twentieth century, Condorcet's spectacular optimism seems hardly to have been a more durable view. The essential distinction to be drawn between these two views is that the Malthusian has been linked historically with conservative political conclusions, while progress in the political and moral sphere has been associated with industrialization and economic growth. These links, I will argue, are not inevitable.

W. Stanley Jevons, who first published *The Coal Question* in 1865, during Britain's industrial age, was a follower of Malthus. For Jevons, however, the fundamental resource shortage was not food and the root of the problem was not population per se. Instead, the problem was that all industry required energy and there was, in his view, no viable substitute for coal-fired steam. Wind energy was too irregular and insufficient; energy from the sun was impossible to harness. "And while the sun annually showers down upon us about a thousand times as much heat-power as is contained in all the coal we raise annually," Jevons wrote, "yet that thousandth part, being under perfect control, is a sufficient basis of all our economy and progress."[5] Petroleum, in essence "distilled coal," was in limited supply.[6] It offered some possibilities, as did water power, but both were taken to be limited, the latter because of the need to dredge and the inconvenience of winter freezing. "We cannot revert to timber fuel," Jevons argued, "for 'nearly the entire surface of our island would be required to grow the timber sufficient for the consumption of the iron manufacture alone.' "[7] Coal, by contrast, had "all those characteristics which entitle it to be considered the best natural source of motive power." But, alas, coal would not last forever. "If our coal were gone, or nearly so, and of high price, we might find wind, water, or tidal mills, a profitable substitute for coal. But this would only be on the principle that half a loaf is better than no bread."[8]

Jevons was not optimistic about the resource-limited future. Studying the average rate of increase in coal consumption from 1854 to 1864, he concluded with great care that the rate of growth seemed to be 3.5 percent and that "the consumption of the last ten years is half as great as that of the previous seventy-two years!" His calculations of coal demand and supply in Britain led him to assert, "we cannot long maintain our present rate of increase of consumption . . . we can never advance to the higher amounts of consumption supposed. . . . the check on our progress must become perceptible within a century. . . . the cost of fuel must rise, perhaps within a lifetime, to a rate injurious to our commercial and manufacturing supremacy; and the conclusion is inevitable, that our present happy progressive condition is a thing of limited duration."[9]

Thus Jevons, as few of his contemporaries, imagined a day when industrial civilization might be forced to return to less efficient sources of energy and saw that progress was not necessarily a straight-line advance toward the perfection of the human race in the luxury to which those in 1865 England were becoming accustomed. But Jevons did not imagine that anything positive could emerge from the limitations he foresaw. The tone of his book was set by an epigraph from Adam Smith: "The progressive state is in reality the cheerful and the hearty state to all the different orders of the society; the stationary is dull; the declining melancholy." He sounded like a British-nationalist Condorcet when he wrote, "Our empire and race already comprise one-fifth [corrected in the 1906 edition to one-fourth] of the world's population . . . and by our guardianship of the seas . . . by the example of our just laws and firm constitution . . . we stimulate the progress of mankind in a degree not to be measured."

Britain, through the greatness of its industry, arts, and politics, was moving the human race ever forward. Near, perhaps, one day to perfection? No. In his final lines, Jevons exchanged the mask of Condorcet for the mask of Malthus: "But the maintenance of such a position is physically impossible," he wrote. "We have to make the momentous choice between brief but true greatness and longer continued mediocrity."[10] And, one assumes, an eternal future of a humble existence for all.

As on Malthus, we look back on Jevons with both admiration and amusement. In this age of staggering wealth, the overstatements of each certainly hamper the argument that the human future is now limited by resource depletion. But the view that human population is ultimately bounded by our ability to produce food is now common, and the view that industrialization is ultimately limited by diminishing energy resources was equally hard to doubt through the 1970s and early 1980s. One might argue, however, that both Malthus and Jevons were not only unduly pessimistic about technological possibilities but also too convinced that political, social, and economic progress are determined solely by a quantitative measure of output, whether agricultural or industrial. Simple and affordable means of birth control leave population a not necessarily insoluble social problem. Economic output can advance in quality even if energy supplies remain constant or slowly decline. Social, cultural, and political progress (even in the absence of perpetual leadership from Britain) may well continue once a reasonable minimum level of economic output has been attained. Malthus and Jevons, just as Condorcet and Marx, accepted a single-minded and economically driven concept of progress that today seems too simplistic.

Soon after Malthus wrote considerable agricultural advances were made and Europeans began to find their way in large numbers to the New World. Soon after Jevons wrote the Age of Oil began. Pessimistic predictions about overpopulation and decline in energy resources were either ridiculed or ignored until the boom era that followed World War II—and up until the late 1960s and early 1970s, those who wrote about resource depletion were often viewed as no more than neo-Malthusian eccentrics. Those who discussed such matters during the postwar boom of the 1940s and 1950s can now be seen as precursors of a coming change in public consciousness. The most important early figures in what might be called the ascetic dimension of environmentalism were Harrison Brown, Fairfield Osborn, and Samuel Ordway, Jr. Their works fall within a neo-Malthusian tradition whose view is that overpopulation, in combination with modern industrial techniques, will ultimately deplete resources and outstrip agricultural production. The neo-Malthusian's concern was broader than that of the earlier conservationist's, who worried most about the depletion of wilderness, forests, and to a lesser extent soil quality. Neo-Malthusians were concerned with the supply of all natural resources.

Fairfield Osborn, writing in 1953, argued, "Quite apart from food supply, there is the other question as to the adequacy of the earth's store of minerals, chemicals, and petroleum, as well as other energy producers, to meet the expanding demands of our industrial civilization." But Osborn's principal fear was for adequate food, given rapidly rising populations in every part of the world. In *The Limits of the Earth*, he concluded, "the goal of humanitarianism is not the quantity but the quality of living."[11] *Our Plundered Planet* (1948) concluded in a similar vein: "Man must recognize the necessity of cooperating with nature. He must temper his demands and use and conserve the natural living resources of this earth in a manner that alone can provide for the continuation of civilization. The final answer is to be found only through comprehension of the enduring processes of nature. The time for defiance is at an end."[12]

Perhaps the most interesting of the early neo-Malthusian works was Samuel Ordway's *Resources and the American Dream*. Ordway's book is neither complex nor technical—it is a gently polemical rejection of the American Dream conceived as an "ever-higher level of living." Ordway articulated a "theory of the limit of growth" for the consideration of "all the scientists and industrialists who have yet to come to grips with the problem."[13] Industrial society each year uses more resource capital than is created. "If this cycle continues long enough, basic resources will come into such short supply that rising costs will make their use in additional production unprofitable, industrial expansion will cease, and we shall have reached the limit of growth. If this limit is reached *unexpectedly*, irreparable injury will have been done to the social order."[14]

This assertion was reminiscent of Jevons in its suggestion that things seem to be going well now, but a day will come that will see the end of it. It was reminiscent of Malthus in that it linked economic prosperity and the stability of the social order. But Ordway's view of the process was more complex than either Malthus' or Jevons'. For Ordway, no particular resource was in and of itself the limiting one. And if decline in resource availability were planned for, he argued, it might not prove harmful in any important way. Ordway seems to have felt that humanity would be better off were we not so materially oriented—a good life and a balanced civilization would do with less by way of industrial output, as much by choice as by necessity.

"Our natural resources on which prosperity depends may be so managed as to remain available for continuing use," Ordway hoped. "Our needs can be supplied if our wants are bridled, and our cupidities curbed. The false ideology which worships unlimited expansion must go. Man must cease to depend for happiness on wealth-consuming gadgets." Ordway argued that we can do without machines and products that "are designed to create, and then to occupy, increased leisure time."[15] The automobile was at the head of his list of such goods—even though Ordway did not have access to detailed calculations of the hours devoted to traveling to and from work in this allegedly time-saving form of transportation and the proportion of working hours devoted to producing, fueling, servicing, repairing, supplying, and parking it.[16] Ordway was also clearly uncomfortable with "radio and television sets blaring imprecations to buy more machine products, 90-page newspapers, pulp magazines and Mickey Spillane's by the millions."[17] One wonders what his reaction would be to the more fully evolved media and advertising industry of the 1980s. Ordway conveyed a yearning for peace and civility, balance and restraint, but he explicitly rejected the concept of a "return to the farm." He also rejected "Malthus' theory of inevitable misery." Goals should be revised, consumption altered voluntarily, land use planned, and distribution of raw materials rationed cooperatively by industry and government. In the end such changes would entail "a better life, though a different kind of life, in the continuing realization of liberty and the pursuit of happiness."[18] For Ordway an ever more materially oriented society was impossible in the long run. But he also felt that materialism had already gone too far—for many or most North Americans, more by way of material goods was as likely to destroy the quality of life as to enhance it.

Ordway's predictions of absolute limits on growth, like those of Malthus before him, have been proven wrong on many specifics. Consider the words of Bernard James who, on his reading of Ordway, drew an absolutist conclusion: "If Samuel Ordway is correct in noting that high grade copper resources will be largely gone in fifty years, and lead, zinc, and tin before 1980, one need be no pessimist to predict with confidence that our present 'quality of life' will decline abruptly and that the shock will send a shudder through the planet."[19] Metal resources are actually one of the less vulnerable supports of a growth-oriented industrial society. Copper in particular is being replaced by silicon, a massively abundant element the efficiency of which is orders of magnitude higher than that of copper. (Furthermore, the slag heaps of old copper mines may soon be mined bacteriologically for whatever copper is needed at the more modest levels of demand which are anticipated at present.) But what is important about Ordway's and James's perspective is not their specific predictions of scarcity but their vision that we can "escape" from Malthusian inevitability if we cease to embrace the concept of inevitable, eternal, material and economic progress. The recognition that there are limits to material growth is, for Ordway, less important than the point that the North America of the 1950s had already reached consumption levels where more was no longer necessarily better. Ordway was one of the first to reject both Malthusian pessimism and the view that only economic growth can lead to progress.

More detailed in its account of resource availability is Harrison Brown's *The Challenge of Man's Future*. Brown's chapter on energy supply (published in 1954) is particularly interesting. In 1950 he noted that per capita energy consumption in the United States was equivalent to one ton of coal per person per year, and he predicted that by 1975 total energy consumption in the United States would double. Regarding the long term Brown accepted the perspective of M. King Hubbert, whose 1949 *Science* article was perhaps the earliest to anticipate the end of oil. Hubbert saw the fossil fuel era as a very brief event within the span of human history (see chapter 4). Graphically placing the few centuries of fossil fuel use into a ten-thousand-year picture, he made the rise and the fall of fossil fuels appear startlingly abrupt. In 1954, Brown concluded that there were two alternatives to fossil fuels: nuclear and solar energy. He expressed no preference but concluded that either technology could sustain a population of some seven billion persons.

In contrast to Ordway, whose path out of Malthusian inevitability involved ethical and aesthetic choices, Brown retained some technological optimism. He anticipated a day when liquid fuels would be produced from wood or other forms of vegetation, such as sugarcane. Like most others in the 1950s, he was highly optimistic about nuclear energy. With considerable foresight Brown anticipated a new phase of the industrial revolution: "the replacement of a very large proportion of the human operators of the machines by mechanisms which possess faster reaction times, can make operative selections more rapidly, and can make the necessary process adjustments more efficiently."[20] Despite his faith in technology, however, Brown concluded that industrial society was fundamentally unstable. Humanity would ultimately revert to an agrarian existence or proceed to a totalitarian one unless we could abolish war, learn to utilize new energy resources, and achieve population stability. "The greater the population density of an industrial society becomes," he wrote, "the more elaborate will be its organizational structure and the more regimented will be its people."[21] Brown argued eloquently for population stabilization, for a balance between societal organization and political decentralization, and for the preservation of wilderness areas and the protection of soil quality. "Although our high-grade resources are disappearing we can live comfortably on low-grade resources," he believed. We can feed all humanity adequately and we can stabilize population, but "with the consumption of each additional barrel of oil and ton of coal, with the addition of each new mouth to be fed, and with the loss of each additional inch of topsoil, the situation becomes more inflexible and difficult to resolve."[22]

Together Osborn, Ordway, and Brown expressed a foresight uncommon in their time. Many of the most sophisticated arguments of the 1970s environmental movement can be found in their writings. But their view was not taken to heart in the postwar era, during which energy use in North America doubled several times, nearly every form of material consumption accelerated, and globally the rate of population growth continued to increase.

With the publication of *The Limits of Growth* in 1972 neo-Malthusianism spoke with a technocratic voice. This book reported in popular style on a computer simulation of the planetary economic and resource future. Although the details of the simulation, and even its technical soundness, have been roundly refuted, *Limits*' perspective touched a nerve.[23] The multiauthor book argued that humanity will in the not-so-distant future face a series of integrated crises—whether in sequence, alternatively, or simultaneously was not certain—of overpopulation, pollution, nonrenewable resource depletion, capital stock maintenance, and/or food shortage. "By making simple extrapolations of the demand growth curves," its authors explained, "we have attempted to estimate, roughly, how much longer growth of these factors might continue at its present rate of increase. Our conclusion from these extrapolations is one that many perceptive people have already realized—that the short doubling times of many of man's activities, combined with the immense quantities being doubled, will bring us close to the limits to growth of those activities surprisingly soon."[24] In brief, the earth is nearing its maximum carrying capacity for our species, particularly at the level of prosperity to which a modest majority is becoming accustomed. The exponential growth of the short list of essential variables—population, resource use, and so on—must "soon" come to an end.

Unlike Malthus and Jevons, *Limits* saw multiple factors constraining the growth of both population and production. *Limits* was far more flexible than Malthus in its view of the projected future, but it offered little of Ordway's perspective that, in rich societies, stopping economic growth might be both possible and desirable for its own sake.

Four simultaneous technological policies are introduced in the world model to avoid the growth-and-collapse behavior of previous runs. Resources are fully exploited, and 75 percent of those used are recycled. Pollution generation is reduced to one-fourth of its 1970 value. Land yields are doubled, and effective methods of birth control are made available to the world population. The result is a temporary achievement of a constant population with a world average income per capita that reaches nearly the present US level (1972). Finally, though, industrial growth is halted, and the death rate rises as resources are depleted, pollution accumulates, and food production declines.[25]

In the end "technical solutions" are not enough: only social and political change can help us avoid near total collapse. The changes called for are unfortunately vague considering the gravity of the authors' view of the future. They urge reduced family size and "new choices" in goods, services, and food. But they do not make clear what, if any, specific changes will suffice to avert the projected collapse. The authors only reiterate, "the application of technology to apparent problems of resource depletion or pollution or food shortage has no impact on the *essential* problem, which is exponential growth in a finite and complex system. . . . even the most optimistic estimates of the benefits of technology . . . did not in any case postpone the collapse beyond the year 2100."[26] Only population stability and the end of economic growth, apparently, allow any hope of postponing disaster.

Many of *Limits'* specific predictions were taken apart by the numerous critics who rapidly came forward following its publication. Particularly doubtful were the authors' estimates of absolute quantities of nonrenewable metal and mineral resources: they assumed that known reserves constituted all ultimately available supplies. Of course, the size of metals reserves varies directly with price: seawater or even ordinary sewage can be a source of gold if the price of the metal is high enough. Additional reserves are often not sought until available supplies are quite low. Furthermore, substitutions often occur with new technologies. Silicon, for example, was substituted for copper in fiber-optics-based communications, a change not foreseen when *Limits* was written. In this way a resource at its limits can almost overnight become a substance of little or no value. Advances in processing technologies can also open up vast new sources of materials—for example, our ability to extract nickel from the laterite ores of the tropics has vastly expanded reserves of the metal. And we have yet to tap such exotic sources of metal as seabed nodules, which contain magnesium, manganese, and nickel, among other materials. Some even anticipate that the asteroids will be a source of metal.

As David Brooks pointed out, a large proportion of the earth is metal; iron and aluminum are particularly abundant, and there is little prospect of depleting the supply of these ores in the imaginable future. "Except for a few substances," Brooks explained, "notably crude oil and natural gas, which are discretely different from the rock masses that contain them, the quantities of mineral materials in even the upper few miles of the earth's crust approach the infinite. A single cubic mile of average crustal rock contains a billion tons of aluminum, over 500 million tons of iron, 1 million tons of zinc, 600,000 tons of copper."[27] Nitrogen, a nonmetallic resource of great importance now derived largely from fossil fuels, is one of the most abundant elements on the planet. The transfer of nitrogen-fixing capabilities from one plant species to another is another possibility not foreseen by the authors of *Limits*.

But criticisms of *Limits* went wide of their mark in the longer view—something the authors themselves had stressed. Their attempts to predict the life expectancy of mineral resources were simply wrong, but their argument that soon one or more of the five variables they identified must stop growing exponentially is far harder to refute. Despite their use of computers, the authors made no explicit claim for predictive precision. Rather, the book expresses the idea that ultimately there are multiple limits to material growth. It is crucial at least to guess at, if not to determine, those limits well before they are reached. "A population growing in a limited environment can approach the ultimate carrying capacity of that environment in several possible ways," they wrote. "It can adjust smoothly to an equilibrium below the environmental limit by means of a gradual decrease in growth rate. . . . It can overshoot the limit and then die back again in either a smooth or an oscillatory way. . . . Or it can overshoot the limit and in the process decrease the ultimate carrying capacity."[28] In more technical language this is the same concern that Ordway had expressed two decades previously. The accelerating expansion of the Sahara, the danger of permanently poisoning the Great Lakes, the impact of acid rain on Western European and North American forests, the continued overcutting of forests everywhere, and the depletion of global fish stocks are recent examples of the third result: excessive expansion that has led to reduction in carrying capacity.[29] These reductions may be temporary, or they may be irreversible.

Upon its publication *Limits* struck a chord in the public consciousness that Brown, Osborn, and Ordway were unable to reach. By the 1970s the runaway character of global population growth was difficult to deny, and pollution was rapidly gathering the attention of the media and the public. *Limits* brought these issues together in a chilling way. Whether or not its factual details were accurate, it helped bring the public to an awareness that industrial society was both undesirable in the excess it had attained and unsustainable in anything like its present form. *Limits*, despite all its errors, presented a believable case that was taken in several directions by economists, philosophers, sociologists, and political scientists.

Events that followed immediately upon the publication of *Limits* brought its claims home with great force. Curiously, the most important of these also led to a partial solution for many aspects of the multiple dilemma *Limits* had portrayed—a solution *Limits* had not anticipated. The first OPEC oil-price increase, and the ensuing crisis mentality surrounding all energy sources, suggested that energy, not minerals or food, might well prove to be the limiting resource. That is, the availability of energy may determine, for example, the limit of our ability to locate, extract, and process minerals. Because of limits on our energy supply, we may never even begin to approach the limits of the earth's other nonrenewable resources.[30] Energy extraction and use also contributes hugely to pollution.

One solution to a range of environmental problems would be to raise energy prices sharply, thereby reducing demand. Doing so, however, would bring out in high relief the inequities of the modern world. Many would continue to drive large automobiles without much notice, while others would fall victim to the price of heating a home or producing their food. As energy prices rose in the 1970s, most other prices rose as well. That these would be the results of the price increase was not as clear in 1970, when *Limits* was being written, as it is now.

Two important features of the neo-Malthusian outlook of *Limits to Growth* have not received widespread attention. First, the restraints discussed there were restraints on physical materials: energy, food, minerals, and so forth. This is not the same as an ultimate limit on economic growth, something the authors of *Limits* did not discuss. Certain forms of economic output are limited quantitatively—there will be less steel from iron ore, perhaps—but economic activities that use little energy and few materials are free to expand indefinitely, and in some industries a decline in quantitative output can be made up in price increases.

Second, *Limits* proceeded more in terms of maximums than in terms of optimums, it used "musts" instead of "shoulds." Tales of global doom at the time attracted much attention, but they are not necessarily a sound means of inducing long-term social change. Statistics do not automatically suggest policy changes. Limits are hard to demonstrate without specifics, but specifics generally prove to be wrong. And if the case is believable but no solutions are offered, it invites pessimistic surrender. If the situation is hopeless, why not enjoy the moment? Why not burn the last few gallons of oil in a barbecue of endangered species? Why not drink the last grain supplies, rather than eating them?

David Brooks and Alma Norman offered an elegant answer to this problem.[31] They denied with great clarity that shortages of non-fuel mineral resources are likely to cause "drastic reduction in human welfare" in the imaginable future. The near-term future of humankind is not, in their view, limited by resource supplies. Substitutions are almost always possible and prices will significantly affect demand. We can continue rapidly increasing our consumption of almost everything except perhaps energy for a century or more. But our lives would clearly be of lower quality. Brooks and Norman updated Ordway's point and developed it effectively. Air and water pollution levels, they noted, are determined largely by total output, caused by the decision to force extra output from the land or from the economy. Wilderness is destroyed worldwide with every increment of growth. The world is increasingly organized and ever more crowded. With further growth social and sociopsychological breakdowns might well become even more common. In the end, our society is not forced by physical limits to change. We must choose, but the choice is not automatic, forced by hopeless situations brought on by greed or error. The Malthusian perspective is neither necessary nor helpful in engendering positive change. An environmental perspective and policies must seek to create a *preferable* world. Real political and moral choices are involved, and neither disaster nor paradise is certain.

The public imagination was stimulated, however, by perspectives less objectively reasoned and hopeful than those of Brooks and Norman. Of these more catastrophically oriented viewpoints, none stands out more clearly than that of Paul Ehrlich, detailed in his bestselling book, *The Population Bomb*. Ehrlich's book, the most widely read of numerous similar tracts published between 1965 and 1975, is crucial to an appreciation of the intellectual history of environmentalism.[32] In it Ehrlich argued that the root cause of most environmental damage was excessive growth in human population. He made his case without any sense of the perspective offered by Brooks and Norman, one that saw environmental decisions as choices involving the quality of life. Erhlich, even more than the authors of *Limits*, was inclined to doomsaying. He was not content to argue for a better future, an optimum future. Either humanity changes its ways, or mass starvation is the price we will pay. Neither technical breakthroughs nor social adjustments, other than an end to population increase, were, in his view, of any great use. Indeed, he felt, in 1968, that it might already be too late to avoid this fate on a scale well beyond the human suffering of the past.

Ehrlich was at his raging pessimistic best in *The Population Bomb* and was absolutely explicit about the cause of the virtually inevitable coming tragedy: "Suppose we do not prevent massive famines," he wrote. "Suppose a billion people perish. At least if we have called enough attention to the problem, we may be able to keep the whole mess from recycling. We must make it impossible for people to blame the calamity on too little food or technological failures or 'acts of God.' They must at least face the essential cause of the problem— overpopulation."[33] The governmental action he proposed was equally dramatic. For the United States, Ehrlich advocated "luxury taxes" on "layettes, cribs, diapers, diaper services, expensive toys" as well as other economic disincentives to reproduction. "Once the United States has adopted sane policies at home," Ehrlich anticipated, "we will be in a position to take the lead in finding a solution to the problem on a world scale."[34] He openly advocated triage— food aid not to the poorest nations but only to those with both an aggressive population control policy and clear hope of obtaining food self-sufficiency. Population control in developing countries must involve action far more drastic than that proposed for the United States: "When he [Chandrasekhar] suggested sterilizing all Indian males with three or more children, we [the United States] should have applied pressure on the Indian government to go ahead with the plan. We should have volunteered logistical support. . . . sent doctors to aid in the program by setting up centers for training paramedical personnel to do vasectomies. Coercion? Perhaps, but coercion in a good cause."[35] Ehrlich also insisted that his proposed U.S. Department of Population and Environment have "the power to take whatever steps are necessary to . . . establish a reasonable population size in the United States."[36] But he did not explicitly propose compulsory sterilization for Americans.

However drastic were the proposals of Paul Ehrlich, those of Garrett Hardin were even worse. Hardin seriously proposed issuing licenses for reproduction, to be sold on the open market. Many of the poor might thus be unable to reproduce, while the wealthy could have as many children as they wished. The total number of licenses—and therefore children—would be controlled to assure population stability. Incredibly, Hardin paid little attention to the question of what would happen in the case of unlicensed pregnancies or children. Hardin has also been a supporter of triage—letting the poorest of nations simply perish. As in a war emergency, he would help only the moderately wounded, not the starving. Hardin called his plan "lifeboat ethics," viewing it as appropriate to a situation wherein all will perish if some are not evicted. Hardin is a Malthusian born again with the "hope" that through brutality the human population can be stabilized. Hardin's position arises from the fear that overpopulation threatens not just hunger for most, but unlivable conditions for all.

To understand Hardin one must examine two of his central concepts: carrying capacity and the tragedy of the commons. Carrying capacity is the maximum population that a given quantity of land of a given character can sustain. If that population is exceeded, not only will some of the population perish, but the carrying capacity of the land will decline, in some cases precipitously and/or irrevocably. This view brings Hardin to the position, similar to that of Malthus, that the only possible kindness lies in cruelty. The carrying capacity of the world either has already been exceeded or is very near to being so. Hardin calls this a "tragedy of the commons," after a parable he revived from a pamphlet written in 1833.[37] As the parable has it, the commons is a shared land on which each herder has the right to graze as many animals as he or she wishes. But the limited carrying capacity of the commons is ultimately exceeded as each individual herder adds additional animals without considering the long-term results. If individual, short-term decisions dominate, the commons will be destroyed, since the individual gain from an additional animal always seems greater than the loss that is shared by all. Hardin sees the only solution as "mutual coercion, mutually agreed upon by the majority of the people affected." "Freedom in a commons," he concludes, "brings ruin to all."[38]

But, as Peter Stillman noted, it is hard to imagine herders characterized by short-term rationality continuing to protect the commons once imminent disaster is averted. Nor is it likely that such a society would choose a strong central government to act ecologically in the long-term general interest:

Those who argue for a strong central government assume that the ruler will be a wise and ecologically aware altruist; they conveniently overlook that their authoritarian ruler, if he is (like everyone else in the society) "a rational, self-interested individual," will not act to solve ecological problems. . . . he will perceive (or quickly learn) that ecologically-sound policies . . . go against the rational self-interest of each individual; and thus for the ruler to impose ecological solutions would be for him to act contrary to his own rational self-interest by increasing popular discontent, undermining consent, and reducing popular obligation.[39]

Both Malthus and Hardin assume erroneously that people will not come to understand the need for population constraint, that coercion is more effective than any other means, and that rulers will be consistently more ecologically minded than the citizenry. Both Hardin and Ehrlich assume that the United States keeps the developing world alive and can act as a ruler-nation, somehow reaching into every bedroom on the planet. These authors move from an appropriate concern with population growth to insensitive attitudes that provoke more outrage than action.

Many environmentalists objected strongly to Ehrlich's and Hardin's claims regarding population levels and their consequences. Barry Commoner debated at length with Ehrlich the causes of pollution and ecological damage. Is it population, standard of living, or something else to blame? In *The Closing Circle*, written as a refutation of Ehrlich's view, Commoner argued that it was, overwhelmingly, something else: faulty technological choices, technologies chosen to maximize profits rather than to minimize environmental impacts:

The basic reasons for environmental degradation in the United States and all other industrialized countries since World War II are drastic changes in the technology of agricultural and industrial production and transportation: we now wash our clothes in detergents instead of soap; we drink beer out of throwaway bottles instead of returnable ones; we use man-made nitrogen fertilizer to grow food, instead of manure or crop rotation; we wear clothes made of synthetic fibers instead of cotton or wool; we drive heavy cars with high-powered, high-compression engines instead of lighter, low-powered low-compression pre-war types; we travel in airplanes and private cars and ship our freight by truck instead of the railroads for both.[40]

Commoner claimed that "most pollution problems made their appearance, or became very much worse, in the years following World War II."[41] His list of such pollutants included phosphates, nitrogen oxides, tetraethyl lead, mercury, and synthetic pesticides. He itemized the increases of these particular substances in the environment and compared those increases with the expansion of population and affluence in the same period (1946–1970). Commoner found that pollution levels had risen 200–2,000 percent, while U.S. economic production had expanded by 126 percent. Some of the expansion could be accounted for by greater affluence per capita and population increase. The larger increases in pollution, Commoner argued, were caused by changes in production technology. As in *Science and Survival*, Commoner proceeded from the biological to the economic and political: "The lesson of the environmental crisis is . . . clear. If we are to survive, ecological considerations must guide economic and political ones." His proposed solution was collective and political rather than individual or biological: "the needed productive reforms," he wrote, "can be carried out without seriously reducing the present level of *useful* goods available to the individual; and, at the same time, by controlling pollution the quality of life can be improved significantly." Commoner went on to reject the extreme populationist notions of Garrett Hardin and characterized Hardin's view as, essentially, barbarism.[42] In short, Commoner is anti-Malthusian—in his view population growth will contain itself in due time and he seems to imply as well that standard of living need not be lowered.

The debate between Commoner and Ehrlich was central to the intellectual history of environmentalism.[43] In response to Commoner's book, Ehrlich reiterated his view that population growth was the principal source of environmental pressure. Later he also laid stress on a second factor: the affluence, or the life-style, of the rich within the richest nations. Commoner stood by the position he had taken in *Closing Circle*: neither population nor affluence is the principal cause of environmental damage; rather, the surface cause is faulty technological decision-making and the root problem is the capitalist economic system.

Ehrlich's rebuttal was effective. He pointed out that Commoner's list of technologies and his measures of damage were selective and that they exaggerated the rate of increase in environmental damage. Ehrlich also argued that at the higher levels of output required by larger populations and greater standards of living, many earlier technologies might well have proved as damaging as have the new ("faulty") technologies. Since the new technologies were selected to increase output and reduce production cost per unit, the damage may be as much a function of the quantity of output as of the technological choices made. For example, switching from new synthetic fibers back to cotton and wool, at 1970 production levels, might result in the overgrazing of marginal range lands and lead to soil depletion, heavy use of agricultural chemicals, or both. In this case one must concur with Ehrlich, though in others (disposable containers, leaded gasoline) Commoner's point regarding techological choices seems correct.

One unspoken difference between the two environmentalists was Ehrlich's orientation toward the so-called third world and Commoner's orientation toward the developed economies. The developing nations, Ehrlich and Hardin would have it, are locked in an updated Malthusian dilemma of numbers and land. The carrying capacity of the land is being diminished by overgrazing on marginal lands, salinization of the soil through excessive irrigation, destruction of complex forest ecosystems to make more land available for grazing, or attempts to grow crops on lands unsuited for the purpose. Commoner did not respond in detail to these arguments, preferring to focus primarily, though not exclusively, on the industrialized world, where population appears to be approaching stabilization and the chief ecological and resource problem, in 1970 at least, was pollution.

We can conclude, then, that both Commoner and Ehrlich made valid points. All three causes of environmental damage—technology, affluence, and overpopulation—contribute to the problem; no single cause is dominant. It would be unduly optimistic to suggest that stabilization or correction of only one of the factors might be sufficient. A more reasonable solution, given the scale of the problem, must employ balance, restraint, and change. Global stabilization of population is necessary as soon as possible, but eliminating the most hazardous technologies and regulating or ameliorating others is needed as well. And surely there must be some way to restrain excess consumption. In the end there probably is not a single principal cause of ecological damage. Any such single-issue view is properly labeled Malthusian in its single-mindedness, even if it does not match Malthus' hopelessness.

The Commoner–Ehrlich debate casts light on the ideological nature of environmentalism. If the principal sources of environmental damage were found to rest with economic choices easy to blame on a particular economic or political elite, environmentalism would fall clearly on the political left. But if the principal sources of damage can be reduced to individual choices such as family size or consumer habits then environmentalism moves closer to the political right, especially if the problem is seen to originate with the habits of the poor or those in poor nations. This view of environmental problems leads to solutions that will cost the poor and perhaps the middle classes at least some life choices, if not actual income. Ehrlich, in a later book, *The End of Affluence*, implied that real economic costs, perhaps even survival costs, were inevitable for large numbers of North Americans in the near-term future. The solutions, in all his works, rest more with individuals than with governments. Ehrlich distrusts collective action, as we can see in the concluding paragraph to *The End of Affluence*:

> The time has come to face up to the basic imbalances in our society and, through personal and (to whatever degree possible) political action, begin to loosen the tightest bonds of interdependence. When and if the real crunch comes, you will get precious little help from Washington or your state capital. If you are fortunate enough to live with good friends or relatives as neighbors, you may find assistance and cooperation there.

And presumably your family will do what it can to help. But the one person you can depend on with complete assurance is yourself.[44]

By the publication of this work Ehrlich had seen the United States and many developed nations achieve replacement-rate birth levels wholly on a noncoercive basis; he was correspondingly more restrained with regard to the sociopolitical implications of population growth. His focus in *The End of Affluence* was on individual readers, adapting to the "new era of limited resources." Government was useless: "Failure to achieve a comprehensive national minerals policy has been one of the most elementary—and stupid—errors made by the U.S. in the past few decades, perhaps exceeded only by our failure to establish population, food and energy policies."[45] In the end, argued Ehrlich, Americans must assume that politicians will miss the boat.[46] The appendix, in keeping with Ehrlich's inclination to individual solutions and to hysteria, contains detailed instructions on "food storage for self-sufficiency." By contrast, Commoner, although he might give insufficient attention to population problems, has always managed to sound calm and reasonable.

This portrait of contemporary Malthusians' tendency to panic emerges more clearly from a fuller reading of the extensive body of work produced by Garrett Hardin. Hardin envisioned three phases of population control: a voluntary phase, an educational phase, and a coercive phase. The goal of the voluntary phase, "no unwanted children," is admirable indeed. Hardin felt it could be achieved by integrating an array of birth control methods with the availability of abortion on request. "Abortion on the request of the woman can be justified as a necessity for the emancipation of women," he wrote. "A century ago we got rid of compulsory servitude; now we must get rid of compulsory pregnancy, and for much the same reasons." But, Hardin concluded, "birth control is not population control—it is only if the number of children wanted is compatible with population stability—that is two or fewer per woman."[47] It is this message that is the essence of the educational phase. Hardin was convinced in 1970 that this second phase was necessary, that globally a system which only avoided unwanted children would not be sufficient. In India, he noted, couples seek to produce two male children—if practiced universally this would double the world's population in twenty-eight years; India had indeed achieved such a birth rate.

Few environmentalists dispute the need for either of these phases, so long as they are carried out with sensitivity and decency by local authorities. And Hardin is at his very best when he discusses the need for population education in the United States. He opposes conveying to young girls the idea that motherhood is mandatory. Women must be able to lead "psychologically rich and respected" lives without having children: "A significant part of our success in population control will come as a 'fallout' from making it possible for more women to become scientists, artists, machinists, businesswomen . . . even . . . professionals in (community) child care. We not only have too many children, we have too many poorly taken care of. We need to pay women to fulfill this role, so important to the nation, instead of expecting them to be unpaid slaves. Paradoxical as it may seem, if we pay them well for taking care of children, they will probably breed less."[48]

Extending women's rights and opportunities is essential to environmentalism, an important part of its logic as a comprehensive political ideology. But Hardin goes off the mark when he proceeds to what he calls the "coercive phase" of population control. His conviction that such a phase is necessary is not argued effectively in terms of carrying capacity—in fact, it is plainly specious: "Some think this phase will never be needed. . . . I think not, for the purely Darwinian reason that *voluntary population control selects for its own failure*. Noncooperators outbreed cooperators."[49]

Hardin, a geneticist by training, seems here to have grossly overestimated the powers of heredity. What better lesson in limiting family size, one might counter, than growing up in a large family of often ignored children? If the inclination toward large families is utterly hereditary, how do we explain the sharp reductions in average family size in the developed nations over the last century or so? This trend continues today; in many countries reproduction is *below* replacement rates—even in some countries (such as Eastern Europe) where the state intervenes actively to *promote* reproduction.[50] The evidence suggests that where some economic development has taken place, reproductive coercion is unnecessary. Furthermore, in countries developed or otherwise, coercion is not effective.[51] Permits for childbearing, compulsory sterilization, and Hardin's own scheme to control the sex of unborn children and legally limit the number of females are destined to provoke nothing but outrage and generate resistance to what otherwise might be freely chosen—modest family size resulting in population growth at or below replacement levels.

Hardin was, however, at his persuasive best in extrapolating present rates of population growth to scenarios of terrifying and absurd futures. What would happen, he asked, if population were to continue growing at the 1960–70 average rate? In 615 years, Hardin calculated, human beings would occupy every inch of land area on the earth if everyone were standing. If anyone were to lie down, someone would have to swim. In an additional 62 years, assuming things continued as before, the seas would be full of humans as well. Thereafter, as Hardin put it, "let us not be niggardly in our imagination. We don't all have to stand up on the same plane. We can build buildings. . . . We can burrow into the earth. How far can we go? Who knows? In the limit, we could convert all the materials of the earth into human flesh."[52] This would be achieved, he calculates, in the year 3527 A.D.—far less time than from the Golden Age of Greece to the present.

Elsewhere, to make his case complete, Hardin demolished the use of emigration to outer space as a solution to population problems. Launching one day's population increment at present levels would cost, he calculated, on the order of $369 billion. This was near to the total gross national product of the United States at the time of writing, and nothing suggests that the cost of such departures would be lower today.[53] However one feels about space colonization, it is not a practical solution to population problems. They must be dealt with on this planet.

Hardin's point is a profound one—growth at present rates cannot continue indefinitely. The views of Commoner and others notwithstanding, concern about population is indeed an important part of environmentalism. But Hardin was too eager to solve the problem of population through coercive means. His solutions are every bit as frightening as his scenarios of population-out-of-control. On the more positive side, perspectives like Hardin's, so long as they are clearly seen as outrageous, can serve to place more sensible inquiries into proper perspective. The hysterical aspects of his views have been criticized by many, including Janet Besecker and Phil Elder, who wrote a response to Hardin's widely read essay "Lifeboat Ethics: The Case Against Helping the Poor," published in *Psychology Today* in 1974.[55] Hardin's article borrowed directly from Malthus, substituting "food aid" for the English Poor Laws. The starving of the world would better look after themselves, Hardin asserted, in terms of both food production and population control, if such aid were not forthcoming. Besecker and Elder replied that food aid is not too great a "sacrifice" but too little—what is required is nothing less than a global effort to raise the standard of living in the poor countries, even at the cost of lowering the standard of living in the developed world. "As more than just the subsistence needs are met and as literacy increases, a population's fertility declines," they argued.[56] If a global effort is made to lower birth rates and raise living standards in the developing countries, human population may never exceed the earth's carrying capacity. *But*, Besecker and Elder claimed, humanity—or at least those characteristics that make the species worth preserving—would *not* survive the insensitive coercion that Hardin urged in the name of survival.

Hardin failed to consider the moral implications of the present maldistribution of wealth on the planet. Besecker and Elder noted, for example, that the production of a meat-based diet requires many times more resources—land, water, and energy—than are required by an equivalently healthy vegetarian or semi-vegetarian diet. North American dogs and cats are presently valued more highly than the children of the poorer countries. "Hardin seems to believe that the wealthy nations are entitled to the resources of the world because their populations are increasing at a decreasing rate," they note. "But their per capita consumption is increasing at an increasing rate and shows no more signs of abating than does the Indian population. That exponentially increasing consumption dooms the race . . . just as surely as any exponential increase in population."[57] Why does

Hardin not suggest a more sensible scheme, one advocating the eviction of North Americans from the lifeboat? It would cost far fewer persons and would achieve for the species considerably more time to bring about population stabilization than would avoidable starvation in the so-called third world.

If energy is the most limiting of resources, the heaviest consumers of energy, not the lightest consumers of food, are the greatest threat to long-term human survival. The energy-rich, in general, also produce more weapons and are thereby as likely to destroy the species as is population growth, if not more. And any scheme deliberately to starve the poor is likely to lead to war. Humanity shares one planet, and any talk of evicting certain of its inhabitants is not likely to produce the cooperation that is the only basis for survival in a nuclear age. The lifeboat is most likely to sink if the inhabitants are all thrashing about attempting to evict each other.

In addressing the issue of population growth, sensitive environmentalists need to ask three questions:

1. What is an optimal human population?
2. What, other than coercive means, might be done to lower birth rates so as to achieve population stabilization?
3. Can stabilization be achieved near enough to the optimal level that that level can be attained gradually and humanely?

How does one determine optimal population? The answer depends, of course, on what one values most highly. If everyone required an uncluttered view of the sea in a warm climate, or long daily walks in scenic wilderness, humanity would long ago have passed the optimum. As Hardin put it, "The question is, which do we want: the maximum number of people at the minimum standard of living— or a smaller number at a comfortable, or even gracious, standard of living?"[58] Besecker and Elder, too, were concerned that serious costs will be borne before population can be stabilized—perhaps, for example, the existence of abundant wilderness. If the earth's carrying capacity is reached, then there will already be far too many human beings to live in terms of anyone's notion of graciousness, and a humane population reduction will not likely be a short-term proposition.

An inquiry into the earth's maximum capacity is necessary before considering the other two questions. This was addressed in another 1970s environmental debate, paralleling closely the debate between Commoner and Ehrlich, concerning food-producing capabilities. To my knowledge it was not a direct debate, but it can be reconstructed here as if it had been. In 1974, Lester R. Brown published *By Bread Alone*, and in 1977 Frances Moore Lappé and Joseph Collins published *Food First: Beyond the Myth of Scarcity*. Brown's book took a pessimistic view of the food-production capacity of the planet. Lappé and Collins, by contrast, were convinced that present and near-future population levels can be fed adequately without assuming dramatic technological breakthroughs in agriculture. But in their view feeding the hungry will require radical changes in land ownership, wealth, food distribution, and individual and collective decisions about crops and diets.

Brown's *By Bread Alone* systematically examined the four basic resources that underlie food-producing capability: land, water, energy, and fertilizer. He stressed that little new arable land is available anywhere in the world; what remains is of lower average quality than that now in use. Thus potential new farmlands will require, on average, more water, energy, and fertilizer if they are to yield as highly as do existing agricultural lands. Even if these additional resources are available, other conditions, such as climate, will make food production on such land uncertain.

Brown discussed four crucial issues related to agricultural land use: (1) the destruction of prime farmland for nonagricultural uses, especially in the developed countries; (2) the futility of clearing jungle lands for agricultural use (the soils and other factors make such land inappropriate for agriculture); (3) the reduction in soil quality (especially tilth) caused by overuse of land and excessive application of agricultural chemicals; and (4) the expansion of desert in several areas of the world through overgrazing. Brown concluded that there is little hope for expanding food production by farming additional land. Indeed, he argued, it will take a great effort in many places to maintain present agricultural lands, let alone find more.

Irrigation, Brown demonstrated, has been one of the principal methods of expanding agricultural capacity in this century. In 1900 there were 100 million acres in irrigation, by 1970 up to 460 million. But the rate of increase of expansion has peaked; the annual rate of increase from 1950 to 1970 was 2.9 percent, the estimated rate for the balance of the century is 1.1 percent.[59] In many places water tables are now dropping, elsewhere soil salinization, induced by irrigation, is increasing. Water is becoming a more limited resource in agricultural development. Large-scale desalinization of seawater for agricultural purposes would require too much energy to be economical. (This factor has been magnified considerably by the increase in energy prices that occurred following the publication of Brown's book.)

Discussing the relationship between energy use and agriculture, Brown wrote, "The experts maintain that, if all the world were to adopt the protein-rich U.S. diet and food-producing system, and if petroleum were the sole source of energy for agriculture, *all known world reserves of petroleum would be exhausted within a mere twenty-nine years*."[60] He concluded that energy too will severely limit expansion of agricultural capacity. But, he noted, the greatest waste of energy in the food system occurs not on the farm, but in food processing and delivery systems—in the wasteful overpackaging of food in developed countries and, perhaps most spectacularly, in the North American penchant for using two-ton automobiles to move ten-pound bags of groceries.

Finally, Brown identified fertilizer as a resource that may, in some cases, be approaching its limit as well. Fertilizers are limited on two fronts: by availability, especially in the case of nitrogen fertilizers derived from fossil fuels, and in terms of usefulness. Each successive application of fertilizer to the same crop on the same land is less effective in increasing yield. At some point—reached sooner when the cost of energy is rising faster than the price of food—further fertilizing will no longer be economical.

Brown tended to give insufficient credit to the possibilities of agricultural innovation. Even Hardin granted that carrying capacity (at great cost to Malthus' reputation) had increased enormously in the centuries since Malthus' death. Brown allowed that crop species might be altered to make better use of fertilizer, but he did not account for more dramatic genetic alterations. We soon may be able to create food plants that can grow in colder climates, opening land in colder regions for agricultural use. Or we might develop species that thrive on oversalinated lands, or even that can make use of seawater. Some plants already grow in salty soil—the task is to transfer this capability to high-yield edible plants. Scientists are also at work attempting to transfer nitrogen-fixing capabilities to additional plant species, which will reduce the need for petroleum-based nitrogen fertilizers.

Such technological breakthroughs, however, do not completely refute Brown's pessimism. They have not yet been achieved, though since 1974 they have come much closer. Each will carry costs as well. If we use salinated soils, for example, irrevocable steps will be taken—at that point *only* the new crops could be grown. Opening marginal lands, in colder regions, to cropping exposes their thin, vulnerable soil cover to erosion by wind or water. The transfer of nitrogen-fixing capability does not decrease the need for other nutrients or water, nor does it stop the waste of nonrenewable energy resources in the processing and distribution sectors of the food system. These are not arguments against proceeding; they are, however, a reminder that population stabilization must become and remain a high priority, whatever the technological possibilities in agriculture. One needn't make the Malthusian error of ignoring technological innovation to see that such innovation will always carry some costs—probably in the continuous need for increases in environmentally damaging and nonsustainable energy and material inputs into the agricultural production process.

The new possibilities are no reply at all to many of the limits to food production Brown and others have pointed out. There will be no new prime land, especially near markets. Fish catches globally have peaked and fish farming is probably too energy intensive in many locations. Some of the best agricultural land is still being removed from agricultural use. Soil quality continues to decline globally because of the excessive demands of human food needs. Additional demands will only add additional pressures, and future gains will be made uphill against diminishing clean energy options.

Let us briefly now consider Lappé's and Collins' position, which directly challenged the view that the earth's carrying capacity is very near to being exceeded. Brown and others argued that the extent of hunger is evidence of how near we are to that carrying capacity. Lappé and Collins disagreed. Whatever the ultimate capacity, hunger today is in their view a problem in distribution, not in agricultural capability. In *Food First* they argued, for example, that more land and effort in the poor countries is devoted to feeding the rich nations than land and effort in the rich nations is devoted to feeding the world's poor.[61] The developing nations are net *exporters* of food. Vast acreage there is devoted to growing coffee, tea, cocoa, sugar, rubber, sisal, tobacco, cotton, and bananas, almost all of which is exported to the rich nations. But most of these products are unneeded luxuries—they add very little nutrition to anyone's diet, rich or poor.

The more Lappé and Collins looked at global food inequities, the clearer it became to them that hunger usually results from economic and political exploitation rather than an insufficient capacity to grow food. In some countries the best fertile lowlands are used to grow bananas for the rich, while domestic food is grown on the most marginal lands. This puts the soil and ecology at great risk. The erosion-vulnerable hillsides are all that is left for peasants trying to grow food for themselves. Jungles that support myriad plant and animal species are clearcut to raise cattle for North American fast burgers. Or rainforests are cut for wood exports and abandoned. Lappé and Collins claimed that virtually every region of the world is potentially self-sustaining. Contrary to Hardin, it is not "we" who should stop aiding "the poor nations"—it is they who should stop supplying us.

The primary solution, Lappé and Collins argued, is land redistribution. This would alter cropping patterns and bring into production land now held by large owners seeking to force up the prices of particular export commodities. Small holders would be more likely to produce food for domestic consumption. Furthermore, small farms are generally more efficient than large farms, in part because owner-producers more freely supply labor. In addition to land redistribution, Lappé and Collins noted two other necessary changes. Those in the developed nations should consume more plant protein directly, rather than feeding most of it to animals. High-fat, animal-protein-based diets are not only unhealthy,[62] they also are ten to twenty times less efficient in terms of land, water, and agricultural energy. How else does China feed a billion people with such limited use of land and energy than by emphasizing plant products? Finally, the developing nations must make the political changes necessary to stop importation of luxuries and military hardware in favor of greater imports of agricultural, industrial, and forestry expertise and the capacity to make simple equipment suitable for the small-scale production of food.

The arguments of Lappé and Collins, in conjunction with a somewhat greater degree of technological optimism than Brown allowed, lead one to conclude that the earth is not yet at the limit of its food-growing capacity. The best counterargument is that a population which doubles every thirty-five years (1970s figures) will soon absorb almost any achievable increase. And Lappé and Collins, perhaps just as much as Brown and Hardin, overstated their case. In fact, most of the arable land in the third world is already in food crops, and most of that food is locally consumed. Domination of agricultural resources by luxury export crops is most pronounced in certain African and Latin American countries. There is some latitude, but not such that the populations can double again and again without stretching the earth's resources severely.

In some cases luxury crop exports can earn a country the foreign currency with which to import grain. Some land used for coffee, for example, cannot be used for grain. Thus neither Malthusian hopelessness nor unfocused moral outrage is an appropriate attitude toward world hunger. We cannot know with precision the carrying capacity of the earth, but a prudent person will conclude that our numbers probably cannot double many more times without exceeding it. One ought also to conclude that the lack of new prime agricultural land and the scarcity of both fossil fuels and water for irrigation are fundamental changes in the human condition. The genetic alteration of plants, if successful, can be used only to buy time for humane, noncoercive stabilization of the global population. We cannot allow the ghost of Malthus to return yet again in another few decades.

We do not know whether there will be enough time for noncoercive stabilization to occur. Given the looming decline in supplies of conventional fossil fuels, it appears unlikely (see chapter 4). Nor can an optimal population level be determined authoritatively. I conclude that it is that level which can be attained without coercion, starvation, or nuclear war, with a maximum global effort to restrain birth rates voluntarily and to provide food and security to the poor. For any hope of preserving wilderness and the habitats of other species, this level should not greatly exceed the one additional doubling that now seems inevitable. Population is projected at ten billion in the year 2050—let us work toward stability by that point.[63]

Since the early 1970s there has been some basis for hope that this is possible. First, birth rates in most developed countries have declined to below replacement levels. Populations in the rich countries are growing now only by virtue of the fact that the generation presently of childbearing age is quite large. If birth rates stay level as the post-baby-boom teenagers mature, the populations of many countries will begin to decline, excepting whatever immigration is permitted. The 1980–85 average birth rate in the United States was 1.6 children per woman (15.9 per 1,000). Canada's present birth rate of 1.7 children per woman resulted in a government report as hysterically pro–population growth as Ehrlich and Hardin are anti–population growth.[64] The report labels the situation a "baby-bust" and finds it especially alarming given that the so-called baby-boom generation has already attained childbearing age.

One can anticipate more reactions of this sort but ˖˖˖ can nonetheless celebrate with enthusiasm the importance of this change, common to almost all developed nations.[65] Besecker and Elder noted that a typical North American consumes fifty times more resources than a typical Indian and calculated that the consumption of the North American population was equivalent in resource-use terms to that of a population in excess of 12.25 billion Indians. Declining numbers in the rich countries—achieved wholly on a voluntary basis, despite the reward systems of most governments and despite dire warnings from some religious leaders, are a tribute to the intelligence of the citizens of those countries. China too is now moving toward population stabilization at an impressive rate, strongly urged by its leadership. (It is not clear how much coercion has been used there.) Only our second question regarding population seems important in the face of this achievement in so many nations: what can and must be done to achieve *global* population stabilization?

The answer to this question improves considerably the prospects for an environmentalist ideology of a progressive character. This point is taken up in more detail later. Suffice it to say for now that voluntary birth-rate restraint (Hardin's voluntary/educational phases) is associated with at least eight factors:

1. An assured food supply
2. Reduced infant mortality rates
3. Literacy
4. Rudimentary health services
5. A social insurance system
6. Urbanization
7. Rising economic expectations
8. Women's rights, including opportunities for work outside the home.

Insecurity about food, child mortality, and income during old age are incentives to childbearing; alleviating these worries will reduce birth rates. Providing the means to limit birth—literacy and health services, including birth control methods—is also necessary. Opportunities for women, especially for education and work, limit the birth rate. In most developing countries women with university degrees have fewer children even than the average woman in the developed world. Finally, there is no doubt that urbanization is coming to these countries shockingly fast already. But the list, with some cultural variations of course, is appropriate in all countries, developed or developing. It simply advocates providing basic human needs—food, shelter, education, health, freedom, and hope—regardless of age or sex. The task of environmental protection cannot be separated from that of providing for other human needs. Malthus and Hardin are profoundly wrong in more ways than one. Malthus saw the problem, but missed the solutions, both technological and sociopolitical; Hardin underestimated the ability of the poor to learn and to act upon a hope for something considerably less than the graciousness of Santa Barbara.

About the same time that Ehrlich was writing *The End of Affluence*, two other authors produced important works, one of which was read quite widely. Robert Heilbroner's *Inquiry into the Human Prospect* and William Ophuls' *Ecology and the Politics of Scarcity* were sophisticated inquiries into the political implications of a neo-Malthusian perspective. The conclusions of these authors recall to mind some of the draconian views advocated (rather than lamented) by Ehrlich's *Population Bomb*. Neither Heilbroner nor Ophuls viewed population as the single cause of environmental deterioration and resource depletion, but both were profoundly pessimistic about long-term human prospects. After reviewing population growth, resource availability, food-growing capabilities, and energy prospects, both authors concluded that neither material growth, energy growth, nor economic growth can continue at the rates of the recent past. Both economically and politically, they argued, North America and the world as a whole are in for very difficult times in the foreseeable future. Ophuls and Heilbroner respectively wrote,

> Once relative abundance and wealth of opportunity are no longer available to mitigate the harsh political dynamics of scarcity, the pressures favoring greater inequality, oppression, and conflict will build up, so that the return of scarcity portends the revival of age-old political evils, for our descendants if not for ourselves. In short, the golden age of individualism, liberty and democracy is all but over.[66]

> Given these mighty pressures and constraints we must think of alternatives to the present order in terms of social systems that offer a necessary degree of regimentation as well as a different set of motives and objectives. I must confess I can picture only one such system. This is a social order that will blend a "religious" orientation and a "military" discipline. Such a monastic organization of society may be repugnant to us, but I suspect it offers the greatest promise for bringing about the profound and painful adaptations that the coming generations must make.[67]

Heilbroner, reflecting on *The Human Prospect* a year later, would not soften significantly his regretful view that authoritarianism would inevitably return along with scarcity.[68] Only a mass movement toward self-discipline, an uncommon degree of social unity, or a political genius would mitigate the return of repressive force. (We will look more closely at some of the resources and economic issues underlying the political conclusions of these books in the chapters to follow.)

In striking contrast to these two works, and in a tone similar to my conclusions regarding population, are the writings of Richard J. Barnet, particularly *The Lean Years: Politics in the Age of Scarcity* (1980). The ominous title notwithstanding, one might conclude that if Barnet is typical, a modicum of hope somehow infiltrated environmentalists' political assessments during the late 1970s. Barnet reviewed the same issues Ophuls and Heilbroner had, and with regard to resource prospects he was similarly pessimistic. But Barnet explicitly counted himself out of both neo-Malthusianism and neo-Hobbesianism: "In today's world the heirs of Malthus preach what they call 'lifeboat ethics,' claiming the same monopoly on realism that fortified the dismal preacher when he pronounced his death sentence for the poor. . . . Despairing of human altruism to subordinate the quest for personal enrichment to the common good, the heirs of Hobbes have seized upon the dangers of ecological catastrophe to legitimate the modern-day Leviathan."[69] Barnet's basis for rejecting both Malthus and Hobbes contains part of the key to understanding the position of an environmental politics on the political spectrum: "Democracy is under severe attack at the moment when gathering evidence suggests that popular participation is a survival value. Major structural changes cannot take place in any country without the mobilization of the whole people. The solution to the energy crisis in the U.S., for example, requires a degree of public understanding and participation which our political institutions do not know how to achieve."[70]

Barnet's view makes clear that pessimism about resource depletion need not result in a politics of pessimism. If he is correct, then neither the individualistic hoarding of Ehrlich, the coercive populationism of Hardin, nor the profoundly regretted authoritarianism of Heilbroner and Ophuls is appropriate. Indeed, all may be counterproductive. Grim solutions are not necessarily more realistic than hopeful ones. Perhaps both altruism and democracy must prevail, especially if hard times are to be characteristic of humanity's future.

four

The Energy Crisis:
Limit and Hope

Between the neo-
Malthusian bleakness of Paul Ehrlich and Garrett Hardin and the
guarded hopefulness of Richard Barnet's *The Lean Years*, the historic
event most central to environmentalism was the energy price shock
of 1973 and 1979. This additional limit, paradoxically, seems to have
ushered in a more positive outlook on the future. To see how the
energy crisis led to optimism, we must look closely at the writings
of Amory B. Lovins.[1] Lovins has concentrated his attention on one
dimension of environmental concern—energy supply and demand—and has done so in such a timely and hard-hitting fashion
that he has altered the way many people think about this issue. The
quality and quantity of Lovins' output has been nothing less than
amazing: seven books and numerous articles, all about energy, in a
nine-year period (1974–83). Lovins' works, taken together, set out
the view that environmental problems are predominantly problems
of energy.

Lovins portrays humanity at a historic crossroad. The era of fossil
fuels has peaked and before us lie two paths: the hard energy path
(which we are now following), and the soft energy path (SEP), the
one Lovins describes as the most desirable, indeed the only possible,
alternative. The advocates of a hard energy path (sometimes called
the business-as-usual approach) do not tend to think seriously about
the long-term future of energy supply and demand. When the overly
optimistic claims for nuclear power popular in the 1950s (for example, that it would provide electricity too cheap to meter)[2] proved

false, hard energy path advocates called for declining supplies of oil to be supplemented with coal, "frontier" or "offshore" sources of fossil fuels, fossil fuel extracted from oil shales and oil sands, large-scale hydroelectric power, and nuclear power. All these sources (except hydroelectricity) are nonrenewable. All involve large-scale, capital-intensive operations. And all involve grave risks to the environment, risks that Lovins and others have documented with great care, especially in the case of nuclear power. In contrast, SEP advocates would have us use only renewable sources of energy, diverse and simple sources carefully matched to end-use needs. It is generally assumed by SEP advocates that such energy sources are environmentally benign, but this is not part of Lovins' original definition of the SEP.

Like Barry Commoner, Lovins sees environmental problems as deriving from faulty technological choices. But for Lovins the most dangerous mistakes have been made with regard to energy technologies. Coal, burned in conventional ways, causes air pollution, acid rain, and climatic changes. Extraction of coal involves considerable environmental problems as well. Extracting oil from shale and sand pollutes the water and diminishes the water resources needed for other purposes.[3] Conventional oil and natural gas are, Lovins believes, too valuable to burn: they should be reserved for use as petrochemical feedstocks (i.e., to make materials such as plastics and fertilizers) for the long term as quickly as the transition can be made. Oil and gas that cannot be extracted without damaging sensitive ecosystems are probably best left in the ground. Fossil fuels should be used sparingly; they should be considered "transition fuels," a bridge to renewable energy resources. Since we can only build one fossil fuel bridge, Lovins emphasizes that we should know what will be on the other side.

The conventional array of options to oil and gas energy involves even greater environmental damage per unit of energy than is caused by extraction and use of the energy sources currently used. This is significant, because conventional oil, in particular, is by no means environmentally harmless. Oil is at the base of the petrochemical industry, whose products are often found to be hazardous; oil refineries have been associated with serious environmental damage;

and drilling for oil contributes more than is widely recognized to problems of hazardous waste management. Smog, caused by oil-based energy, is still with us, and the automobile adds a significant share of nitrogen oxides to acid rain.[4] But whatever the environmental effects of conventional oil and gas, it pales in comparison to the likely result of replacing them, at current levels of energy demand, with some combination of hard path sources. Conventional oil and natural gas are relatively benign compared to all the most visible options on the horizon, especially those for electricity and portable liquid fuels. Even assuming no further growth in energy demand, considerable technological advances and enormous pollution abatement expenditures will be necessary to hold pollution at present levels in the future. Lovins is too cheerful to set the problem in quite these terms, but such a perspective can be arrived at from his writings.

Lovins himself has been more interested in communicating the positive character of the SEP option. The soft energy path, he writes, "has three main technical components: (1) using much more efficiently the energy we've got, (2) getting it increasingly from soft technologies . . . and (3) intelligently using fossil fuels for a transition." First priority is given not to energy supply, but to demand. Energy demand is not determined in the heaven of consumer sovereignty as it was in perspectives on energy prior to Lovins'. In a hard path, Lovins concludes, "there is a presumption that the more energy we use, the better off we are. That is, energy is tacitly elevated from a means to an end in itself; whereas in the soft path how much energy we use to accomplish our social goals is considered a measure, not of our success, but of our failure." Lovins optimistically claims that continuous increase in energy demand is all but over, and that energy demand and supply will stabilize in the developed nations at or below present levels. "Clearly if our long term energy needs are going to be roughly where they are now or a bit less, rather than soaring heavenwards, then soft energy technologies can do a lot more a lot faster than we thought they could."[5]

The end of growth in energy demand and supply is not a regrettable failure of progress. The future Lovins envisions is not at all draconian; indeed, life in the energy-limited world will be generally better. Economic growth will not stop—Lovins ridicules those who think that growth in GNP and in energy demand march in lockstep. Society and economy must and will simply learn to use energy more efficiently. As Barry Commoner put it, *productivity* has more than one meaning, and energy productivity should be seen as at least as important as labor productivity.[6] If energy demand is level or declining, fossil fuels can gradually be replaced not by dirtier energy sources, but by cleaner ones; not by depletable sources, but by renewable ones. And not only do SEP sources allow for superior environmental protection, they will lead to economic, political, and social gains as well—at least relative to the direction we have been heading as conventional oil and gas become more difficult to find and extract. This shift in perspective is central to an understanding of the evolution of environmentalism as a whole: it has helped to create an environmentalism free of the bleakness of Malthusianism. I examine the importance of this new perspective later in this chapter.

Energy in an SEP is supplied by *soft technologies*, which have five important characteristics.

1. Renewability is crucial to the logic of Lovins' vision. All non-renewable energy sources will ultimately be exhausted. The low cost of fossil fuel, foolishly subsidized by governments for decades, has helped create the illusion that the supply is endless. We have gained insight into the nature of the illusion as oil supplies have peaked. Humanity, Lovins argues, must gradually return to renewable *flows* of energy as a basis for society and economy. We must not remain overly dependent on fixed *stocks* of energy.

2. Soft energy path supply technologies are varied and diverse. There are dozens of possible sources of renewable energy, each applicable to specific tasks (although each by itself is inadequate as an answer to the energy crisis—there is no "quick fix" source, no single massive renewable source available). Low-grade heat energy is available from sunlight, even in cold climates. Hot spots in the earth provide substantial quantities of geothermal energy extractable as heat or electricity.[7] The heating and cooling capability of near-surface earth and rock can be utilized everywhere on land. Even in the dead of winter, an expanse of triple-glazed window can be con-

structed to distribute heat energy from the sun into a house. Partially buried houses, built into south-facing hillsides, can be designed to allow natural light into all living spaces. With proper insulation, air-to-air heat exchangers, and a small wood stove and/or electric heat pump, they need neither furnace nor air conditioner. This demonstrates the elegant simplicity of soft technologies. Without mechanical heating and cooling devices, additional capital costs of such buildings are low, there are almost no additional maintenance costs, and the lives of their inhabitants are, if anything, improved—while demand for nonrenewable energy supplies is reduced radically or even eliminated.

Some things we use energy for are not so easily transferred to renewable sources. High temperatures (in excess of 150° C) are more difficult to produce, as are large quantities of portable liquid fuels. But a number of technically viable options are coming forward, several of which were economically competitive in selected locations in the early 1980s.[8] Electricity can be generated from wind, water, waves, and tides; in turn it can produce industrial-grade heat. Biomass of all kinds can be used to produce alcohol, which serves as a portable liquid fuel. Organic wastes, often now a cause of pollution, can be transformed into both fuel and fertilizer. Ocean current temperature gradients can be used to generate electricity (this has recently been proposed on a large scale for Hawaii). The ultimate soft technology is solar photovoltaics, if they can be made more economical over the coming decades. Each of these technologies uses renewable energy sources only; even a partial list of such sources is impressive in its diversity.

3. Soft technologies are easy to understand and often accessible to persons with little technical expertise. Many are particularly suitable for use in less developed regions. Indeed, perhaps the simplest of renewable energy technologies—wood heat in airtight stoves— has been widely adopted in the past ten years in such places as the Eastern provinces of Canada, rural New England, and Appalachia. The Canadian government was startled to find that money provided under its grant program to convert homes from oil as a source of heat paid for conversion to wood almost as often as conversion to

electricity or natural gas. The technology involved in burning wood advanced considerably in the 1970s.[9]

4. Soft technologies are matched in scale to end-use needs. Lovins has been particularly concerned with the massive scale of hard path technologies. "We are used to hearing that energy systems must be enormous to be affordable," he wrote. "And there often are some real economies of scale in construction. But there are often some real diseconomies of large scale which we haven't properly counted before."[10] One uneconomical aspect of large-scale energy projects is the cost of distributing energy from central sites to dispersed consumers. Unfortunately, this cost becomes proportionately greater as energy use becomes more efficient. Some utilities have claimed that it is uneconomical to hook up new superefficient homes—their tenants do not buy enough energy to pay for the connection costs.[11] Nuclear power projects, which tie up large amounts of capital for up to a decade before they sell any electricity, have recently nearly bankrupted several major North American utilities.[12] Soft energy sources, by contrast, are geographically dispersed. With greater dependence on these sources, other aspects of society and economy would tend to decentralize as well—a transition that would be welcomed for a variety of reasons.[13]

5. Lovins identified soft energy sources as "matched in energy quality to end-use needs," calling this characteristic the "most important part of the definition of soft technology."[14] He divided total energy demand into four categories or "qualities." The first category is heat of less than 100° C. In the United States this category comprises one-third of all energy demand, much of which can be met using solar technologies. An additional one-quarter of demand is for heat greater than 100° C, most of which is for temperatures just above that point. Often water can be preheated with solar energy so that only a final increment of heat energy need come from another source. A third form of energy, another third of U.S. demand, is for energy in portable liquid form, used for transportation. Only 8 percent of the total demand is for "premium" electrical energy, the highest form. Thus, tasks that require electricity make up only a small portion of energy demand. Only 8 percent of our present use

of energy goes to operate computers, appliances, communications and electronic devices, lights, and industrial electric motors. This proportion of energy use Lovins calls electricity-specific demand; it includes needs that cannot be filled easily by other means. Using electricity, an especially expensive form of energy, to perform other tasks is wasteful in several ways. Lovins compares the use of electricity to heat homes or water to "cutting butter with a chainsaw." In 1977, the United States used 13 percent of its energy in the form of electricity, and that proportion was growing rather than staying constant or declining to what Lovins considered a more appropriate level. The appropriateness of soft technologies to their uses is important in Lovins' rejection of the "all-electric" energy future.

It is Lovins' broad, long-term view that has contributed most to the worldwide energy debate of the 1970s and 1980s, as well as to the development of a politically viable environmentalism. Lovins' notion of hard and soft paths has opened up a new view of both the past and the future. He more than anyone else has seen the full importance of the peaking of the fossil fuel era. He has retained his breadth of vision in detailed debates about the relative environmental and economic merits of offshore oil, synfuels, and nuclear power, leading many to realize that, ultimately, society must return to sources we have left behind. We must steer away from both international confrontations over oil exports and the equivalent dangers associated with dependence on nuclear energy. The energy transition, Lovins argues, is the most important issue that humanity must face, now and for the next century.

To appreciate Lovins' contribution we must look also at earlier efforts toward soft technologies. Lovins was by no means the first to realize the technical potential of solar energy. Solar architecture has at least a twenty-five-hundred-year history, as Ken Butti and John Perlin have illustrated. Active solar hot water heaters were a major industry in Florida as early as the 1920s and 1930s. This industry foundered as low-cost electricity was made available, even though it remained economically competitive. It failed for technical reasons that made electric water heaters slightly more convenient.[15]

The Resources for the Future Conference in 1953 marked the first full articulation of the energy view that came to public consciousness in the 1970s. The discussions of solar energy that took place are striking in their insights, given the energy-unconscious era in which they were made. Maria Telkes of New York University commented that "for each $100 spent on atomic energy development only a fraction of a cent has been spent on solar energy development." But even these small expenditures had produced some impressive results. H. C. Hottel of M.I.T., whose research group had built solar collectors achieving an impressive 35 percent efficiency, believed that "proposed uses of solar energy can be understood or visualized by the layman, whereas advanced knowledge is needed to understand atomic energy." George Lof, another leading solar pioneer, detailed the design of flat-plate collectors and collector systems with electrical backups, adding that, in general, "expensive converted heat in the form of electrical energy" was not necessary to heat homes.[16] (One lapse in the energy foresight of the 1953 conference participants stands out as well. In an introduction to a section on energy conservation, the editors of the conference proceedings noted that "automobiles and the gasoline they burn have become more efficient than they used to be."[17] The oncoming age of the gas guzzler proved them wrong.)

Some conference participants anticipated millions of solar-heated homes by 1975, but Telkes did not believe such a development would occur so fast. Had it happened that way, of course, Amory Lovins' 1976 article advocating an SEP, published in the distinguished journal *Foreign Affairs*, would not have seemed so revolutionary. Several of the participants in the 1953 discussion argued for immediate solar energy, use and energy conservation in order to reserve oil, coal, gas, uranium, and thorium, for other uses that could not be readily met with solar energy for developing countries, or for future generations. Needless to say, their advice was ignored; during the decades that followed precisely the opposite pattern of energy production and use prevailed throughout North America and the developed world.

Discussion of solar techniques at the 1953 conference was very sophisticated. It was noted that Bell Laboratories had achieved 6 percent efficiency on direct conversion of sunlight to electricity; and there was even some discussion of advanced biomass conversion techniques, using, for example, algae. But very little was subsequently done to advance these capabilities, especially with regard to commercial developments taking advantage of solar, wind, or biomass energy possibilities. In 1975, use of active solar energy technologies for nonagricultural purposes was probably less than it was in 1945.

Thus Lovins' case regarding the need for solar energy and conservation was hardly new. But in the 1970s more people were prepared to listen—because OPEC had shocked the world into realizing that there were almost no low-cost alternatives to oil. People also listened more carefully to Lovins because they were no longer as naive about nuclear power as they were in the 1950s.

In the 1960s, nuclear power was considered the leading long-term alternative to fossil fuels—that is, among those few who thought that an alternative would be necessary. Even in the early 1970s many people—including some environmentalists—remained sympathetic to nuclear power. Tiny Bennett and Wade Rowland, for example, wrote, "We have at our disposal now—in fact, have had for some time—virtually unlimited energy in the form of nuclear power. The last, relatively minor, problems involved in its practical exploitation are being straightened out."[18] But Amory Lovins was at his eloquent best in his case for solar energy and conservation as alternatives to nuclear power. Pronuclear environmentalists, after he began writing, were clearly an endangered species.

Lovins' attack on nuclear electricity was based on five arguments:

1. More electricity is not needed—it is an inefficient way to supply demand for lower grades of energy.
2. Nuclear power is hazardous to the environment.
3. Nuclear power is inextricably linked to nuclear weapons.
4. Nuclear power will result in a variety of social and political problems.
5. Nuclear power is not economically viable without massive governmental subsidies and protections.

Lovins and many others in the 1970s argued strenuously that nuclear power is the most fundamental technological error in human history. Nuclear power, Lovins stated, inevitably results in forms of pollution that at present we have little or no capacity to handle—indeed, we will probably never develop such a capacity. Nuclear power plants are prone to dangerous malfunctions that sooner or later will result in loss-of-coolant accidents and perhaps core meltdowns. In addition, radioactivity has been and continues to be unintentionally released into the environment, especially in the extraction and processing of nuclear fuels. (Significant hazards exist at virtually every uranium mine and mill in North America.)[19] Concern with the danger of nuclear war and nuclear accidents is clearly the intellectual source of Lovins' work. He sees loss-of-coolant accidents, problems associated with reprocessing, and terrorism and sabotage involving nuclear facilities as virtually inevitable.[20] Mistakes occur with every technology, but with nuclear power mistakes carry too high a price. The technology is, in a word, unforgiving.[21] Lovins quoted J. T. Edsall: "I believe that the confident advocates of the safety of nuclear power plants base their confidence too narrowly on the safety that [it] is possible to achieve under the most favourable circumstances, over a limited period of time, with a corps of highly trained and dedicated personnel. If we take a larger view of human nature and history, I believe that we can never expect such conditions to persist over centuries, much less over millennia."[22]

The dangers of terrorism, sabotage, and nuclear war are even more problematic for Lovins than nuclear accidents or environmental damage. Lovins has focused on "fallibility problems" associated with the nuclear industry rather than on "routine events," which in an early paper he identified as "heat release and associated biological and meteorological problems, visual impact, transport and land use impacts, scheduled releases of noble-gas and other radioactivity from nuclear facilities, exposures of transient nuclear workers, the high incidence of lung cancer among some underground uranium miners, and the escape of 226Ra-bearing particles or daughter products into the air and water from improperly managed uranium mill tailings."[23] These problems, alarming as they sound, pale in comparison to the less predictable catastrophes to which nuclear power facilities are particularly vulnerable: accidents on a scale no other industry could have, and terrorism, sabotage, and theft.

Many experts believe that the most critical problem of civilian nuclear power is likely to be that of safeguarding inventories of strategic materials against theft and subsequent illicit manufacture of crude but convincing nuclear weapons. . . . Possible nuclear thieves, or instigators of theft by agents, include terrorist groups, nonnuclear states, lunatics, criminal syndicates, and speculators—a diverse range with some strong transnational connections and with a history of impressive persistence and sophistication.[24]

Perhaps Lovins' best and clearest work (written with L. Hunter Lovins) is *Energy/War: Breaking the Nuclear Link*, which begins, "the nuclear proliferation problem, as posed, is impossible." The authors discussed the rapid spread of nuclear weapons capability through a flourishing "ambiguous nuclear cooperation"—ambiguous because weapons technology proliferates in the name of peaceful nuclear energy technology. Nuclear technologies flow from the United States, West Germany, and France to such unstable countries as South Africa, Libya, Iraq, South Korea, Brazil, Argentina, Israel, and Pakistan. Proliferation is "the transcendent threat of our age," in the authors' view leading "by inexorable logic to the necessity of phasing out nuclear power." Quoting Cousteau, they insist, "we must learn if we want to live at all, to live without" both the peaceful and the warlike atom.[25] This position recalls Barry Commoner, whose political activism likewise rose from a deep concern with the dangers of nuclear weapons. Commoner was active in the early opposition to nuclear weapons testing and in publicizing the environmental and health effects of strontium–90. The origins of environmentalism are inextricably bound up with opposition to nuclear weapons.

Almost as frightening as Lovins' discussion of terrorism, nuclear accidents, and weapons proliferation is his enumeration of the steps that might be necessary to prevent them. In *Non-Nuclear Futures* Lovins quoted nuclear scientist Alvin Weinberg, with whom he later engaged in an extended debate: "Some thoughtful advocates of fission technology, such as Weinberg, have discussed 'the social mechanisms that seem to be required if we concede that we shall always be dealing with huge amounts of 239Pu'—for example, 'a cadre, that, from now on, can be counted upon to understand nuclear technology, to control it, to prevent accidents, prevent diversion in Uganda as well as in the USA, in Ethiopia as well as England.' "[26] Many agree that the control of nuclear power requires a "techno-logical priesthood" of experts who must stand apart from society. Lovins argues that it is unlikely such people could maintain stan-dards of design, construction, and maintenance exacting enough to prevent accidents. And the existence of such a powerful and separate group, the work of which would be little understood by the majority, would pose a threat to democracy. The political importance of the sharp contrast between the "technological priesthood" and the "el-egant simplicity" of soft technologies is crucial to Lovins.

But technical experts are not the only threat that nuclear power poses to democracy. A plutonium-based economy might require a paramilitary component to secure against theft, terrorism, and the clandestine production of nuclear weapons. Lovins fears that such a society would consider it necessary to infiltrate potentially threat-ening groups and to spy on private citizens, especially nuclear in-dustry employees and opponents. In this view he has not been alone. Russell W. Ayres, writing in the *Harvard Civil Rights / Civil Liberties Law Review* in 1975, concluded that the recycling of plutonium would place severe strains on the Fourth Amendment to the U.S. Consti-tution, which protects private citizens against unreasonable searches of person or property. The possibility of theft of plutonium would also promote the growth of wiretapping, informing, and other covert surveillance in the nuclear industry. In an economy based on plu-tonium, the vision of many nuclear industry advocates, transpor-tation of the fuel would involve vast numbers of people, just as transportation of oil does today. The level of scrutiny required for such an economy led Ayres to conclude, "It is surely within reason to demand that all other sources of energy be proven unworkable or unacceptable and to demand significant long-term reduction in the consumption of energy before implementing an energy program with such dire effects on law and liberty."[27]

This sums up my view of the nuclear industry, though I see a range of "dire effects" beyond those on law and liberty. Although I do not exclude the possibility of limited use of a "once-through" nuclear electric system, in conjunction with conservation and renewable resource use, I do not believe we should go further. Reprocessing is very dangerous to the environment, and Ayres and others are convincing with regard to its threat to liberal democracy. In spite of my guarded optimism, I do remain skeptical that high-level nuclear wastes can be safely disposed of without separating plutonium from the expended fuel. Serious environmental and weapons-related risks thus seem an inevitable adjunct of nuclear power. Another concern of those willing to support the limited use of nuclear electricity is that nuclear energy might ultimately supply a large enough proportion of energy demand that the temptation to recycle plutonium will become irresistible when uranium supplies begin to decline. Future uranium importers, faced perhaps with a hostile and powerful "UPEC," may not be able to resist opening the Pandora's box of plutonium recycling.

Critics of a plutonium economy often sound no more alarming than do the statements of nuclear proponents regarding nuclear industry security. Some advocates of nuclear power are concerned enough about the terrorist threat to society, and to the nuclear industry in particular, that they approve of broadly repressive measures to prevent terrorism. Threats to civil liberties are, of course, a risk of most anti-terrorist activity, but the possibility of nuclear terrorism may invite particularly persistent threats, in part because of widespread public fear of all things nuclear.

Proponents of nuclear power are, of course, very cautious in their public statements about nuclear terrorism. First, they do not wish to invite the very acts they fear; second, they do not wish to frighten the public into opposing expansion of nuclear energy. Nonetheless, one pronuclear member of the U.S. Congressional Joint Committee on Atomic Energy advocated capital punishment for crimes involving nuclear materials and called for psychological testing of large segments of the population, worrying about the "underpaid, underpromoted worker in a reprocessing facility with a large debt and a nagging wife."[28] Clearly many will feel it necessary to monitor the personal, psychological, and financial affairs of nuclear industry employees. It will be hard to disagree and difficult as well to draw the line at a particular group of persons or a particular industry. This threat to privacy and civil liberties (of which there is considerable evidence) sets many thoughtful people against the Faustian bargain of nuclear power—even if they are convinced that the environmental risks of nuclear energy are worth taking.

Lovins' best case against nuclear power is his demonstration that it is the marketplace that has ended the expansion of the nuclear industry.[29] Only in the "centrally planned economies" of France and the USSR is "bureaucratic power sufficient to override . . . economic realities."[30] (Lovins neglects to include Ontario among the jurisdictions willing to defy the economic realities of the nuclear electric industry.)[31] The task of preventing the weapons proliferation that might be associated with the expansion of nuclear power is thus no longer what it was once imagined to be: "nuclear power is simply not commercially viable, and questions of how to regulate an inexorably expanding world nuclear enterprise—the focus of present (proliferation) policy—are moot. The relevant question is rather how to manage, and turn to non-proliferative advantage, the gradual contraction and disappearance of nuclear power under the irresistible force of market economies."[32]

Lovins' case against nuclear power over the decade has shifted from an emphasis on noneconomic problems to an enumeration of the economic weaknesses of the nuclear industry. Lovins' economic nonviability argument predates the spate of defaults on nearly completed nuclear plants. He insisted early on that the nuclear option, even with massive research and development subsidies, simply could not compete economically with simple improvements in energy efficiency. Energy conservation and renewable sources of energy will win in the marketplace, in Lovins' view, if the competition is a fair one.

Fair competition requires that the utilities *charge what new energy sources cost, without averaging them together with already-paid-for sources.* Conservation is cheaper than the new sources of energy, but it is not cheaper than energy sources constructed with the labor, capital, and materials prices of 1900, 1920, or 1950. Fair competition also requires that the full social and environmental costs of all technologies be included in the price consumers pay for energy. If competition took place in this way, the contest would not be as close as it is. But even without such adjustments, nuclear power is failing.

What must be done to make the competition between new hard path energy sources and soft technologies, including conservation, a fair one? Current pricing patterns are holdovers from an earlier era when each new unit of energy was cheaper than all preceding units. Newer, larger hydroelectric dams produced electric power at far lower cost than existing sources of supply. To encourage more rapid development of these cheaper supplies, the largest energy consumers were charged less per unit than were small customers. Incentives to conserve were nonexistent—the more energy an industry used, the lower its average energy costs.

In determining prices for electricity, the lower costs associated with already built plants are averaged with costs of newer construction, in order to keep prices low and demand high. This practice makes sense only if expansion is seen as desirable in and of itself. But nuclear power should be viewed as, at best, a risk worth bearing, certainly not as a goal in itself. Marginal cost pricing (charging users the full cost of new supplies) and flat or inverted rate structures (charging large users as much or more per unit than small users) would raise energy prices considerably for some. The marketplace would then sort things out and teach us to adapt and conserve (although the strategy would include, one hopes, some aid for the poor). The casualties of this market discipline, in Lovins' view, would include the nuclear power industry. Lovins occasionally sounds for all the world like Adam Smith reborn as an environmentalist.

Lovins, in 1980, referred to a 1978 U.S. Department of Energy estimate of the difference between rolled-in (averaged) prices for energy and prices corresponding to the "costlier components of the 1978 fuel mix," which included "Canadian gas, Alaskan oil and recently commissioned power stations."[33] In 1979 OPEC raised its prices to match the cost of all the visible alternatives to their product. World oil and energy prices followed suit. But the price increases were not always passed on fully to the consumer. Some energy prices were still averaged, rather than set at the margin.

Before OPEC achieved much of what Lovins was calling for, the gap between rolled-in and short-run marginal prices in the United States was estimated to be $66.3 billion dollars, $20 billion of which was in the price of electrical sources of energy and $32.3 billion in gas and gas liquids.[34] When oil prices rose, gas and electricity were substituted at prices just below that of oil. The prices charged for gas and for some sources of electricity then approached the marginal cost of production more closely. But even those higher prices were not sufficient to cover the escalating costs of nuclear construction when interest rates shot up.

The increase in demand for all energy sources, including electricity, declined sharply. For five consecutive years there was an absolute decline in demand for oil. And the cost of new nuclear power became so high that *even when averaged* it raised electricity prices to the point where the demand plants were built to meet tended to vanish upon their completion. New orders for nuclear power plants stopped in the late 1970s; by the early 1980s several nearly completed plants were abandoned.[35] With economics on his side, Lovins was heard in the highest government circles. (His earlier arguments involving radioactive pollution and world peace had commanded far less attention.)

Amory Lovins is not interested in the restrained, careful, or limited use of nuclear energy. He wants nothing less than to "put the nuclear genie back in the bottle."[36] The soft energy path and nuclear power are mutually exclusive alternatives to oil; they "exclude each other by logistical, cultural, and institutional competition. . . . Though they are not technically incompatible, they are deeply incompatible in all the other ways that matter, and we cannot do both at once."[37] I find the paths' exclusivity difficult to demonstrate. But let us leave that question aside for the moment.

What is striking about Lovins' perspective is his optimism in the face of problems that have set others to speculating about the end of humanity. Lovins not only sees a set of environmentally benign alternatives to fossil fuels, he sees it in the context of a free market. Government need only remove the economic and political barriers and thereby impose economic reality on those who would promote other options. Creative individuals will then find a thousand diverse, dispersed, creative solutions to our energy problems.

With Lovins' participation or advice SEP studies have been prepared for most developed nations. Perhaps the most advanced has been done for Canada, province by province—it was popularized under the title *Life After Oil: A Renewable Energy Policy for Canada*. An excellent study for West Germany was done by Lovins and several others.[38] For Canada, the best supply options over the fifty-year planning period are energy conservation (economically the best single alternative to oil), wood-based methanol, passive solar, wind, and small-scale hydroelectric power. To understand Lovins' perspective one must grasp the broad purpose, methods, and results of these studies.

All the studies address a single question: is an SEP feasible? Can advanced, high-energy economies function exclusively on energy from renewable sources? In the mid–1970s asking such a question seemed mad. Maybe someday we will turn to solar and so forth, the experts would say, but there are many better options available now. Or, they would argue, the technologies necessary for solar power are off in the distant future, not yet proven. Renewables are interesting as "supplements" but can never be sufficient in themselves. Scientists have even claimed that we left renewables behind more than a century ago for very good reasons: they cannot provide enough energy, when we want it, where we want it, at a cost that would allow our economy to remain at a high level of productivity. Many people still think that the idea of an SEP is irrelevant to any but intellectuals with nothing better to do than speculate on long-term possibilities.

Studies of soft energy paths, therefore, were not designed to address the desirability or likelihood of an SEP. These are largely political matters. SEP studies are almost exclusively concerned with technical and economic feasibility. In developed nations, renewables now provide less than 10 percent of total energy demand. Could they supply 100 percent, not "someday," but soon, in fifty or fewer years? At a reasonable cost, taking into account the future price of oil and other nonrenewable alternatives? Using only proven technologies, technologies that work now? Finally, can it be done without making developed societies over? Will we still have cars, color televisions, dishwashers, washing machines, and so on? The SEP studies were carried out under these conditions. The Canadian study even assumed a threefold increase in per capita air travel over fifty years, despite the fact that this is generally the least energy efficient mode of travel. For country after country it was demonstrated that an SEP is feasible.

Canada is big, cold, and rich and by some measures has the highest per capita energy consumption in the world. In another sense, however, Canada is an easy case for an SEP, because there is a great deal of land per capita and much water, forest, and wind. Renewable energy sources are necessarily dispersed, and in Canada there is a great deal of room in which to disperse sources of renewable energy. But its size also requires that a great deal of energy be expended in transporting both people and goods. In the Canadian study the calculations were done separately for each province and later integrated so that feasibility of an SEP could be demonstrated on a province by province basis. This is a wise strategy for a country noted for its tendencies to provincial autonomy in political, cultural, and economic matters.

Life After Oil, a popular version of the eleven-volume Canadian SEP study, was published in 1983. The study took the population growth rates forecast by the Canadian government and built two different scenarios for economic growth: a high-growth assumption, 4.3 percent per year, and a low-growth assumption, 2.6 percent. In fact, since 1978, the year the study was based on, the economy has not achieved even the low-growth scenario in many years, and the government's population growth projections have declined as well. But slow economic growth has negative implications for a SEP as well as the obvious positive one that less economic activity generally means less energy demand. "A less prosperous society may be reluctant to experiment. And many of the changes in the soft path occur only when the existing capital stock, from cars to factories, is replaced with newer, more efficient designs, something that occurs more slowly with slower economic growth."[39]

This tells us a great deal about SEP energy planning. The necessary changes can take place only over the long term—fifty years is probably a minimum time frame. Nor is feasibility likelihood. Implementing an SEP requires replacing or substantially modifying virtually the whole capital stock of our society—appliances, automobiles, housing, even cities. Some of these things are rapidly enough replaced in any case. But in housing, for example, only about 2 percent of existing stock is added per year. After fifty years, new designs would amount to only 50 percent of all housing, unless many buildings were torn down—and this assumes that 100 percent of new buildings would be of the new designs. A soft energy path is thus feasible in a fifty-year time frame only given a large measure of optimism. A beginning is urgent if energy conservation in an advancing society is not to be replaced by forced limitations on energy use and economic decline. But any hint of Malthusianism is decidedly not a part of Lovins' perspective and style. He fears only desperate attempts to force expansion of hard path options. In Lovins' view only a society in panic would choose nuclear power, so worry about supply is better kept quiet.

In the Canadian study SEP planners made another false assumption—that oil prices would rise at an average rate of 2 percent per year for the full fifty-year period. Writing in 1983, the authors noted, "the recent decline in world oil prices, unless offset by steep future increases, effectively extends the dates of our scenarios by about ten years—so the economy we have described for . . . 2025 . . . would be closer to 2035. This effect would be more marked on the supply side . . . than on the demand side where so much conservation is already cost effective."[40] Energy price increases are very important to the development of an SEP. But it is never suggested that such increases ought to be imposed. In fact, the authors of the Canadian study cautioned that future price adjustments on oil are likely to be difficult: "the scenarios in our analysis may have given a misleading impression of smooth curves seamlessly connecting 1978, 2000, and 2025. In fact, transitions in energy supply and demand . . . occur in a series of shocks, spurts and lulls. Price changes are highly erratic, especially in regulated and cartelized energy. . . . The path may be soft, but it will not be smooth."[41]

The authors of *Life After Oil*, like Lovins, take a noninterventionist approach to economic policy. They seem to fear too much that if oil prices lurch upward, considerable hardship may result. They seem to assume that the market is beyond human control and that regulation interferes with the effectiveness of the market rather than enhancing it.

Can we not demand that an SEP be both feasible and likely and also smooth? Can we not legislate slow, steady price increases for essential energy commodities? If world prices were low, we could raise the domestic price by adding energy taxes, saving the money for the day when subsidies are necessary. Or perhaps we could negotiate a slow, steady increase with oil suppliers. After all, price lurches hurt producers of oil as well. These possibilities lie outside the deliberately drawn boundaries of the SEP studies, but are perhaps more important than Lovins and others have thus far allowed.

That critical comment aside, let it be clear here that Lovins' work has broad appeal. It involves conceptualization of considerable genius. It has been praised by both the moderate political left and the moderate political right, by pacifists and by a former chairman of the U.S. Joint Chiefs of Staff.[42] Lovins has managed to accept the status quo side of much generally contested political turf while challenging radically the way we see the world and its future. Thus much of Lovins' work—and this is true of much of environmentalism in general—stands outside or beyond the left–right political spectrum. Lovins has raised issues that traditional politicians on every side have ignored for years.

The West German SEP study, which the Lovinses helped write, is the only one to attempt systematic extrapolation of its conclusions to the world as a whole.[43] The authors wished to draw conclusions regarding the impacts of an SEP on the accumulation of CO_2, which dangerously affects the global climate. Their opportunity to extrapolate also arose from the following peculiarities of the Federal Republic of Germany (FRG):

1. In the study's base year, West Germany's economy had the highest percentage of GNP derived from industrial production (50.7 percent).
2. West Germany was "already one of the most energy-efficient industrial countries in the world."

3. The FRG has a relatively rigorous climate (in a global comparison).
4. The FRG is a net exporter of "embodied energy" (energy contained within exported goods and services): the processed goods they export, on average, require a higher proportion of energy in manufacture than do their imports.
5. It is more difficult for established, mature, economies like that of the FRG to put new, more energy efficient technologies into place than it is for rapidly developing economies to make such a transition.

This final assumption seems debatable—poorer countries may not be able to add to capital stocks at all, let alone add those of relatively efficient design—but otherwise the case for global extrapolation from the FRG study seems reasonable.

A comparison of the West German and Canadian studies suggests that the latter was indeed conservative in its estimates of the potential of energy efficiency and renewables. For example, the West German study concluded that "despite a 4.6-fold increase in global economic activity during 1975–2080, and despite a doubling of world population, total energy needs for all three future years (2000, 2030, 2080) are *below* the 1975 level, dropping over the next century to less than half the present level."[44] This is based on the use of available, cost-effective technologies. The figures for the FRG in particular suggested that over the full life of the study a five-fold increase in energy efficiency per unit of GNP is possible.

Amory Lovins, perhaps more than anyone else, has grasped the full importance of the energy crisis of the 1970s. He has seen that questions of energy supply and demand underlie most environmental and economic questions. Without ample energy, food production would decline, and feeding even the present world population would become more difficult. Without expanding energy supplies, raw materials production might decline, since we have already used up most of the easily accessible sources. Pollution levels are closely linked to energy production and use, energy sources, and transformations of energy-based materials. As David Brooks put it: "Energy—its production, transportation, and consumption—

is the most significant source of pollution throughout the world, and its adverse effects seem to grow more than in proportion to its use. With the exception of certain (not all) renewable sources, the effects of energy use are either ubiquitous, as with heat losses, or cumulative, as with radiation, or both. It is therefore difficult to see how controls other than limitations on energy use can deal effectively with the problem over the long term."[45]

Amory Lovins and OPEC have taught us that—whatever brief revivals we might experience in the future and however many centuries fossil fuel supplies may endure—the 1970s were probably the climax of the fossil fuel era. Global energy consumption has probably already peaked or will do so soon. Humanity now faces a double transition: first from more to less convenient forms of fossil fuel, and then, or perhaps simultaneously, a move away from fossil fuels. This double transition will be one of the most profound events in human history. But again Lovins, seeking to avoid both panic and Malthusianism, does not describe the situation so starkly.

One cannot, however, understand the ideological significance of environmentalism without realizing that since the 1750s, the beginning of the Age of Coal in Britain, fossil fuel use has spread and intensified almost continuously. The study of fossil fuel use is really the study of industrialization itself. Perhaps, then, Karl Marx's apprehension of human civilization was not materialist enough. Coal, hydroelectricity, oil, and natural gas—not some vague and mysterious "forces of production"—have helped bring about modern social relations, capitalist or socialist. And only hydroelectricity, thus far the least important of these, will see humanity through in the long term. Marx's "superstructure" may or may not rest on the forces and relations of production, on machines and organization. But clearly all these things do rest on something fleeting, on a fragile and temporary gift from the dead plant and animal species of eons past. It remains to be seen whether we can move in an orderly way to a more secure and permanent grounding for what is arrogantly referred to as modern civilization.

Prior to the industrialization of Britain, humans everywhere were dependent on renewable energy sources, essentially wood, wind, water, and sun. Without ever tapping those precious supplies of fossil fuel, stored solar energy, humankind produced the temples of Asia, Bach and Mozart, Shakespeare and Omar Khayyam, mathematics and medicine, Gothic cathedrals, the pyramids, Athens and Rome, and Chinese vases (though the last involved overexploitation of wood, the energy source that sustained the industry). Once the fossil fuel era began, humankind quite quickly became dependent on the most accessible and portable of the high mass-energy-density (MED) forms of nonrenewable energy: conventional oil. This was especially true of those nations that industrialized relatively late. The grand era of oil, it now appears, may prove shorter even than the age of coal. Henceforth humans must move to using less accessible sources of energy and less portable forms of energy. We have, in a matter of decades, used up the largest portion of the high-MED forms of fossil fuel. Nature's achievements of endless millennia will be gone in a flash of human need, ease, and whim.

Should humankind survive the transition from conventional oil, we will come to respect and appreciate the founders of OPEC, whose self-interest has promoted our well-being. Earlier energy transitions, from wood to coal and from coal to oil, took perhaps thirty years on average, but the double transition that faces us now is clearly of a different order. Lovins has demonstrated that the transition to either nuclear energy or an SEP cannot be that rapid, because it is a transition to lower-quality fuels, not higher, from relatively accessible and inexpensive sources to relatively inaccessible and expensive sources.[46] (In this context, nuclear power can be seen as based on a fuel source of such "high quality" that we must build very elaborate and expensive precautions around it.) And this transition, unlike those before it, will be slowed by the massive socioeconomic edifice we have built on impossibly cheap energy sources.

The rapid rise in oil prices from 1973 to 1980 set into motion the beginnings of a transition toward a post-oil and ultimately a post–fossil fuel human society. Few people believe that, given current population levels and standards of living, we can return to exclusive dependence on renewable sources of energy. But Lovins has convinced most environmentalists that such a transition is not only desirable but inevitable.

Lovins has pointed environmentalism in the right direction. Indeed, without his work, environmentalism might never have developed broad ideological appeal. Most environmentalists agree that energy is *a*, if not *the*, limiting resource. But, though energy may bound the human future in many ways, Lovins has shown that energy limitations do not foreclose the continuing development of economy, society, and polity. There will always be modest but adequate supplies of perpetual, clean energy. Even such transition fuels as coal can be burned cleanly in fluidized-bed furnaces.[47] Pollution levels can be kept down. Some forms of economic growth can continue indefinitely, albeit perhaps at a more modest rate. If widespread recycling is utilized to conserve energy, many problems associated with nonenergy resources will also largely take care of themselves. Lovins' perspective thus allows us to begin constructing a politically saleable environmentalism.

But Lovins at times makes the solutions sound a bit too easy. One of the principal weaknesses in his argument is spelled out in Roderick Nash's article "Trouble in Paradise."[48] A leading conservationist whose principal environmental concern is the preservation of wilderness, Nash rejects the prospect of coastlines and mountaintops cluttered with windmills and endless acres of land devoted to biomass-derived fuels. And indeed there have been several other instances of environmentalist opposition to small-scale, renewable energy supply projects.[49] *Life After Oil* concluded that even in Canada, whose population density is one of the lowest in the world, the land needed to supply renewable energy is considerable.[50] Unanswered questions remain. Is small-scale, renewable energy use, in aggregate, still benign? Doubtless more so than coal burned with limited protection and far more so than unlimited use of nuclear power. But might renewable sources not be more benign if used in combination with selected hard path sources, even in some circumstances nuclear power?[51]

These are very difficult questions, but they may well be on the environmentalist agenda in the long term. Even now Nash, for example, prefers some use of nuclear power, chiefly because it can produce a great deal of energy on a small amount of not necessarily scenic land. (A great deal of scenic land is often required to produce, for example, wind energy.) Nash neglects to mention the wilderness disruption associated with uranium mining and uranium mine tailings that has occurred in northern Ontario, northern Saskatchewan, the Black Hills of South Dakota, Colorado, and New Mexico. But his point cannot be ignored. The SEP studies have assumed continuing economic and population growth, but they may have underestimated the long-term costs of that growth. Most of the studies have assumed that total energy use, despite spectacular gains in efficiency, will remain constant. But SEP sources, at present levels of demand, may well produce considerable environmental and economic stresses of their own. For example, there may be competition between biomass for fuel and for food. If an SEP is pursued in a free market, the rich may drive alcohol-fueled cars while the poor go hungry. The greatest environmental stresses may occur on what was once wilderness or relatively unused land. Large amounts of energy can be gathered from wind and sun only by utilizing large areas of land, often areas not presently utilized. Thus even an SEP will involve real costs. Although we cannot fully anticipate what they will be, it serves no useful purpose to ignore them.

Few environmentalists, however, are open at this time to the use of any nuclear power under any circumstances. This is small wonder given the events at Three Mile Island and Chernobyl[52] and the appalling environmental record of the nuclear industry regarding uranium mining and milling and the reprocessing of spent fuel. Nonetheless, Lovins' case that there can be no "middle" path of any kind in the medium to long term remains unconvincing. I am convinced, however, that the environmental costs of renewable energy can be far lower than those associated with using hard path sources of energy exclusively. Even Lovins and the SEP planners may have underestimated the role energy conservation can play. North Americans have squandered energy absurdly for at least several decades now. The countries of Western Europe have built economies and societies of equal or greater strength and comfort on much less energy per capita or per unit of GNP (often half that in North America). Industry after industry has been more energy-efficient per dollar of output; average transportation use has been lower per unit of passenger-distance; for decades units of energy have been used over several times for different tasks. And, as the West German study makes clear, there is still considerable room for improvement. In addition, oil consumption in the United States declined significantly between 1979 and 1983, but GNP continued to grow at a moderate rate. In 1979, for example, there was no growth in energy demand, but a 2.3 percent increase in GNP. Growth in demand for oil only bounced back very moderately amidst exceptional economic growth, following on a large earlier decline in the price of oil.[53] Thus it is clear how modest the SEP studies have been about the possibilities for energy conservation— perhaps they have been too modest.

Much of Lovins' writing, and most of the detailed SEP studies, were done prior to the 1979–83 declines in North American energy consumption. At the time, it doubtless seemed sufficiently radical to call for no growth in energy demand for the ensuing fifty years. Anything else would have seemed too austere, Malthusian, anticapitalist, or just plain depressing. But now there is reason to think that, if improvements in efficiency take place gradually and the North American population stabilizes and begins to decline, further declines in energy demand are possible. If demand declines by 1–2 percent annually over several decades, or at a slower rate over a longer period of time, renewable sources may prove environmentally benign even in the long run. And there is no reason to exclude the possibility of continued economic growth in some forms even in the face of such a limitation on energy demand. Present conservation possibilities include the following:[54]

Transportation
1. In early 1985 the Petroleum Industry Research Foundation predicted that U.S. gasoline consumption would drop sharply by 1990 due to the increased efficiency of new automobiles relative to those being scrapped. With new price and policy initiatives the potential for reducing gasoline consumption, even without a loss of convenience, is enormous.
2. High-speed rail is faster and more fuel-efficient than air travel from city center to city center on trips of less than

three hundred miles. Switching from air to rail transportation for such trips would reduce energy use per passenger mile by at least a factor of 2.

3. Some automobiles sold today use 30–40 percent of the fuel an average new car uses. It might be cheaper to give such cars to the owners of gas guzzlers than to supply their fuel needs from synfuels plants at presently projected costs.[55] Less fuel would be used if more people either lived nearer their jobs or drove to work fewer days per week. In the future more work will be performed at home using advanced communications devices. Few of these possibilities, other than increased automobile efficiency, were envisioned in the SEP studies. But the enormous current need for portable liquid fuel will almost certainly cause environmental problems even if supplied through renewable sources.[56]

Industry and Commercial

1. The more successful steel industries of the world, those that use continuous casting, use far less energy than other steel technologies—one million BTUs less per ton. It has been estimated that by making greater use of recycled scrap and continuous casting, and by reusing process heat, the steel industry could reduce its energy demands by 50 percent by 1995.

2. Returnable bottles use one-fourth the energy of throwaway bottles.

3. The huge Canadian pulp and paper industry, by using wood wastes as an energy source, could become a net producer of energy rather than the largest industrial user of energy in the province of British Columbia.[57]

4. A ton of aluminum can be produced from recycled materials with less than 5 percent of the energy used to produce a ton from raw ore. (Yet forty U.S. states and most Canadian provinces do not have compulsory container deposit legislation.)

5. Ceramic heat exchangers can recover 75 percent of the energy from exhaust gases—they have by no means been installed everywhere possible.

6. Refrigerators can be made 25–50 percent more efficient for less than a hundred dollars per unit. It may now be technically possible to make refrigerators that use virtually no energy.[58]

Building Construction

1. Super-efficient houses have been constructed in the Canadian prairies, a region even many Canadians consider uninhabitable because of its harsh winters. For some of these houses heating costs have been held to only several hundred dollars per year.
2. The holes in a typical residential dwelling total a square yard. Closing up such holes and encouraging use of smaller automobiles, Lovins estimated, could render virtually all U.S. oil imports unnecessary (at 1979 import levels).[59]
3. High efficiency office towers, such as the new headquarters of Ontario Hydro in Toronto or Gulf Oil in Calgary, use only 20–30 percent of the energy that buildings of more conventional design use.[60]
4. Individual rather than block metering of apartment buildings reduces electricity demand by an average of 30 percent: people are motivated to conserve if they can see concrete results. Time-of-day electricity pricing might cause us to think about when we use electricity and allow reductions in utility back-up capacities.
5. Up to 60 percent of the air conditioning needs of commercial buildings is due to the heat associated with lighting. The use of task-specific lighting, more efficient lights that produce less heat, and natural lighting can reduce this demand.[61]

Throughout this century oil has become more and more central to the struggle for wealth and power.[62] By 1970 nearly all the wealthy and powerful nations of the world were net importers of oil. The actions of OPEC provoked the few nations with prospects of energy self-sufficiency to declare that self-sufficiency was an overriding national goal. Only in the United States and Canada, with their broad array of domestic energy options, was this a relatively short-term goal. But by the late 1970s all the governments of the West knew that concerted action to reduce oil imports might reduce the price of imported oil. Since 1980 this effort has been successful, but it may well prove to have been misguided in the long run.[63] Government support for energy conservation was rarely the result of far-sighted acceptance of any Lovinsesque perspective—conservation was primarily a means of defeating the hated OPEC. Lovins has made clear why lower prices for oil are a profound mistake in the long term. Our best future, environmentally and economically, is one of relatively low energy use and the prospect of a world at war is only increased by severe lurches in oil prices.

Declining oil prices, of course, assure more rapid depletion of global oil supplies. A sudden shortfall in oil supplies may goad government decision-makers to subsidize the expansion of the nuclear industry. Or worse, it might encourage one or more nations to fight for their supplies of oil. Energy conservation will seem less important if further declines in energy prices are anticipated. But neither renewable sources nor nuclear power would be sufficient if energy demand in nuclear-armed nations again began growing rapidly. An orderly transition to renewable sources of energy, and a greater likelihood of peace, will be associated with gradual, steady increases in oil prices.

Many economic benefits are possible from the transition to energy efficiency and renewable sources of supply. Employment opportunities would increase and, ultimately, inflation associated with rising energy prices would decline, especially if energy productivity rose more quickly than prices. Some recent inflation has come from the capital costs of large energy projects, which also contribute to pressure on interest rates. And, as Lovins has made clear, energy price inflation is also a function of its nonrenewability—thus, renewable sources may well provide a cushion against inflation.

My claim that employment will increase with renewable energy use flies in the face of the conventional economic wisdom concerning the effects on employment of energy prices and energy use. But studies have shown that many things environmentalists desire, including an SEP, will increase employment. If accepted, this perspective can facilitate political cooperation between environmentalists and others who seek to increase employment. Prior to

Lovins' work and the concurrent and subsequent development of the jobs-environment literature, the environmental perspective seemed only to harm the employment rate; thus there was little basis for hope that environmentalism might become an ideology of wide popular appeal. I summarize here some of the important but little-known literature on jobs and the environment.[64]

Analysts at the Centre for Advanced Computation at the University of Illinois showed that, with few exceptions, most energy conservation opportunities are more labor-intensive than is energy production.[65] John M. Cogan and his associates at the International Institute for Economic Research studied five alternative programs by which the United States might cope with its energy problems. Each of the programs that raised energy prices (e.g., through deregulation of oil and natural gas prices, taxes on energy imports) or mandated decreased energy consumption also increased employment.[66] In the alternative programs, the total direct, indirect, and substitution jobs (which takes into account the shift in consumer spending from energy to other goods and services) is greater than the number of jobs lost by the cut in spending on conventional energy sources. Indeed, there are fewer jobs per dollar spent on conventional energy than on any other commodity—even when the construction of new plants is included in the analysis.[67] Energy conservation causes a shift from higher-wage jobs in the energy industry to lower-wage jobs in, say, the insulation industry. The turnover of capital seems higher in conservation activities than in energy production; and there appears to be a closer relationship between the rate of production and the rate of labor use.[68]

Canadian studies corroborate those for the United States. David Brooks, for example, investigated the short- and medium-term effects of implementing several specific conservation measures and the long-term effects of adopting a zero energy growth strategy. He found that, in the short term, employment gains from energy conservation are far greater than job losses at energy supply facilities. In the medium term, when construction of new or replacement facilities is involved, the employment gains from conservation still outweigh the losses, although the differences are no longer so large. In the long term, full employment and zero energy growth were found to be compatible, but not for all sectors and not without transition problems. In particular, the simulation indicated that the energy supply and heavy construction sectors would likely suffer employment declines.[69]

Many of the jobs put at risk by changes necessary for environmental protection are already at risk from new technologies, or they are in industries in which capital investment per job is so high that an equivalent investment in any other industry would produce a larger number of jobs. The employment typically associated with conservation is "local, low- to moderately-skilled, and concentrated in or near urbanized areas which are suffering the most acute unemployment problems."[70] Of course, some individuals would still suffer. But with compensation of some sort, the transition might require only development of new skills and possibly relocation. Concern over these effects is the best argument for starting now on the transition, rather than delaying until changes must be made more rapidly.

A time-series analysis of the relationship between energy supply and employment by T. Akarea and T. V. Long also concluded that constraints on energy supply would increase employment. Roger Bezdek and Bruce Hannon found that investment in railroads and mass transit equal to that in highways would result in energy savings of 61.6 percent and additional employment of 3.2 percent. Charlotte Ford and Bruce Hannon found a net increase in jobs from major investment in home insulation, even after allowing for the withdrawal of capital from a mix of other industrial sectors. P. J. Groncki and others found that more than ten thousand continuous jobs would be created by substituting wood heat for oil heat in the New England states—not including the employment associated with manufacturing and installing wood stoves. Finally, Sen. Edward Kennedy reported a study by the Public Resources Center of Washington, D.C., which concluded that the development of conservation and renewables could save much money in energy costs and could result in a net increase of 1.8 million jobs. Numerous other such energy-related studies are reported in three major analytic summaries of this work.[71]

Several studies have shown that mandatory refillable container legislation creates jobs. Indeed, both recycling and pollution abatement tend to be labor-intensive. Increased use of public transportation, particularly buses and trains, not only reduces energy demand and air pollution but generates jobs.[72] Reforestation and less chemically dependent agriculture would also probably increase employment opportunities. A broader environmental view can also be taken of employment, one that considers more than questions of energy supply and demand. The Sierra Club and other environmental groups recently proposed an environmental works program designed both to improve the environment and to be both more labor-intensive than the present mix of public expenditures.[73] Proposed projects included railroad construction, national parks improvements, creation of urban parks, and revitalization of city centers.

Environmentalists have made two additional points regarding unemployment. Social expenditures such as those on health, education, welfare, and the arts have relatively low environmental impacts and create a large number of jobs per dollar.[74] That is, a GNP dominated by human services rather than by the manufacture of goods (particularly primary goods) is less likely to threaten the environment and less likely to suffer high levels of unemployment.[75] This is important to a possible ideological association between environmentalism and more traditional progressivism. The final, and perhaps the most important, environmentalist assertion regarding unemployment is also the most direct possible solution to the problem. Work can be redistributed, shared equitably among all who wish to work. Reductions in work time have been advocated by the German Green Party and by several North American environmentalists.[76]

The environmental logic of this proposal has two essential dimensions. First, both automation and information processing use little energy—especially if there is less need to transport people to brightly lit, climate-controlled workplaces.[77] Robots are not afraid of the dark and do not object to heat and cold as much as people. They do not need cafeterias or washrooms. And they use less space per unit of output since they can work around the clock and on weekends and holidays.

Humans set free from labor and drudgery by automation should be encouraged to spend their free time in predominantly low-energy activities. Energy-intensive leisure activities could be made relatively expensive; energy-light activities cheap or free. But people might simply choose to do better those things we already do in our free time. One can almost infinitely improve on such activities as food preparation, athletics, arts, home repairs, education, and childrearing. One might reasonably hope and expect that this would be the outcome of increased leisure.

Yet we fear the future, even those dimensions of it that appear potentially positive. Environmentalists have long been seen as doubtful about all economic and technological advances. The combination of OPEC and the SEP have allowed environmentalists to break out of that mold. Technology and economic growth are not in themselves a threat to the environment. What is needed are the means by which to choose among new technologies—new economic and regulatory policies that will encourage environmentally sound technological decision-making. A modern politics must be at least two-dimensional. Distributive politics, the politics of left to right, must be complemented by a politics of technological choice based on sound environmental values. We must develop political institutions capable of dealing with both kinds of issues.

Environmentalists now have a positive technological and economic case to make, one that is decidedly different from that which might be made by the traditional left or right. It can be constructed in such a way that there will be economic benefits, though not necessarily more money, for most people. I develop this case throughout the balance of this book.

Since Lovins charted the path, environmentalists have become increasingly comfortable with many new technologies and emerging and potential industries. They have become technologically selective rather than hostile to technological advance—demanding the democratic right to define advance, but no longer doubting that advance is possible. Desirable technologies include computers, telecommunications, and the whole array of information industries.[78] They might also include many forms of biotechnology, especially those agricultural advances that reduce dependence on toxic and/or nonrenewable chemicals. Environmentally appropriate biotechnologies might involve some kinds of genetic alteration of plant species, virtually all aquaculture, and many new uses for microorganisms.[79] Obviously environmentalists emphasize the technologies associated with energy conservation and those renewable sources of energy supply that are relatively benign environmentally. But there is no environmental reason to resist advances in automation and robotics.

The concept of an SEP and the ensuing jobs-environment literature have added considerably to the potential political appeal of environmentalism. The clearest appreciation of this fact can be found in the writings of Denton Morrison: "The tradeoffs of environmental features such as clean air, water, and wilderness for economic features such as efficiency, independence of action, profits, jobs and cheap goods and services were apparent . . . from the beginning, as was the potential for corresponding conflict. . . . But in substantial measure these costs either were not anticipated or were underestimated in the 'apple pie and motherhood' definition of environmental concern that surrounded Earth Day." In his assessment, after the 1973 oil embargo environmentalists were on very shaky political ground in terms of these environmental/economic tradeoffs. "Restrictions on offshore drilling, on the Alaskan and other pipelines, on coal burning, and on auto emissions (which in the early 1970s involved technologies that reduced mileage) in the name of environmental protection were factors environmental adversaries could point to as related to the increased oil imports that in turn increased vulnerability to . . . OPEC." Lovins provided "a positive, programmatic proposal for an alternative energy source based on a renewable resource and on productive processes that would simultaneously reduce pollution and increase employment (especially at the lower skills levels), and that argued that economic growth and energy growth could be de-coupled."[80]

Without the perspective provided by an SEP, environmentalism was locked into a politics of negativism and hopeless confrontation with virtually all the organized political forces of contemporary society. It seemed that the further humanity proceeded into the double transition, the harsher such politics would become. When hard pressed, people might endure hardship, but they would not likely vote for those who seemed to advocate it. Amory Lovins, OPEC, and the many individuals making conservation decisions have shown that there is another way out of energy crises, and thereby out of many other environmental dilemmas.

part two

Science, Values, and Ideology:
Environmentalism in Overview

five

Environmental Science and
Environmental Realism

In chapters 2–4 I set out
the principal concerns of the environmental movement: (1) the preservation of wilderness, endangered species, and wildlife habitat; (2)
pollution; (3) the availability of nonrenewable mineral resources; (4)
the ability to produce enough food for everyone; (5) the long-term
adequacy of energy supplies; and (6) the threat of war in a nuclear
age. Each of these problems might involve limits on human numbers
and/or affluence. Modern Malthusians believe that one or more of
these will inevitably slow, stop, or reverse human progress. Obviously nuclear war can do so in an instant. But none of the others,
I argue, involves such an absolute limit. Latitude remains in each,
though not so much as the extreme technological optimists believe.[1]

Solutions to these concerns do not involve Malthusian limits so
much as choices based in a set of environmentalist values. I describe
these values in chapter 6. Suffice it to say for now that environmentalists agree human societies must make these choices soon—
nature will not make them for us. Barring nuclear armageddon,
humanity will survive to face the burden of its collective freedom.
There is no avoiding the fact that collectively we are responsible for
the quality of the world we leave to future generations. That is, in
a sentence, the perspective from which environmentalism as an
ideology proceeds.

This chapter and the two that follow seek to establish a distinctly
and consistently environmentalist basis for making decisions about
these matters. This involves, first, developing the connection be-

tween environmentalism and scientific knowledge. There are two additional components of collective decision-making. First, we must construct and use an appropriate, consistent, and humanly meaningful set of values. Second, we must examine ways to integrate the facts we approvingly call scientific with the values we sometimes pretend are less important. This integration is the essence of the new politics of technological decision-making. Environmentalism can be seen as one coherent perspective on or ideological view of this new politics. It is an ideology deeply based in environmental science and in a coherent set of environmental values. The whole that results provides a distinctive perspective on contemporary political realities. But before examining this ideological whole we must focus on environmentalism and science.

Few doubt now that environmental concerns have significantly influenced the emphases, and even in some cases the methods, of many of the natural sciences. Beginning with Rachel Carson and continuing with the current alarm about acid and toxic precipitation and the greenhouse effect, scientific findings have spawned environmentalism and pushed it forward. Virtually all the matters discussed in chapters 2–4 derive from the environmental sciences. But it is less well understood that science itself has been influenced by the evolution and wide acceptance of environmental values and that environmentalism, in turn, embodies a highly ambiguous and selective appreciation of the scientific world. It is based in science, but its adherents are often deeply hostile toward many of the products of science, even at times toward science itself.

Natural and social scientists have tended to view their roles as scientists and citizens as separate. Environmentalists, in contrast, have generally seen these roles as irretrievably linked. Not since the nineteenth century, when Marx, Engels, and many others sought (so wrong-headedly at times) to blend science and ideology, has there been so explicit an effort in this regard.[2] Marx and Engels erred in part because they made little attempt to distinguish between the historical outcomes they preferred and those predicted "scientifically" using their methods. And environmentalists have tended to use science to extrapolate fearsome futures, assigning to the political process the task of resisting their scientifically demonstrated scenarios. But problems have developed within an environmentalist blend of science and values because the emphasis has been more often on the natural, rather than the social, sciences.

Environmentalism must blend the natural sciences, values, and social sciences in a distinctive way. No particular set of findings in the natural sciences can determine an ideological perspective. Science, as Max Weber put it, is nothing if it is not specialized. Environmentalism is integrative. The findings of the ecological, toxicological, and resource-related sciences must be integrated conceptually, generalized at a level with which many natural scientists are uncomfortable. This process has been attempted most often by social scientists. Before we examine their efforts, however, let us attempt to understand how foreign the outcome of this task may seem to many in the natural sciences.

Environmental Science and Environmentalism

Almost three decades ago C. P. Snow delivered a famous set of lectures wherein he divided the intellectual world into two camps or cultures. "Literary intellectuals at one pole—at the other scientists, and as the most representative, the physical scientists," he said. "Between the two a gulf of mutual incomprehension—sometimes . . . hostility and dislike, but most of all lack of understanding. They have a curious distorted image of each other. Their attitudes are so different that, even on the level of emotion, they can't find much common ground."[3]

Even though environmentalism has clearly been pushed forward by scientific findings, there is a great gulf between environmentalism as a political movement and much of the scientific community. Environmentalists have been hostile to much of what science has offered society.[4] Likewise, many scientists deeply resent the claims and style of environmentalists. The greatest resistance to *Silent Spring*, for example, was based in segments of the established scientific community.[5] This mutual hostility is closely related to the mutual incomprehension outlined by Snow. But the environmental sciences—including ecology, epidemiology, toxicology—may provide a means to bridge the gap. Or these environmental scientists might at least be able to convey messages from one side to the other.

Nonscientists, in Snow's elegant language, have a "rooted impression that the scientists are shallowly optimistic, unaware of man's condition."[6] Scientists, in turn, see literary intellectuals and philosophers as lacking in foresight and peculiarly unconcerned with "advancing the lot" of their fellow men. Most scientists see no reason why the tragic condition of an individual person should impose limits on the future of the human collectivity. The individual condition and the social condition are sharply distinguished. This subtle line between optimism and pessimism is relevant to an understanding of the extent to which environmental issues have altered the scientific perspective. Snow claims the scientist sees it as his or her duty to contribute to the improvement of the human social condition. But an ecological perspective requires scientists to appreciate limits— immutable biological laws that bind humanity and other species. Surely the scientific optimism particularly characteristic of the physical sciences and engineering has been tempered by the growing ecological sensitivity of the life sciences.

Many environmentalists believe that the blind optimism of these physical scientists and the "linear" (nonintegrative, sometimes hyperspecialized) character of their work are at the heart of many environmental disruptions. But Snow would argue that many environmental problems have been caused not by physical science but by the gulf between scientists and humanists—now a separation as well within the sciences themselves. The new sciences of limits are in conflict with the sciences of progress. The sciences, like the whole modern scholarly and intellectual world, have become hyperspecialized. There are myriad gulfs in language and conceptual perspective. Those who build giant hydroelectric dams and conceive nuclear power plants do not know very much about biology. The environmental movement has helped bring together the multiplicity of specializations, but environmentalists have not thought enough about the central cleavage in the scientific community.

This gap involves two alternative approaches to science. One sees science as an enterprise continually allowing humankind to break through apparent limits. Linked to creative entrepreneurship or the power of the state, this type of science has driven human society and history for several centuries. Its optimism and achievements are almost universally celebrated. Environmental science, in contrast, emphasizes both the limits imposed by nature and the costs associated with technological advance. Environmentalists have stressed over and over that there is "no free lunch."

Even Snow, who noted and regretted the gulf between science and humanism, placed himself on one side of the scientific/environmentalist gap:

> "One truth is straightforward. Industrialization is the only hope of the poor . . . .It is all very well for us, sitting pretty, to think that material standards of living don't matter all that much. It is all very well for one . . . to reject industrialization— do a modern Walden, if you like, and if you go without much food, see most of your children die in infancy . . . then I respect you for the strength of your aesthetic revulsion. But I don't respect you in the slightest if, even passively, you try to impose the same choice on others who are not free to choose. In fact, we know what their choice would be. For, with singular unanimity, in any country where they have had the chance, the poor have walked off the land into the factories as fast as the factories could take them."[7]

Rejecting some dimensions of industrialism, of course, is no longer taken to be merely aesthetic. Pollution is more than ugly; environmentally induced birth defects cripple and kill children as surely as hunger does. Some aspects of industrialization are helpful neither to our well-being nor to the poor.[8] More important, one need not reject science or optimism to argue that humankind should no longer do everything it is technologically capable of doing. We can send people to the moon, alter DNA, and destroy the world. We must learn to guide scientific research and application by political decision-making that is sensitive both to the sciences of limits and to a broad conceptualization of the best future for all.

Environmentalism can be seen as a political movement that seeks to impose upon the physical sciences and engineering restraints based on the findings and judgments of the social and life sciences.

In this battle, many disciplines are divided against themselves. In the life sciences we have epidemiology and ecology in one corner, insensitive biological engineering in the other. Steady-state economics faces off against those forms of cost-benefit analysis that apply discount rates to human lives.[9] But environmentalism can also be seen in many other ways. Let us examine how environmentalism and environmental science might help bridge Snow's gap.

Environmentalism involves, in effect, a scientific revolution, a paradigm shift, in the sense developed by Thomas Kuhn.[10] Science can never again be an activity solely devoted to removing humanity from nature, lifting us out of natural limits—for centuries, if not millennia, its implicit goal. Especially beginning with the industrial revolution, science served to separate humanity from nature, developing machines without considering unintended consequences. Science and technology were the means of accelerating economic advance. But environmentalism fundamentally shifts the purpose of science. The new science can continue to advance productive efficiency, but that efficiency must also be seen in organic and ecological rather than merely in mechanistic terms. Productivity must be measured by its long-term sustainability rather than by short-term increases in output.

Environmental science assumes that every new technology introduces undesirable and commonly unanticipated impacts. The scientific gap can be bridged, however, by a neutral concept of impacts, one that takes into account both positive and negative, short-term and long-term impacts. An expanding research emphasis on the negative impacts of science and technology need not diminish our appreciation of their benefits. We must simply acknowledge that every benefit carries costs. Impacts include both economic costs and benefits and a range of other effects which must be measured in terms of noneconomic values. The more we can learn about those values, the more informed will be our technological choices. Both traditional and environmental scientists must acknowledge the necessity of seeking a reasonable balance between positive and negative effects.

The balance reasonable environmentalists seek involves reminding society that unanticipated costs of negative impacts can be severe, even irreversible. This has happened so often that environmentalists seek to reverse the burden of proof regarding safety of new technologies. Proponents of new technologies and substances should be required to demonstrate their safety. In our court system, people are innocent until proven guilty. But new technologies should be seen as guilty until proven innocent.

On the other hand, environmentalists should grant that nothing is absolutely safe, and that technological decisions must involve consideration of benefits as well as costs. Environmentalists would like such decision-making to be more conscious and democratic than it has been. Someone must speak for other species and for future generations, and we all must be willing to accept less economically desirable options when necessary.

Economics is at the heart of decisions regarding the application and evolution of science, and it is central also to the gulf within science. Scientists have been urged toward economic considerations by both private interests and governments of every ideological perspective. Much of humankind has been freed from resource scarcity by a science guided largely by conventional notions of economic progress. This scientific optimism need not now be rejected, but it does need to be guided by a more complex understanding of progress.

That this change is occurring is itself a measure of the economic progress we have made. We have the luxury of thinking beyond ourselves and beyond the present moment. Human survival, in advanced societies at least, does not require more economic expansion. Earlier, human health was automatically benefited by any such expansion, regardless of negative impacts. Now, however, there is a difference between richer societies and better ones, and we can begin to base the structure of science on this distinction.

The gap between environmental and traditional science can be narrowed by new perspectives on both the limits of and the opportunities for economically defined progress. The perspective guiding both science and society must include both positive and negative impacts of human productive activities. It must integrate our understanding of natural limits with the possibility that limits can be altered by human intervention.

Ultimately the resolution of these two dimensions of the contemporary scientific world is as much cultural and political as it is scientific.[11] It involves as well a new understanding of the meaning of progress. To that end I review in this chapter some important concepts, developed by environmentalists, that allow the competing conceptions of science to come together. This reconceptualization of progress is itself rooted in scientific research, but it generalizes scientific findings to a point with which many scientists feel uncomfortable, a level at which it is difficult to avoid the worlds of values and politics.

The Conceptual Structure of Environmental Realism

Environmentalism is probably best understood as a body of ideas that has been developed by integrating the findings of environmental science and environmental values. That integration occurs at a high conceptual level, but if environmentalism is to be a realistic set of ideas, its conceptual structure must be rooted in both reason and science. Science, too, advances principally at the level of conceptualization and theory. Concepts are our means of understanding the world, the very basis of our grasp of reality, and they are important to both the natural and the social sciences. An aesthetic of simplicity and clarity has inspired, informed, and impelled scientific progress. It is thus doubly important for environmentalism to achieve and articulate a broad conceptual overview. This chapter reviews the conceptual progress that has thus far been made.

The first concept we will consider is overshoot, essentially an ecologically informed update of Malthusianism. Garrett Hardin uses the term in association with the concept of carrying capacity, and biologists use it in their study of the population patterns of various plant and animal species. Many species, in many situations, experience a pattern of population overshoot. Populations of deer or rabbits moving into a new habitat or otherwise finding a sudden increase in food supplies may experience overshoot. Bacteria in wine vats also follow the pattern. Sudden access to an abundance of required resources is followed by a population increase that eventually exceeds the carrying capacity of the resource base. A population crash follows; individuals die off until the population is well below carrying capacity.

The concept has been most systematically applied to human societies by William R. Catton, Jr., whose pessimism about the human future seems at times to exceed even that of Malthus or Hardin. Catton argues that the human population is already in an overshoot situation; at this point we can only understand the reality of the situation in order to "refrain from inflicting futile and unpardonable suffering upon each other."[12] His work is so bleak that it has not attained a very wide readership. Catton's argument is captured in these sentences:

> These final chapters provide no magic recipe for avoiding crash. There is none, when overshoot has already happened. It is in acknowledging that unwelcome fact that this book differs most fundamentally from previous ecological analyses. Facing that fact offers indispensable insights. Even writers deeply concerned with ecological aspects of the human predicament have remained strongly fettered by time-honored cornucopian thoughtways; many books have tried to persuade readers that if we will all become ecologically concerned in the nick of time, we may still avert the natural sequel to our excessive success. We *didn't* become enlightened in time for that.[13]

According to Catton, humankind has arrived at a population level that presumes the continued availability of fossil fuels. What once was an abundance of opportunities has been turned by a human population boom into an indispensable requirement for high levels of energy input. There are already far more people than can be sustained without fossil fuels. Catton begins his analysis with George Borgstrom's calculations of *ghost acreage*—the acres of additional farmland needed to replace that proportion of food that is not produced renewably on any given nation's land mass. To this number Catton adds *fossil acreage*, the number of acres needed to grow "organic fuels with equivalent energy content" to fossil fuels. Catton concludes that "the entire 1970 corn crop, converted to alcohol, could have supplied less than 7.5 percent of that year's domestic demand for motor fuel. It would have supplied only 1.27 percent of total U.S. energy consumption."[14] He follows this line of reasoning through to conclude that even if all existing farms were converted to growing corn-for-fuel, only one-fourth of current energy demand would be met—and no acres would be left for food production. Catton does not allow for other sources of renewable energy, including such existing ones as hydroelectricity and wood. He does not allow for the edible mash that would remain from fuel alcohol production or for any increases in energy efficiency. If his calculations are correct, we should be very concerned about the viability of soft energy paths in densely populated and heavily industrialized countries. But his calculations differ sharply from those of Lovins and others who have carefully explored the science and economics of renewable energy.

Catton examines at length the error of accelerating the drawdown of fossil fuels. This acceleration, he argues, merely cuts into our future. We should expect the worst and act accordingly, as if we have already overshot, although we cannot be certain that we have. The more we depend on resources best left for future generations, the more thorough will be the crash, whatever horrible form it may take. In the nearest he comes to optimism, Catton writes, "if crash should prove to be avoidable after all, a global strategy of trying to moderate expected crash is the strategy most likely to avert it."[15]

Catton's pessimism is clearly misguided in some respects. He seems to dismiss the possibility of an SEP, without a direct and detailed rebuttal.[16] He appears to underestimate the ability of non-industrial societies to sustain dense populations. He also underestimates industrial societies' ability to adapt to energy shortfalls.[17] Catton, in short, assumes energy, particularly fossil fuel, to be more necessary for survival than it is. Nonindustrial nations survive very well on 2 percent of the per capita energy used by North America. Canada now produces more than 10 percent of its energy from renewable sources. Even if one assumes SEP analysts have grossly miscalculated, North Americans and others are in considerably better shape than the irrupted blooms on Catton's wine vats.

But in staggering back from Catton's spectacular pessimism, one should not dismiss overshoot as a useful analytic tool. As applied to energy supply and demand, rather than to population sustaina-bility, it is a useful and important concept. Analysts of SEPs have demonstrated that present energy demand can be met using renew-able sources within fifty years. They have not demonstrated that higher levels of demand can be met without severe environmental damage. And it is impossible to demonstrate that fifty or one hundred years from now we could begin to meet present levels of demand. The further fossil fuel stocks have been drawn down, the more expensive it will be to transform societies and their capital stocks in the ways SEP advocates (or, for that matter, advocates of nuclear energy) propose. If energy demand were to increase in the meantime, such transformations might prove impossible.

The concept of overshoot helps us to see where the potential incompatibility of "mixed" energy paths lies. If renewable energy sources or nuclear energy were added to continuing use of fossil fuels, if energy consumption were to expand again through the use of these new sources, it might prove impossible in the future to move quickly enough to a soft path, or even to a nuclear–SEP hybrid. Energy demand might increase to a point that prohibits a transition from fossil fuels without a crash of some sort. To avoid energy overshoot, renewable supplies must back out nonrenewable sup-plies, and increased efficiency must replace demand; it will not merely free supplies to be used elsewhere.

Catton's application of overshoot provides insights, but it is no substitute for the detailed scientific work associated with SEP plan-ning. Nor does it provide much by way of inspiration toward such work. Detailed SEP studies provide an essential response to those who argue the ultimate inevitability of environmentally risky energy megaprojects. Something much better, they claim, is both techno-logically and economically feasible. The science of SEP planning also responds to the bleaker environmentalist vision associated with the concept of overshoot.[18] Bleak visions of the future are not only (hope-fully) unrealistic but also politically problematic. If the future is as desperate as Catton paints it, there is no argument against gambling everything in environmental terms to avoid it.

The perspective inspired by the concept of an SEP, informed by the ultimate danger of overshoot should SEP implementation be long delayed, moves us toward a balanced environmentalist overview. We now understand that means must be found to halt the expansion in total energy demand and then to see that demand gradually declines to the point where it can be comfortably met from renewable sources. A wide variety of further conceptual inquiries follow. What sort of economy will assure such a shift? What sort of society will assure that the evolution would take place in an orderly way? Clearly it is not just energy use that will change—virtually everything about our society and technology will be altered. What kind of society and economy would continue to be guided by the environmentalist concerns listed in the opening paragraph of this chapter? Three additional concepts are environmentalists' best answers thus far. Together they structure a vision neither of doom nor of paradise. This conceptual structure both integrates the findings of the environmental sciences and provides inspiration for further research.

The first of these concepts, the *steady-state economy* (SSE), is in many ways the most interesting.[19] Its very name directs attention away from nature ("out there") to the core of human society and history: economic activity. It provides a necessary link between the natural and the social sciences. Advocates of an SSE argue that economic growth in the developed economies is no longer a desirable goal. Both population and per capita resource consumption should stabilize. Analysis centers on the economic and social implications of this view.

The name *steady-state economy* seems to beg a fundamental question: precisely what is to remain steady? Some argue that GNP ought to remain stable or decline. But GNP is a crude measure. As E. J. Mishan puts it, "an increase in the numbers killed on the roads, an increase in the numbers dying from cancer, coronaries or nervous diseases, provides extra business for physicians and undertakers, and can contribute to raising GNP. A forest destroyed to produce the hundreds of tons of paper necessary for the American Sunday editions is a component of GNP. The spreading of concrete over acres of once beautiful countryside adds to the value of GNP . . . and so one could go on."[20] Mishan's is one of the earliest voices in the debate on the desirability of economic growth. His mid–1960s publication *The Costs of Economic Growth* characterizes modern industrial societies as afflicted with "growthmania" and either unaware of or indifferent to the costs of growth. Mishan is also a very important contributor to the development of cost-benefit analysis—an economic exercise that in some hands has come to be too quantitative (as opposed to qualitative) for many environmentalists. Nonetheless, cost-benefit analysis allowed us to take the important step of acknowledging that all economic activities have costs as well as benefits, and much excellent research has been done on the quantification of environmental costs.[21]

From 1956, Mishan was "repeatedly afflicted with doubts about the value for human welfare of the growing tide of ... economic expansion" that followed World War II. He does not see growth as an obvious and desirable end of economic policy. In the preface to a 1960 work Mishan foreshadows much of the debate between environmentalists and economists that followed from his work: "There is apparently a strong prejudice among research workers against admitting that the unmeasurable effects are likely to be more significant than the measurable ones, and that in such cases, therefore, any conclusions reached on the basis of the measurable effects only are unwarranted."[22] Risk analysis has attempted to fill the scientific gap implied here, so has environmental impact assessment. Most important, however, Mishan's perspective points to the need to shift the burden of scientific proof—new technologies must be guilty until proven innocent. This, of course, requires political decisions, which in turn require that environmentalism achieve great popular and perhaps ideological appeal within contemporary society. But the importance of unmeasurable effects is sufficient to justify transferring such decisions from the realm of experts to the realm of the democratic citizenry.

Against such a prospect is a phenomenon Mishan calls the "flight from reality into statistics."[23] The public is continually pressured to avoid close scrutiny of the obvious costs of economic expansion; they are encouraged to focus instead on statistics—productivity figures, the balance of payments, or overall growth indices. Most people simply assume that if these numbers are rising "we" all must be better off—or if they are not rising as fast as they are somewhere else, we must be doing badly, we are somehow deprived. In this age of communication and quantification, individuals are virtually unable to be content with a decent job and a comfortable life; they cannot relax and enjoy themselves because they are constantly being told that "these are bad times" for Britain or somewhere else. Mishan's portrait of the mood of 1960s Britain rings true in the 1980s as well. People living in economies of staggering wealth, economies every bit as successful as they were last year, feel as if they and their societies are in desperate straits. When such a mood prevails many feel that government should not help the hungry or fund educational institutions and that industry cannot possibly undertake the major expenditures necessary to reduce pollution. Such things are seen as luxuries that "we" cannot afford. But perhaps, it is asserted, we could pay for these things if only there were a 2–3 percent annual increment of economic growth. It is a curious fact that doing as well as last year, or even almost as well, is not celebrated in the rich nations, or for that matter, by rich individuals.

Mishan's discussion of the "no-choice myth"—every nation must "keep up" or it will "not survive"—is fascinating. Technological changes are not intelligently examined to determine whether they improve the society as a whole. Instead, nations are viewed as "power-houses for producing GNP, it is assumed that more of this is better." And with "rapid growth in the popular channels of communication it is more true than ever before that the sheer weight of reiteration rather than the power of reason influences the attitude of the public."[24] Near-universal ownership of color televisions and national newspapers with computer-generated color graphics only increase the "weight of repetition." One suspects that the overwhelming repetition of the pro-growth message is at least partly conditioned by the possibility that its assumptions are either false or less important than they are made out to be.

What reasons are offered to justify the urgency of "our" need for economic growth? In the 1960s, Britain needed to "improve its balance of payments" in order to "protect the pound." In North America and Britain in the 1980s, the needs to "put people back to work," to "become more efficient, like Japan," and to "rebuild national security" are stressed. Canadians and Americans are also told that the economy must expand to "control the deficit." Only economic growth, it is assumed and asserted, can make these things possible. Mishan also noted that growth is said to be needed for the next generation, to reduce poverty in the world, and to provide for the old and the sick. Mishan rebutted all these claims and was at his eloquent best in rejecting the last: "If within these wealthy countries the public conscience is unpreturbed by the existence of a small minority of very poor people, many of whom are too old or too sick to take care of themselves, we might as well admit it. It is hypocrisy to pretend that the only way to help them is to create more wealth by growing faster when, in fact, the share of the under-privileged minority in the annual increment of output is negligible."[25]

In fairness to growth advocates one must agree that in the event of economic slowdown the rich may indeed enhance their disproportionate economic share at the expense of the poor. A deliberate slowing of growth can even be a weapon to stir waning enthusiasm for new spirals of advance.[26]

We must take particular note of the view that rapid economic growth is seen as the only possible way to put young adults to work. Growth is not currently promoted as a benefit for future generations; it is urged to help the "lost generation" in our midst. It is as if no one should look too far down the road for any reason. Business must be freed from regulation now; a "climate for investment" is an urgent item on the political agenda. Few suggest that whatever work is available should be shared more equitably or that leisure time should be expanded for all. Have we not all contributed to the incredible efficiency and productivity that allows the social luxury of extended leisure for much of the population? This has been achieved without any real loss in production. At present the problem is a highly uneven distribution of social and economic security, not the possibility of free time for some. The distribution and involuntary character of such time are the problems, not its existence. Why are people not composing cases for qualifying, rather than spending sleepless nights worrying that they may be next?

This may strike some readers as outrageous, but I suspect it is far less so than was Mishan's case against economic growth in 1960s Britain. The problem with productivity figures in British industry was not, he wrote, so much an old-fashioned style of management and work as a failure to assign sufficient value to frequent tea breaks. In an era of massive unemployment caused in part by the rapid introduction of office automation and robotics, perhaps Mishan's view should be applied completely (see chapter 9).

Mishan outlines the costs of growth and discusses many issues that became hallmarks of environmental science and environmentalism: pollution and noise pollution, the siting of obvious disamenities like airports (the era of hazardous waste treatment facilities had not yet dawned), and excessive highway building and traffic congestion. He opposes private ownership of automobiles, arguing that it is the only way to control urban sprawl and all of the other now better-known costs of the automobile. He argues in a footnote for the "provisional continuation of a taxi service in the metropolis . . . in order to prevent abuses arising from any exemption in favor of privileged groups such as doctors or ministers of the crown."[27]

Such a resistance to modern society sounds outrageous to most contemporary North Americans. For his part, Mishan considers us armed lunatics.[28] But twenty years later, even some North Americans see that GNP growth is not necessarily a measure of social advancement. Of course, neither does every additional increment of GNP necessarily contribute to social decline. Some forms of economic growth reduce environmental damage, either directly or as substitutes for more harmful activities. And a great many activities have negligible environmental impacts and highly desirable social impacts. Much work in environmental science goes toward determining which impacts are more and less problematic. But we need a more subtle means of appreciating conceptually the import of the myriad isolated impacts.

Charles Taylor, the eminent Canadian political philosopher, came very early to an intelligent appreciation of this issue. Environmental concerns, he observed, "spell the end to exponential quantitative growth . . . there are qualitative changes which we understand as growth because we consider the end result more valuable, even though they involve no greater use of material resources." Taylor discusses three essentially harmless forms of growth: "qualitative growth," which involved no greater materials use; "greater economy," production involving reuse of materials or avoidance of materials use; and "short runs of quantitative growth which make use of renewable or astronomically abundant resources."[29]

A few years earlier, Kenneth Boulding used a tidy phrase that captures Taylor's ideas: "energy and material throughputs." This phrase carries the conceptual core of a steady-state economy; indeed, it must be placed at the center of any clear statement of environmentalism. If the energy and material throughputs of the economy can be reduced, other forms of economic growth can be welcomed. Affluence can be measured, for example, in antiques, fine art, high-quality meals, and more durable and intelligent machines. The goals of this sort of economy are efficiency, quality, service, beauty, and intelligence—not volume and mass of new material goods made from new raw materials. In Boulding's "spaceman economy," "the essential measure of success . . . is not production and consumption at all, but the nature, extent, quality and complexity of the total capital stock, including in this the state of the human bodies and minds included in the system. In the spaceman economy, what we are primarily concerned with is stock maintainance, and any technological change which results in the maintenance of a given total stock with a lessened throughput (that is, less production and consumption) is clearly a gain."[30] The principal goal of this economy, although Boulding does not say so, is not necessarily profit maximization.

The classic environmentalist work *A Blueprint for Survival* uses another phrase to characterize the same change in economic thinking: conversion from "flow economics" to "stock economics."[32] It proposes a number of policy measures designed to minimize raw materials use and thereby to conserve nonrenewable resources and reduce pollution. These measures included (1) a raw materials tax proportionate to the availability of the material in question; (2) an amortization tax proportionate to the estimated life of a product; and (3) a power (energy) tax on the amount of "power" used in a product.[33] The first tax is the opposite of the depletion allowances beloved by pre-OPEC American government and the extensive subsidies granted to raw materials extractors in Canada and other countries.[34] The second tax might be difficult to administer, though the intent is environmentally sound. More and better consumer education and product testing might serve the same purpose. The third tax was imposed quite effectively in the 1970s by OPEC. One can only wish that initially it had been somewhat more gradual, and then predictably and continuously increased.

The meaning of the concept *steady-state economy* now should be clear. The most widely cited definition of the term is that of Herman Daly, who describes an SSE as "an economy with constant stocks of people and artifacts, maintained at some desired, sufficient levels by low rates of maintenance 'throughput,' that is, by the lowest feasible flows of matter and energy from the first stage of production (depletion of low-entropy materials from the environment) to the last stage of consumption (pollution of the environment with high-entropy wastes and exotic materials)." Daly defines both GNP and SSE in terms of physical commodities, but SSE is "defined in terms of constant *stocks* (a quantity measured at a point in time, like an inventory), not *flows* (a quantity measured over an interval in time, like annual sales)." Daly does not see the possibility of further *desirable* growth in GNP: "The steady-state perspective seeks to maintain a desired level of stocks with a minimum throughput, and if minimizing the throughput implies a reduction in GNP, that is totally acceptable."[35] In other words, throughput minimization, for Daly, is far more important than GNP maximization. He does not argue for twin goals of throughput minimization and GNP maximization.

Economic growth (in GNP terms) in Daly's conception of a SSE seems unlikely. Daly's SSE society might improve in other ways, but once a "desired level of stocks" were attained, conventionally measured economic activity would probably remain steady or decline slowly. The reasoning behind this conception of an SSE becomes clearer when one looks at Daly's marvelous concept of "angelized GNP." Discussing the idea of an economy based more and more on services, and less and less on goods, Daly described it as approaching "non-physical 'angelized GNP.' " In his view such a prospect was largely an illusion:

> While it is true that some activities are more throughput-intensive than others, it is not clear that these activities are always services, nor is it clear that the differences are very great once

indirect effects are incorporated . . . . That most services require a substantial physical base is evident from casual observation of a university, a hospital, an insurance company, a barber shop, or even a symphony orchestra. Certainly the incomes earned by people in the service sector will not all be spent on services but will in fact be spent on the average consumer basket of both goods and services.[36]

In assuming an inevitable link between SSE and GNP restraint, *Blueprint for Survival* upholds a view similar to Daly's. But its own recommendations for energy and materials taxes seem designed to allow such links to be broken. *Blueprint* asserts that "Gross Domestic Product (GDP), which is population multiplied by material standard of living, appears to provide the most convenient measure of ecological demand."[37] This flies in the face of Commoner's central point in *The Closing Circle*, that technological choices rather than population and affluence are at the heart of environmental problems. Lovins' work also contradicts *Blueprint*'s claim. A third potential response to the claim that GNP growth itself is a problem is that which Daly belittles with his phrase "angelized GNP." But Daly's assertion is made without sufficient evidence. The expansion of human services, especially if they replace other forms of economic activity, will likely positively affect the environment. Human services do not generally require much energy or material throughput. Why not allow them to expand to take up as much of the GNP as possible? The fourth possible response is the most straightforward: pollution abatement technologies, energy conservation, and renewable energy production all have a long way to go, and these activities too contribute to GNP growth.

A fifth response is possible to the assertion that economic growth and environmental damage are inevitably linked. In the long run there is some connection—not a one-to-one relationship, but a complex, positive relationship. Inevitably, some percentage of economic activity will be goods-related, and nearly all goods production will result in some environmental harm. Infinite economic growth is probably impossible on a finite planet. But there is one nonimpact, highly desired "good" that can be traded for expanding GNP. These trades can be legislated or developed on an individual basis; day-by-day or over a lifetime, by all producers of GNP, rich or poor. The good is, of course, free time.

Advanced communications and automation technologies "produce" time with a minimum of environmental impact. Time can also be produced by decreasing energy and material throughputs or by legislating additional holidays. Filling this leisure time is far easier for most people than our society and its leadership cares to admit. Filling the time without increasing energy and material throughputs may also be easier than one might expect. A little human ingenuity and entrepreneurship, especially on the part of educational institutions, symphony orchestras, the telecommunications industry, and suppliers of low-equipment recreation might suffice.

More time is also needed for many so-called "alternative" technologies and techniques: small-scale, "organic" food production and processing, public transportation, recycling by means of separation at source, and high-level maintenance of homes and machines necessary for energy-efficient functioning and durability. The time for both expanded leisure and expanded maintenance functions must come from reduced work time. Highly equitable distribution of available work time is crucial to the social impact of such a change.

In summary, limits on the expansion of energy and material throughputs, rather than on the expansion of GNP, seem the better goal. One wonders why so many analysts assume that these march in lockstep. The authors of *Limits to Growth*, as well as Ophuls and Heilbroner, made such an assumption; it lies behind the deep gloom of many environmentalist authors. Although there is, of course, a connection between the two meanings of "steady state"—limiting throughputs would restrain GNP growth in comparison to the growth rates that could be achieved given infinite energy and materials. But this should not be alarming news to anyone but economists. A society that forces growth in the demand for energy and materials beyond the levels that can be sustained in the long run is, simply, imprudent. A society that forces GNP growth at any cost, in any form, is, environmentally speaking, inappropriate. An already comparatively wealthy society that does such things is both stupid and greedy. But neither the world nor the capitalist system is yet at the precipice. Growth in GNP can continue if the forms of growth are carefully selected. The selection process may or may not require the detailed intervention of government; a short list of interventions would be an excellent start:

1. Control of the price of energy, or even control only of dominant energy forms, to assure that energy prices will rise slowly, steadily, and continuously
2. Controls on average work time, to assure full employment, or something near to it
3. Environmental protection measures of the sort most developed economies have been moving toward for twenty years or more, with more stringent and more consistent enforcement.

Within such conditions, a variety of economic systems can continue to function. And whatever economic, that is, GNP growth that can be achieved should continue. Growth may not reach 5–10 percent per year, but such expansion is not needed in rich countries. Nor would slow growth or even economic decline be a cause for alarm. The myth of urgent need for economic growth has so infused our society that a more restrained future seems terrifying at first glance. One can only hope that more people will think their own way out of this assumption.

Gideon Rosenbluth of the University of British Columbia took a calm and distanced view of the economic growth debate in 1975, writing, "A surprising feature of the controversy is that many participants write as if the choice were between exponential growth, i.e., growth at a constant proportionate rate, and no growth at all— 'zero growth,' and that this all or nothing choice applies not only to the aggregate but also to its components."[38] This is the key to the double meaning of SSE. Ultimately, economic growth may cease. All will be "angelized" except that which is sustainable from renewable sources of energy supply. Materials also will either be renewable or will come predominantly from renovation, repair, reuse, or recycling. But when this will happen is unknown to environmental science—so too, critically, is the amount of energy that can be obtained from sustainable sources, as well as the GNP that can be supported by that energy supply. It is certain, however, that in North America an economy larger than but different from the present one can be sustained with less energy. And, if SEP analysts are not off the mark, some reasonable proportion of present demand can be supplied from renewable sources without intolerable levels of environmental damage.

Some components of the economy can expand very rapidly. Others might stop growing. Still others might contract. The total might grow slowly, perhaps, as Rosenbluth suggests, at a declining rate; or at a slow and steady rate for a long time; or perhaps unevenly. Or economic growth might halt, but the quality of life could continue to advance and few would then care very much about economic growth. Within an economy bounded by the sort of restraints environmentalists might choose to impose—in the name of health, sustainability, or prudence in a nuclear-armed world—a considerable range of economic outcomes remains possible. The continued doubling and redoubling of energy and material throughputs will soon no longer be possible; nor is releasing toxic substances into the air, water, and land advisable; nor is the elimination of wilderness prudent. Those, essentially, are the limits that environmental science, broadly defined, suggests. Within those limits, all but the most fragile of economic systems can continue and prosper—*if* the conditions (limits, choices) are imposed sooner rather than later.

This reasoning rebuts some of the most gloomy and determinist environmentalist views of the 1970s. Heilbroner concludes that a stationary capitalism, if well managed, "would not seem to present insuperable problems . . . insofar as those problems concerned the maintenance of employment or aggregate purchasing power." But an SSE need not be "stationary," even if resources were stretched to their absolute limits, which I have argued is not likely to happen. Heilbroner worries about a capitalist system in the "absence of an expansionary frontier," and is concerned that in a nongrowth system there would be no way "to satisfy the demands of the lower and middle classes for higher living standards, while protecting the privileges of the upper groups. The solution has been to increase the output of the economy, thereby providing absolute increases in income to all classes."[39] But, again, SSE does not necessarily entail no

GNP growth. Further, even without economic growth, individuals could experience rising standards of living so long as the young began earning at a low level. This situation is commonplace today. Of course, exploitation of youth is not necessarily the best solution. Indeed, one might argue that middle-aged people are more appropriate candidates for semi-voluntary leisure than the young.

Heilbroner and others writing in the early 1970s did not see the many ways real economic growth could continue if energy and material throughputs remained steady or even slowly declined. We need to go a bit further than the view with which Heilbroner ends his third chapter:

> Thus, whether we are unable to sustain growth or unable to tolerate it, there can be no doubt that a radically different future beckons . . . .In place of the long-established encouragement of industrial production must come its careful restriction and long-term diminution within society. In place of prodigalities of consumption must come new frugal attitudes. In these, and other ways, the "post-industrial" society of the future is apt to be as different from present-day industrial society as the latter was from its pre-industrial precursor.[40]

It is clear that Heilbroner believes growth is directly tied to production of energy and processing of resources. But he does not go far enough. The task is not necessarily to reduce the level of industrial activity, but rather to change it—substituting smaller, more complex, more durable industrial products for larger, simpler, less durable ones.

Paul Hawken captured this sort of change in his popular 1983 book, *The Next Economy*. Hawken speaks of an "informative" economy replacing a "mass" economy (*mass* describing both material volume and the lack of product individualization). The new economy will be based on products that are more carefully designed, more useful, more durable, easier to repair, lighter, and stronger. They will also consume less energy. "The mass economy is being replaced by an economy based on the changing ratio between mass and information contained in goods and services. Mass means the energy, materials, and embodied resources required to produce a product or perform a service. While the mass economy was characterized by economies of scale, by many goods being produced and consumed by many people, the informative economy is characterized by people producing and consuming smaller numbers of goods that contain more information."[41]

In the new economy, instead of driving large and not very durable automobiles to the movies, individuals may use well-made video-cassette recorders to tape films broadcast while they are asleep. Their automobiles will last longer, first because they are used less often, and second because durability has become an important criterion in the purchase of manufactured goods. Computers provide access to the world of information; one is just as likely to purchase wisps of energy and data as material objects. As Heilbroner saw, the economy of the future will be profoundly different. But it will not necessarily be smaller in economic terms—which are a measure of what is scarce and what is valued. Durable objects in a society with a steady population will be traded and traded again. What is manufactured will be less often an object than an idea, or proportionately less an object and more an idea. This suggests economic decline only if one is fixed on the forms economic growth took in the mass industrial age.

The concepts of energy and material throughputs and SSE allow us to integrate a very complex assortment of data, to shift from the world of scientific detail to that of political economy, policy and ideology. These concepts and the forms of analysis they suggest can serve as guides to applied, and even relatively pure, sciences. Just as the social science of economics once urged the natural sciences and engineering into new directions, in the era now upon us other sources of extra-scientific or social scientific inspiration are necessary. Only in understanding the world in these new conceptual terms can scientists and the agencies that fund them place into proper perspective the importance of technological breakthroughs in such areas as energy and materials conservation, product durability, toxicology, or biologically based pesticides. Only in the complex calculations of SEP feasibility—both technological and economic—can we come to understand the collective human condition and bridge the gap between the scientific and humanistic cultures, and between technological science and environmentalism.

Two other attempts were made to summarize the key characteristics of society and economy anticipated and/or advocated by environmentalists. Both are at least potentially more adaptive,
complex, and optimistic than either overshoot or SSE. The concept
of the conserver society is more subtle and less ambiguous than SSE,
but somewhat overcautious in its original outline.

The concept of the conserver society was popularized by the Science Council of Canada in its all-time best-selling publication, *Canada
as a Conserver Society: Resource Uncertainties and the Need for New Technologies*. The best summary of this concept is the carefully developed
definition contained in the report:

> A Conserver Society is on principle against waste and pollu-
> tion. Therefore it is a society which
> —promotes economy of design of all systems, i.e., "doing
> more with less"
> —favours re-use or recycling and, wherever possible, reduction
> at source;
> —questions the ever-growing per capita demand for consumer
> goods, artificially encouraged by modern marketing techniques,
> and
> —recognizes that a diversity of solutions in many systems,
> such as energy and transportation, might in effect increase
> their overall economy, stability, and resiliency.
> In a Conserver Society, the pricing mechanism should re-
> flect, not just the private cost, but as much as possible the total
> cost to society, including energy and materials used, ecological
> impact and social considerations. This will permit the market
> system to allocate resources in a manner that more closely re-
> flects societal needs, both immediate and long term.[42]

This definition includes many of the goals of environmentalism and
many of the findings of environmental science, and it also suggests
means by which these goals might be achieved, such as full-cost
market pricing and restraints on modern marketing techniques.

However, it should be noted that the paragraph skirts the question of population level, probably because this is an issue about
which even quasi-autonomous agencies of government are cautious.

Indeed, the *Conserver Society* is cautious throughout. It points out that the conserver society "questions the ever-growing per capita demand for consumer goods," but it lays more stress on how a conserver society would provide enhanced opportunities for many business sectors.[43] Obviously the authors sought broad support for their concept, and they were indeed successful in articulating an intelligent "centrist" environmental position.[44] It must be recalled in particular that the Science Council is an agency of a government that has for several centuries promoted an economy based on resource exports. The notion of a society based on resource use restraint is, in Canada, at least novel, if not subversive.

The *Conserver Society* sidestepped the issue of nuclear power. But, although the report did not explicitly mention renewable energy sources within the definition of a conserver society, the authors emphasized them throughout the report. Pressures within the government and the scientific community may have contributed to this seeming discrepancy. In association with the publication of the *Conserver Society*, the Science Council engaged Amory Lovins as a consultant and some years later published an excellent review of renewable energy technologies.[45]

The conserver society seeks to "avoid waste and pollution" and to alter the economy in order to maximize reuse of resources, even when the particular resource is not in short supply: "Materials that are inherently abundant, such as iron, aluminum, silicon, carbon, calcium, magnesium, sodium, cannot be regarded as globally limited, from the standpoint of depletion, even in the long term. Their excessive use, however, still presents costs, in the form of energy consumption, environmental impacts, and the other costs mentioned above. There is, therefore, still a strong case for conservation and more efficient use." It rejects the notion that conservation means "going backward" in time or that it entails decreased prosperity. "To suggest that moving toward a Conserver Society means regression, or moving 'back to the woods,' is totally misguided."[46]The report both emphasizes new business and employment opportunities and focuses on the meaning of Pierre Dansereau's excellent phrase "joyous austerity." The *Conserver Society* captures the conceptual meaning of environmentalism; it is an elegantly simple blend of science and values.

A 1983 follow-up to the *Conserver Society* clearly placed the conserver society in a centrist position on economic growth.[47] It noted with enthusiasm a 1979 public opinion survey by the Canadian Ministry of the Environment, which indicated wide public support for "an alternative involving continued growth but also involving resource conservation and recognition of environmental limits."[48] This option fell between more stringent conserver options (including an SSE) and more status-quo or growth-oriented options. One suspects a bit of a have-one's-cake-and-eat-it-too factor in play here, but it is just as reasonable to attribute to the public an inclination to intelligent moderation. The point is that environmentalists and the wider public may come to similar positions through concepts like the conserver society.

The Conserver Society Revisited took a position generally supportive of both biotechnology and electronics, even associating both these technologies, and the conserver society, with the ongoing transformation of industrial society. Thus the Science Council's position is close to that of Hawken. *The Conserver Society Revisited* also linked its proposed model for socioeconomic evolution to Nikolai Kondratiev's theory of economic long waves.

> It has been suggested by numerous analysts, both within and outside Kondratiev's theoretical framework, that a few of the new technologies—biotechnology, microelectronics, computer-assisted design and manufacturing—will be basic to the continued economic viability of industrial societies. These technologies are also strongly compatible with the transition to a Conserver Society. To these technologies should be added, from a Conserver Society perspective, those of improved energy efficiency, renewable energy supply, and resource recovery and separation.[49]

This is indeed far from the view that economic growth is impossible or undesirable. It is also a long way from the pervasive gloom of the mid–1970s environmentalists. A "new vulnerability" is seen in industrial economies, but the conserver society as conceptualized here suggests that the worst outcomes, both environmental and economic, can be avoided. I share with these authors the view that the energy and resource limitations we face will not lead to a static society. On the contrary, they may propel many aspects of the socioeconomic transition that is already occurring. (I do not, however, share the extreme optimism of such analysts as Peter Drucker, who is so happy with recent declines in energy demand and in the price of raw materials that he forgets fossil fuels are not a renewable resource.)[50]

The fact of nonrenewability stands at the center of the last conception of environmentalism and environmental science that we will discuss: the *sustainable society*. The cover of Lester Brown's book summarizes this perspective: "We have not inherited the earth from our fathers, we are borrowing it from our children."[51] Rather than building his concept of environmentalism around avoidance of waste and depletion, Brown chose to emphasize the notion of sustainability, the maintenance and use of the earth's renewable resource base. He stressed the protection of land and soil quality, sustaining biological resources against the pressures of overpopulation and industrialization, the use of renewable energy sources, and the need for population stabilization. In combination, *Building a Sustainable Society* and *Canada as a Conserver Society* convey virtually all the major themes rooted in the findings of the environmental sciences. The two concepts of sustainable and conserver societies together capture the essence of moderate environmentalism.

The notion of a sustainable society has recently been effectively linked to some of the more traditional concepts of economic theory by Robert Hamrin in *A Renewable Resource Economy*. Hamrin seeks ways to bring economics back to its base in natural resources, to develop what he calls "genuine supply-side economics." Hamrin, like Brown, takes a moderate environmentalist position on economic growth: "The concept of sustainable growth encompasses the necessity of continued economic growth to meet basic human needs around the globe while also underscoring that the growth must be of such a nature that it can be sustained indefinitely by respecting nature's boundary conditions."[52] He goes on to note that the concept of sustainable growth should address issues of intergenerational equity, must determine sustainable rates of regeneration of renewable resources and encourage recycling to the point where virgin nonrenewable resources merely supplement existing resource stocks. The capacity of the environment to absorb various kinds of pollution must continuously be taken into account as well. Traditional economics has too often treated environmental issues as externalities and ignored resource issues by blithely assuming that the opportunities for substitution were infinite.

Particularly useful is Hamrin's discussion of "rationality" as used in traditional economic analysis. "Rationality implies a degree of foresight about future gains and costs and an ability to weigh them against each other which are just not possessed by the economic actor. Belatedly, we are recognizing that in a world of uncertainty . . . human economic behaviour is much more irrational and erratic than that assumed in a theoretical world of equilibrium." Nothing in the economic world is more uncertain than the extent of future resource scarcities. Future supply, demand, and price cannot be predicted with accuracy. Hamrin quotes Allen Kneese, who argues that this uncertainty "creates a systematic incentive to produce too much of a nonrenewable resource in the present at the expense of production in the future."[53]

Traditional economics makes many false assumptions about market efficiency, but none is more important than this one. We must discover ways to leave in place the real efficiencies of markets while inserting nonmarket values such as intergenerational equity and sustainability. Futures markets, unfortunately, only work well under conditions of limited uncertainty. But in some matters, assumptions that err on the side of stability must be made. Energy price increases, for example, should perhaps be imposed politically, along with increases for other key nonrenewable resources. That done, the market may be the best means of sorting out the consequences—at least for those who have a range of options.

To the Conserver Society's "joyous austerity" Lester Brown added two other important phrases: "voluntary simplicity" and "conspicuous frugality." Each suggests that environmentalism involves nothing less than an attempt to alter the value structure of modern

Western society. Environmentalism thus conceived calls for more than economic efficiency and the most obvious policy consequences of the environmental sciences. It articulates and promotes a set of values higher than traditional economic values, be those private or collective, accumulative or distributive. Economic values are not rejected outright by other than a minority of environmentalists. Indeed, some claim that an environmentalist political economy would result in enhanced economic performance, especially in terms of employment levels and long-term resource management. However, in the end environmentalism seeks to return economic values to a secondary status. Economic success cannot be purchased at the price of ecological insecurity. Economic growth becomes, for environmentalists, a means rather than an end.

six

Environmentalism as a System of Values

As we saw in chapter 5, many of the central themes of environmentalism can be expressed in terms of integrative concepts. We have also seen that environmentalism both derives from scientific findings and provides a new perspective on the natural sciences. Environmentalism can be understood in part as a new scientific paradigm. But it can also be seen as a set of values or as a political ideology (discussed in chapter 7). Of course, if environmentalism is a political ideology it must include a set of values and claims regarding the role of science in society (however *science* might be defined). But it is important to place considerable, if not primary, emphasis on environmentalism as a set of values.

In agreement with Samuel Hays, I see environmentalism as a potential revolution in social values, a broad change associated with post-World War II economic developments in the wealthy nations. As Hays put it,

> We are at a stage in history when new values . . . have emerged to give rise to new preferences. These are characteristic of advanced industrial societies throughout the world. . . . They reflect two major and widespread social changes. One is associated with the search for standards of living beyond necessities and conveniences to include amenities made possible by considerable increases in personal and social "real income." The other arises from advancing levels of education which have generated values associated with personal creativity and self-development, involvement with natural environments, physical

and mental fitness and wellness and political autonomy and efficacy. Environmental values and objectives are an integral part of these changes.[1]

Some environmentalists, particularly in the mid–1970s, felt obliged to deny that environmental values had a significant political dimension. Political solutions were rejected in favor of personal changes, particularly in one's habits as a consumer.[2] Achieving environmental goals solely in this way is only marginally more plausible than achieving socialism through large-scale voluntary charity.[3] Nonetheless, environmentalism as a set of values has an autonomous logical validity apart from the political process, and it ought to be set out separately from environmentalism as an ideology. More important, since politics itself rests on values—it has been defined as "the authoritative allocation of values"—one cannot see clearly the political implications of environmentalism without delineating first its value priorities.[4]

What, then, are the central value assertions of environmentalism? The following have consistently been emphasized in the writing of environmentalists and are implicit in their actions.[5]

1. An appreciation of all life forms and a view that the complexities of the ecological web of life are politically salient.
2. A sense of humility regarding the human species in relation to other species and to the global ecosystem.
3. A concern with the quality of human life and health, including an emphasis on the importance of preventative medicine, diet, and exercise to the maintenance and enhancement of human health.
4. A global rather than a nationalist or isolationist view.
5. Some preference for political and/or population decentralization.
6. An extended time horizon—a concern about the long-term future of the world and its life.
7. A sense of urgency regarding the survival of life on earth, both long-term and short-term.
8. A belief that human societies ought to be reestablished on a

more sustainable technical and physical basis. An appreciation that many aspects of our present way of life are fundamentally transitory.

9. A revulsion toward waste in the face of human need (in
   more extreme forms, this may appear as asceticism).
10. A love of simplicity, although this does not include rejec-
    tion of technology or "modernity."
11. An aesthetic appreciation for season, setting, climate, and
    natural materials.
12. A measurement of esteem, including self-esteem and social
    merit, in terms of such nonmaterial values as skill, artistry,
    effort, or integrity.
13. An attraction to autonomy and self-management in human
    endeavors and, generally, an inclination to more demo-
    cratic and participatory political processes and administra-
    tive structures.

Needless to say, not all environmentalists accept all of these values.
Most environmentalists find many of these values central to their
outlook on life, but the list is not a catechism.

The first three items on this list are closely linked. The first, which
can be summed up in the word *ecology*, is the most basic of environmental tenets. The second and the third items are corollaries of
the first. But the fourth and fifth, and sixth and seventh items might
seem to contradict each other. The eighth and ninth values are compatible, and the tenth, eleventh, and twelfth follow in part from
them. The thirteenth value can be seen as the most acceptable and
practical means to achieving the previous twelve. This kind of analysis brings us to a more complete understanding of environmentalism and its potential as a more consistent and coherent set of
values and, thus, a stronger political movement. Let us consider
these values one at a time.

In chapter 2 we saw that the first of these environmental values
links environmentalism to its historical antecedent, conservationism.
Since the latter half of the nineteenth century conservationism has
been an influential intellectual and political movement, springing
from deep concern with threats to the quality and even the viability

of the natural world, especially the forests of Europe and North America. The ideas of such people as Henry David Thoreau and John James Audubon were widely communicated and shared. The political initiatives of John Muir, a preservationist, and especially Gifford Pinchot, a rational planner, were important in high political circles. The conservation movement advanced the careful, efficient use of natural, renewable resources, while radicals like Muir looked beyond resource use—we owe the existence and much of the continuing beauty of North America's National Parks to them. But mainstream conservation reflected the gospel of efficiency so central to the thinking of the Progressive Era.[6]

Environmentalism goes beyond conservationism in several important ways. As David Brooks and Doris McMullen put it, conservation focuses on the "resources being used as raw materials for industry—in other words, on what was going into the production system."[7] What these authors call the "third" environmental movement (the first two comprising what I call conservationism) shifted concern from the inputs to the discharges of production systems. Pollution, environmentalists pointed out, damages the biosphere's ability to sustain life, is poisonous to humans, animals, and plants, and destroys resources. Environmentalists think in ecological terms, seeing a threat to any one species as a threat to the whole web of life. Many of humanity's intentional and unintentional interventions, environmentalists maintain, are not only immoral or wasteful, but suicidal. The continuity and diversity of the web of life are essential parts of our being, morally, spiritually, intellectually, and physically.

One consequence of this view is that environmentalists, in defending human health and ecological well-being, demand a shift in the burden of scientific proof regarding the safety of chemical substances. Suspected pollutants and toxic substances, they argue, must be presumed dangerous to the ecosystem or to human health until they are demonstrated safe. Not only reverence for life but the fact that errors in such matters often carry irreversible consequences require that we err on the side of safety, not on the side of risk.

Humanity is not above nature—we are a part of the natural world. As living beings, we are vulnerable. And we are the only species whose activities put at risk virtually all life as we know it. This destructive power has several dimensions, including nuclear war, toxic wastes, and climatic alteration. The simple weight of our numbers and our needs for space and food also threaten the existence of thousands of species of plants and animals. Our new powers place on us responsibilities that seem beyond our present moral capacity. Thus perhaps the first priority of environmentalism is the rapid development of a global ecological consciousness. Difficulties with such an effort lie in the fact that such a consciousness often clashes with the heretofore almost universal support for unrestricted economic growth.

Perhaps the clearest single expression of this central value of environmentalism can be found in John Livingston's *One Cosmic Instant*. Livingston, one of Canada's leading naturalists, makes clear the error of imagining that the human species is somehow separate from nature. Western society, he argues, has consistently given every appearance of indifference to the nonhuman environment. Species after species has been driven to or near to extinction and more are threatened every day. But "most significant of all, perhaps, has been the unchanging traditional assumption that although the loss of these animals may well have been regrettable, it was inevitable and unavoidable in the context of the advancement of human progress. It was sad that these things had to happen but, after all, what was at stake was human welfare, and in the final analysis human welfare comes first. That's only 'natural.' "

Five hundred years later, humanity still has not learned the lesson of Copernicus' finding that the earth and the solar system revolve around the sun; the sun does not revolve around "our" planet and our species. We must depart, Livingston concludes, "either from the narrow and egocentric cultural course we have adopted, or . . . from the blue planet itself. If we are not yet capable of identifying the specific threads in the fabric of our beliefs which have sustained the entire tapestry upon which the myth of human dominance is emblazoned, then it may be too late already."[8]

Lynn White, Jr., and others have traced the roots of that myth back into the Judaeo-Christian past.[9] Humanity has given itself dominion over the beasts of the field and over everything else on this planet. This arrogant self-appointment is rooted deep within our religious, philosophical, and ethical past. William Leiss' *The Domination of Nature* probes for the origin and meaning of the assertion of human mastery over nature. He finds it commonly associated with the belief in scientific rationality and "linked both logically and historically with capitalist or bourgeois society"—and further, while the need to dominate nature originated with capitalist society, it has reappeared under socialism. Leiss credits to Sir Francis Bacon a recovery of the "divine" bequest for a more modern and secular age. "Bacon provided the formula whereby the idea of mastery over nature became widely acceptable, a formula which also was easily secularized as the cultural impact of religion gradually diminished." Leiss characterizes these words of Bacon as the essential "formula" for domination: "For man by the fall fell at the same time from his state of innocence and from his dominion over creation. Both of these losses however can even in this life be in some part repaired; the former by religion and faith, the latter by arts and sciences."[10] In this new perspective, science was no longer seen to contradict religion but to work hand-in-hand with religion for the salvation of humanity. This new view opened the way for the scientific revolution, secularization, and the notion of progress itself. Not until the mid-twentieth century did it occur to many that humanity might not be up to the task of mastery. Only recently have we realized that after humanity's brief reign the natural world may never recover its former glory.

The central value of environmentalism is, then, respect for the laws of nature, the conclusion that ecology is more fundamental than human wants and needs. The natural world must be given every right that humanity grants to itself—some environmentalists, for example, argue that trees should be granted legal standing in human courts.[11] Humanity surely cannot escape the jurisdiction of nature's court—we may be in grave danger of receiving a severe sentence soon.

From this respect for nature, whether rooted in fear or love, follows elimination of the human-created hierarchy of the universe. Love of nature and recognition of natural limits lead to humility about the place of the human species. Humility, indeed, can be singled out as the second environmentalist value and a corollary of the first. Livingston's *One Cosmic Instant* is subtitled *A Natural History of Human Arrogance*. He concludes his first chapter,

> Conscious change of direction toward the environmental ethic will mean the practice of a kind of artificial selection—choosing certain positive elements in our traditions, and rejecting negative elements. The selective process will not be easy, for it will demand something that is foreign to us—humility. It will demand unprecedented humility in the face of the encountered facts of the biosphere and the cosmos. It will demand willingness to see ourselves in the perspective of time of infinite duration and of events of unimaginable magnitude.[12]

Our terrestrial home is no more than a dot in the vastness of space, and the biosphere on its surface is a mere "film of dampness," delicate and slight. Human history is, thus far, but a brief instant. This view, of course, is consistent with the Judaeo-Christian tradition. Whether vastness is called nature or God, humility is an appropriate attitude toward it. Humility in the face of the infinite expanses of time and space and our frailty and mortality leads to a kind of dualism in the character of most human societies. On one side is the desire to "conquer nature," to root out the terror of emptiness, vastness, coldness, and silence. On the other is respect for and a sense of unity with all the living things of this planet.

Both aspects of this dualism are captured elegantly by H. V. Nelles in his history of the development of hydroelectric power at Niagara Falls. The extraction of power from Niagara was portrayed by its promoters in terms of magnitude and mystery. "Publicists and newspaper reporters drew upon familiar agricultural images, such as 'tamed' and 'harnessed' and freely mixed the military metaphors of 'conquest' and 'triumph.' . . . The reputation of this Wonder of the World, the frightening rush of its dark waters and the fearsome roar of its cascade, were known to every citizen. . . . On the one hand the engineer was locked in mortal combat *against* the forces of nature, yet at the same time he consciously strove to be in harmony *with* nature's mysteries."[13]

Arrogance was probably necessary to the construction of those first "mighty" dams, but humility is clearly the order of the day now that we appreciate the full environmental costs of many such engineering projects. No sense of relationship with nature or its mysteries was present in those who poisoned the now toxic Niagara.[14]

The fulfillment of human needs, desires, and whims has had higher and higher natural costs. David Ehrenfeld, reflecting on these costs in *The Arrogance of Humanism*, noted the widespread use of the word *hopefully* with respect to human action.

> Why bother with "hopefully" if we actually have the power to rearrange things as we see fit and remake any thing or process that does not serve our purposes or take our fancy? . . . The major reason for the prevalence of hopefully = let us hope is that deep within ourselves we know that our omnipotence is a sham, our knowledge and control of the future is weak and limited, our inventions and discoveries work, if they work at all, in ways that we do not expect, our planning is meaningless, our systems are running amok—in short, that the humanistic assumptions upon which our societies are grounded lack validity.

Humanism Ehrenfeld defines as the view that all the problems of human interaction with the environment are readily soluble, either through technology or through political and economic adjustments. Ehrenfeld and others despise what they see as human arrogance and are deeply pessimistic about the future of our species, along with most others. Thinking of a favorite piece of baroque music that reminded him of the sea, Ehrenfeld wrote, "It saddened me because it reminded me that in my century nothing is totally free of the taint of arrogance. We have defiled everything, much of it forever, even the farthest jungles of the Amazon and the air above the mountains, even the everlasting sea which gave us birth."[15] There are, for these environmentalists, too many humans wanting too many things. We are too technologically able and too ignorant to forgo anything that seems, in the short-term view, easy to get.

But this humility and even pessimism do not lead many environmentalists to negative attitudes about human health. Environmentalism is bound up with the recent rapid growth in preventative personal health care. The expanded use of "natural" foods, the decline in consumption of red meats, and the increased consumption of fresh vegetables and whole grains are all a part of this change. So too is increased participation in such physical activities as jogging, cycling, cross-country skiing, swimming, sailing, and windsurfing, as well as personal and political struggles against tobacco addiction. All of these changes are linked in one way or another with the environmental movement.

However contradictory they may seem to humility and pessimism, fitness and preventative medicine are corollaries to the first environmental value, the love of all life forms. Arrogance toward the natural world can lead also to lack of respect for one's own body. Is it not arrogance to believe one's health is invulnerable, whether to pollutants, occupational hazards, automobiles, overeating, or tobacco?

In the 1970s and 1980s many who knew nothing of respect for the wider environment learned a great deal about taking care of their own bodies. Some of them then became alarmed about air quality, realizing that their gains from exercise were greatly diminished by air pollution.[16] Many who endured the horrors of breaking nicotine addiction were outraged to learn that secondary smoke threatens their health.[17] Others were distressed to learn of environmental threats to their carefully balanced diets.[18] Samuel Hays also notes the links between health concern and environmentalism in a recent article.

A new view of health constituted an equally significant innovation in environmental values, health less as freedom from illness and more as physical and mental fitness, of feeling well, of optimal capability for exercising one's physical and mental powers. The control of infectious diseases by antibiotics brought to the fore new types of health problems associated with slow, cumulative changes in physical condition, symbolized most strikingly by cancer. . . . All this put emphasis on the non-bacterial environmental causes of illness but, more importantly, brought into health matters an emphasis on the positive conditions of wellness and fitness.[19]

The emphasis on wellness and its preventative maintenance clearly shifts the focus of health from medical treatment of disease to lifestyle changes and environmental protection.

Another clear link between an ecological perspective and a concern for healthy living is the interest in better and more natural diets. The earliest connection was made by Frances Moore Lappé in *Diet for a Small Planet*, which has now sold well over a million copies.[20] *Diet for a Small Planet* argues convincingly that whole grains, fresh vegetables, and fruits are not only better tasting but healthier and more ecologically appropriate than the typical North Amercian diet. Dozens of similar books have sold well in North American for nearly twenty years now.[21] The ecological connection—the fact that these healthy foods require less land, water, and energy to produce than meat—is more explicit in Lappe's writing than in most of the others.

Several authors drew another link between diet and ecology in their discussions of additives and trace environmental contaminants in our food. Linda Pim and the Canadian environmental group Pollution Probe produced two excellent books on this subject. *Additive Alert* discusses the health implications of substances intentionally and legally added to foodstuffs in Canada; the book contains a product and brand-name guide to the use of such additives. It notes that Statistics Canada estimated 117 million pounds of food additives are used each year in Canada—about five pounds per person annually. Pim's second book, *The Invisible Additives*, discusses trace quantities in food of pesticides, livestock drugs, natural toxins, packaging leachates, and pollutants from the air, water, and soil. Pim stresses the importance of a societal shift to a more ecological agricultural system.

Two California-based investigative reporters, David Weir and Mark Schapiro, made another connection between ecology and healthy living in *Circle of Poison*, which traces the effects of the U.S. government's willingness to permit export of hazardous pesticides banned in the United States.[22] Those chemicals are usually exported to countries without a scientifically sophisticated regulatory apparatus, and they are often used by farmers or farm workers unable to follow the complex rules for their relatively safe application. In some developing countries, empty pesticide drums are used to collect rainwater for drinking! Finally, the biggest users of these expensive chemicals are large farms that produced food for export to North America. In coffee, bananas, pineapples, tea, and sugar the circle of poison is thus completed.

These books make clear the extent to which we humans are bound up with the ecosystems we have blithely threatened. The best strategic approach to dietary health in a contaminated world, some conclude, is to focus on foods low on the food chain, in which fat-soluble contaminants are not concentrated. One might also choose foods from local producers whose agricultural practices one knows, or organically produced foods. Unprocessed or only minimally processed foods are also recommended. In short, one eats a bowl of oatmeal with fresh fruit, not a plate of bacon or a bowl of Count Chocula.

The connection between personal health and environmental hazards has led many to realize that there is no wholly personal route to better health. There is little point in jogging, rowing, or cycling for miles in polluted air. Eating a healthful meal may not help if one's glass of wine has been filtered (legally) through asbestos.[23] Regularly eating vegetables grown "organically" in certain urban locations carries considerable risk of lead poisoning. Finally, taking good care of oneself at home can be offset by the risks of a hazardous workplace. The concern with personal health has thus created a truly impressive potential for expanding ecological and political awareness.

The perspective gained from such books as *Circle of Poison* points as well toward a fourth value associated with environmentalism: a global perspective. Pollution does not respect national and other political borders. Much of the acid rain that falls in New England, New York, and Eastern Canada originates in Ohio, Indiana, and Illinois. Acid rain in Scandinavia comes from Great Britain. Pollution in the Danube is less acute in the countries where it originates. Much of the northern hemisphere received fallout from the Chernobyl nuclear catastrophe.

Nor do resource shortages affect economies in isolation. The economies most severely hit by the 1970s increases in oil prices were neither those of producers nor those of large consumers of oil—they were the economies of the poorest countries, who use small but critical amounts of imported oil in agriculture and in a few modest industries.

Environmentalists see that the earth is a commons. Solutions to many environmental problems must be undertaken on a global scale. In the early 1980s environmental issues rose to the top of diplomatic agendas despite the fact that few of the dominant political figures of the day were anything but hostile to environmental concerns. Ronald Reagan discussed acid rain with the prime minister of Canada. Major treaties on toxic substances and other environmental issues were signed in Europe,[24] and after Chernobyl even Russia was drawn into diplomatic discussions of environmental issues.[25] That environmental decision-making is entering the diplomatic sphere suggests that local, even national solutions to the most pressing problems on the environmental agenda are no longer possible. Environmental politics is international politics.

The titles of recent environmental works frequently reflect the global perspective of the movement.[26] The cover of Ophuls' *Ecology and the Politics of Scarcity* features a classic photo of the earth from space. Kenneth Boulding captures this sentiment in his phrase "spaceship earth." In a recent speech the noted U.S. environmental activist Gus Speth argued that the most prominent environmental issues are increasingly problems of a global scale—acid rain, the destruction of tropical rainforests, the spread of toxic substances, or the greenhouse effect.[27]

But environmentalists have been equally insistent that environmental solutions must involve greater decentralization. (It must be noted that while this is consistently stated, it has not always been articulated as clearly as many other environmental values.) Decentralization sometimes refers to dispersal of populations, though neither suburbs nor strip development in the countryside are advocated. It also is sometimes said to involve localizing political decision-making and reversing the trend to political centralization prominent in most nations for a century or more. Of course many intellectuals, not just environmentalists, have long opposed both centralized political power and excessive urbanization; environmentalists have not added as many new insights here as they might (see chapter 9).

Decentralism is perhaps the most explicitly political value on our list, with the possible exception of those that urge restraints on consumption. And many environmentalists strongly express decentralist values. Energy Probe, an environmental organization based in Ontario, urged the breakup of Ontario Hydro, a large and historically significant publicly owned utility.[28] Many environmentalists are also self-proclaimed anarchists (albeit of a gentle variety).[29] And the soft energy path clearly necessitates considerable residential decentralization, just as "organic" agriculture requires more labor— thus rural repopulation—if production levels are to be maintained. Such publications as *Harrowsmith, Rain,* and *Mother Earth News* emphasize environmental concerns in the context of a preference for rural settings and virtues. The body of literature on building one's own autonomous and rural solar home and/or returning to the land is massive and has not been without effect.[30] Governmental demonstration projects such as the Ark in Prince Edward Island were popular in the 1970s and suggested that homes should allow a greater range of functions, even aspiring to self-sufficiency in energy and food production.

The environmental expression of the themes of self-management, self-reliance, autonomy, and decentralization clearly challenge contemporary industrial society. Yet these values are manifest in many ways *within* that society. Here environmentalism shares common roots with the New Right: both seek a return to a wholesome—and perhaps mythological—past. Self-sufficiency in energy, shelter, and food has obvious appeal in economically unstable times, especially in societies dominated by large international corporations and bureaucratic governments. Sustaining oneself and one's family using renewable resources, one can imagine a secure future for one's descendants—perhaps the ultimate luxury in difficult economic times. By stressing the values of decentralism and autonomy, environmentalists have reached the popular consciousness.

But there is an important caveat with regard to the relationship between decentralization and environmentalism. However strongly environmentalists prefer a decentralized, self-managing future, environmentalism's effect in advanced industrial economies has often been to broaden and strengthen the powers of central government. The national bureaucracies of the United States, Canada, and Western Europe over the past twenty years have grown disproportionately in the environmentally relevant areas of energy, environment, and resource management. But many politically sophisticated environmentalists, including most of those on the left, do not view growing governmental power as undesirable. They distinguish between autonomy and self-reliance as personal goals and the need for political control of centralized economic power.

The contradictions between the "anarchist" and "localist" utopias of Bookchin and other environmentalists and the burgeoning bureaucracies cannot be ignored. But one cannot simply dismiss the growth of national environmental bureaucracies as a betrayal of the cause. Were regulatory powers not established on a national basis, pollution "havens" would abound—some jurisdictions would choose a massive industrial tax base over a clean environment, and surrounding areas, if not whole nations, would soon bear the costs. National, even international environmental standards and regulations make a great deal of sense. Local enforcement might be more effective, as might locally based recycling or energy conservation programs, but there are limits to the environmental slogan "think globally, act locally."[31] Acting locally is perhaps less intimidating, but it is sometimes insufficient.

Another problem of environmental decentralism concerns the question whether geographic dispersal of urban populations is environmentally appropriate. The back to the land movement of the 1970s faded rapidly and the "electronic cottage industries" of Toffler's "third wave" have been slow to materialize.[32] Of course subsistence organic farming, renewable energy, and/or "telecommuting" are good for the environment. But many find subsistence farming on marginal land unsatisfying, and long-distance commuting to work is decidedly not an environmentally appropriate lifestyle. I examine some of the environmental benefits of urban living in chapter 9. Suffice it to say now that such ways of life are not necessarily inappropriate environmentally and can sometimes be preferable.

In the long run the most environmentally appropriate geographic distribution of population would likely involve both modest increases in urban population and a modest trend toward true rural living. There would be more housing downtown in large urban centers; true rural life would not include extensive commuting. Daily or even weekly commuting to a city from a more natural setting is not a life pattern that will be sustainable in the long term. But more and more people might be able to choose not to work for extended periods. At that point and in those cases an environmentally appropriate rural life would become feasible for them.

But this issue is distinct from political decentralization. The latter is often compounded with such other issues as the need for simplification and greater participation (discussed further below). It is also bound up with concern over the complexity and secrecy associated with regulation, including environmental regulation. In environmental matters, complexity and secrecy arise from government's unwillingness to act decisively—for example, banning a short list of obviously hazardous chemicals for all or most uses. The unwillingness to act leads to elaborate and expensive regulatory and inspection systems. Second, some industries and some environmental bureaucracies seek to keep their activities from the public eye.[33] Most of their reasons—"trade secrets" and "proprietary rights," for example—are simply smokescreens for the comfort of silence.[34] An open and democratic government can be every bit as beautiful as a small one, and it may be a good deal easier to achieve.

There are numerous important opportunities for environmentally compatible forms of political and economic decentralization. Increased local political initiative and enhanced local political and economic autonomy will play fundamental roles in any political success environmentalism as an ideology might garner. Some recent evidence suggests that environmentalism, combined with local initiative, can significantly affect economic recovery in depressed regions.[35]

The sixth value on the list is less a value per se than a perspective.

Environmentalists tend to think in terms of the long-term future; their time horizon is extended. This characteristic distinguishes environmentalism from the prevailing ideology of technocratic (interest-group) liberalism. Those who merely balance existing interests are content to bury toxic wastes in ways that render them harmless only for a matter of decades. A century of safety is an extravagance; to politicians a century might as well be forever. Elected governments rarely see beyond the next election. Only environmentalists seem to ask about the long-term effects of, say, hydrogeology, bioaccumulation in food chains, or genetic changes in populations. For an environmentalist, there is really no such thing as disposal of toxic wastes—there is reuse, or containment, or destruction, or forgone need. "Disposing" of the toxins merely defers problems, it does not resolve them.

Time horizon may be the single most important distinction between environmentalists and others. Environmentalists want products to be durable and repairable. They want materials to be recycled or, if organic and nontoxic, returned to the soil. Environmentalists want to know that there will be future generations of virtually all life forms on the planet: human life in a world where this is unlikely seems morally outrageous. In this environmentalism is a very conservative sensibility—it embodies a feeling for flow and order moving from generation to generation. The flow from the past through oneself into the future is life itself.

Many of the issues related to the extended time frame of environmentalism are discussed in such works as Ernest Partridge's edited collection *Responsibilities to Future Generations.*[36] Therein the issue of nuclear power, and particularly nuclear wastes, is discussed extensively. Environmentalists wonder whether one generation has the right to put all future generations at risk in order to meet its own energy needs. They also realize that depletion of fossil fuels places future generations at risk, albeit risk of a less dramatic sort. They are prepared to forgo present energy use, and to forgo economic growth if necessary, to contribute to greater future security. In short, an environmental perspective does not ignore an issue simply because its constituencies and victims are unborn. Thereby environmentalism stands apart from the perspectives of either interest-group liberalism or most traditional varieties of socialism.

In 1963 Lynton Caldwell noted that environmentalism provides in several ways a distinctive focus for public policy. One of these is its long-term view of what might be in the public interest.[37] The importance of a long view was discussed even earlier by Fairfield Osborn—the opening chapter of his *Our Plundered Planet* (1948) is entitled "The Long View." Osborn wrote, "There is a value in what some people call 'the long view.' Perhaps we can best comprehend the human situation today if we first peer through the long vistas of space and time. Who knows? Perspective sometimes provides its own insight."[38] John Livingston, speaking of how to bring society closer to an environmental ethic, writes, "It will demand willingness to see ourselves in the perspective of time of infinite duration and events of unimaginable magnitude."[39]

A long view conveys immediately that, although there are dozens if not hundreds of alternatives to oil and natural gas, we are not likely to find an easier energy source. And from a long-term point of view, one sees much more clearly that there is no really effective way to extract radioactive or most other toxic substances from the environment. One also sees that there is a limit to the number of human beings that can be sustained comfortably on this planet, if we are to share it with other species. One sees no guarantees that humanity will survive the next few centuries—or even tomorrow—and one appreciates the profound destructive power of nuclear weapons and the necessity for their elimination.

Large-scale energy projects require at least a decade from the planning stages to the production of energy; thus long-term planning is imposed by these technologies even on liberal and conservative governments. The *Harvard Business Review* emphasizes the need for a U.S. industrial strategy. Something of a long-term perspective is increasingly a part of advanced industrial societies, whether environmentalist or not. But environmentalists go further. For example, although soft energy path possibilities seem to some an opportunity to return to the free market and Jeffersonian liberalism, an SEP must also be planned within a fifty-year time horizon. The many small projects in a SEP may open the way to entrepreneurship, but the goal of producing most or all energy from renewable resources involves such major societal changes that long-term planning is essential. In conclusion, both in their sensitivity to problems and in their proposed solutions, environmentalists significantly extend the sociopolitical time frame, distinguishing themselves thereby from much of the conventional political spectrum.

Not in contrast to their long view but because of it, environmentalists are stricken with a sense of urgency. Everything is a crisis—there is an environmental crisis, an energy crisis, a pollution crisis, a crisis in our forests, and a crisis of world hunger. Much of this anxiety, of course, is based in the way the contemporary media sell news. News must seem new and urgent. Television newscasters will not report that the Cuyahoga River is in its n-thousandth day of total pollution; nor will newspapers tell us that humankind has now used 61.587624 percent of the world's supplies of oil. But whether the product of a mass media age or not, the concerns of environmentalism have almost always been conveyed in terms of great urgency.

William Ophuls lists five reasons for not setting out "formal solutions to the political dilemmas of ecological scarcity." Any transition would undoubtedly take decades, he writes, and "the hour is very late. Now that everyone can recognize the evils of ecological scarcity, it is probably too late for a nicely planned transition to a steady state."[40] The natural world itself, in Ophuls' ominous view, will impose many of the necessary changes and will demonstrate soon the advisability of many others. Like William Catton, Ophuls concludes that overshoot has already occurred. So too does Paul Ehrlich and, to a lesser extent, David Ehrenfeld.

Urgency is common among environmentalists. But is this urgency compatible with the emphasis on a long view? Yes. The compatibility lies in realizing the magnitude of the changes called for and the slow progression of change. Environmentalists also fear that needed changes will not occur until they are absolutely necessary. Ophuls writes, "nearly all of the constructive actions that could be taken at present (for example, drastically restricting the use of private automobiles) are so painful to so many people in so many ways that they (the constructive actions) are indeed totally unrealistic."[41]

Shortly after this was written the second wave of OPEC-induced oil price increases provoked, if not legal restrictions, at least very real economic constraints on automobile use. But the following price collapse suggests that the necessary changes cannot be achieved through the market acting alone. One can anticipate a future involving lurches from energy restraint to expansion and back again for at least the next several decades. Now that the sense of urgency has passed, both governments and individuals seem to have forgotten that fundamental changes still must be made and that they will be far easier sooner than later.

Few people realize that a century from now there will be less automobile use than there is today. They do not think to forgo trivial trips now in order to make a more necessary future trip possible for their children or grandchildren. More radically, whole societies might forgo excessive automobile use now in order to achieve less costly heat tomorrow. Such changes are in order in many countries unless we begin soon to replace all our housing stock with energy-efficient designs. These changes, as we saw in chapter 4, will require up to a century to accomplish. We can achieve them in an orderly and humane fashion if and only if we begin very soon and proceed steadily.

In the interplay between a long view and a sense of urgency one finds another environmental value—the desire for sustainability of human economic activities in terms of environment and resources. Forests should be harvested no faster than they can be replanted— forest ecosystems must be sustained. Metals must be produced with an eye both on the supply of the ores and, crucially, on the energy needed to extract and process the metal. (Metal produced from recycled materials, of course, requires far less energy.) In general, environmentalists prefer renewable to nonrenewable resources, particularly as regards the most vital resource, energy. Amory Lovins' work urges dependence on renewable energy sources alone. Lester Brown's *Building a Sustainable Society* subsumes most of the concerns of environmentalism under the conceptual umbrella of a sustainable society. Achieving sustainability involves a long-term transformation of many basic aspects of our industrial economy. The environmentalist transformation emphasizes, for example, protection of prime agricultural land and utilization of biomass wastes as sources of energy and enhancers of soil quality. (Such wastes are valuable as fertilizers even after methane gas is extracted from them.) Pyrolysis would allow the production of both alcohol and fertilizer from sewage, manure, or crop wastes. As John Helliwell demonstrates, much of Canada's massive forest industry could become energy self-sustaining by using forest wastes as an energy source. Environmentalists also urge that toxic wastes be seen as chemical feedstocks.[42] Perhaps even more radically (in the technological sense), several environmentalists advocate that electronic communications systems replace reliance on far more energy intensive transportation systems.

Ecologically speaking, industrial society must transform its production processes to make them more energy and materials efficient, in a word—sustainable. The effects of such a transformation on the distribution of wealth and work will not be consistent. Some jobs will be lost, and a smaller number of unionized industrial jobs will be replaced by a greater number of now nonunionized service jobs. The demand for sustainability also will clearly place some limits on current economic output. For example, globally we may be harvesting close to the total sustainable output of many species of fish—some fish have been harvested at well beyond sustainable levels for years now.[43] Acid rain and hydroelectric dams further threaten fish stocks. Options include enhancing fish stocks by improving fish farming operations and altering dietary habits, thereby decreasing the demand for animal protein of all types.[44] The point remains that sustainability implies limits on production.

Globally, humans are cutting more wood than we should—at great cost in some places. Some of those costs were documented a century ago by George Perkins Marsh. The forests are further threatened by acid rain and by the nearly pointless clearcutting of vast tracts in the Amazon regions of Brazil.[45] Pressure on forests is also associated with their recreational use. Environmentalists, ever conscious of sustainability, must look long and hard at their own advocacy of a return to renewable sources of energy. In the developed economies, less than 10 percent of total energy demand is met from

renewable sources. How much more can be supplied on a sustainable basis from wood? Many developing countries already face severe, even desperate and destructive shortages of firewood, used
for heat and cooking.[46] But better forest management can increase
yields, especially in such nations as Canada, whose forest mismanagement is rapidly becoming a negative example for the developed
world.[47] The limits to sustainable production are thus not fixed, but
we should take better care of our renewable resources.

Humankind in many places is seriously mismanaging the earth's
agricultural resource base. In many developed economies, especially
North America, prime agricultural land has been taken over for other
uses, eliminating the possibility of later agricultural use, perhaps
forever.[48] The urban and suburban configurations that have been
created on such land may not survive the decline of oil. Yet this
continues to happen fifteen years after OPEC's first warning. Near-
urban recreational and prime agricultural land may well be the most
important long-term resource we have. But even in jurisdictions
where more than 95 percent of the land base is not of such a character
or quality, it is this small portion of prime land that is used for
parking lots and shopping malls, while city cores languish for lack
of business. Agricultural land is also threatened by a wide range of
bad farming practices often characterized in summary as industrial,
rather than ecological, agriculture.[49]

All of this has been thoroughly documented and is now widely
known. But little effective action has been taken.[50] Numerous intelligent policies have been proposed to protect agricultural land.
For example, government might purchase development rights from
near-urban farmers, leaving them free on retirement to sell their
farms as farms, without loss of equity. Those who wish to pass the
land on to their children would gain a retirement nest egg without
selling the farm.[51]

A more ecologically benign agriculture, sustainable in the long
term, is not necessarily less productive per acre in the short term,
but it might be.[52] However, it is reasonable to anticipate that it will
be more productive per acre in the long term. It is more labor intensive and thereby might lead to somewhat higher food prices. But

when energy prices rise again, much if not all of that economic disadvantage will probably be reversed. Sustainable agricultural practices require present investments to protect future yields.

We have had the technical knowledge to manage forest, farms, and fisheries for decades, if not centuries. And most people know— or sense—that contemporary society is in many ways unsustainable. That is why *Limits to Growth*, despite its many factual errors, struck a tender nerve. But little has been done toward achieving long-term sustainability.

Kenneth Boulding's claim that most people do not think beyond their own children is correct. As he put it, unless an individual identifies with a whole community and its long-term future, conservation of resources seems irrational. Boulding's answer to the question, "Why should we not maximize the welfare of this generation at the cost of posterity?" is twofold and succinctly captures the inner logic of sustainability. He suggests that individual welfare depends on one's ability to identify with a community in both time and space. It makes a difference in terms of environment whether that community is seen to be family, town, region, nation, species, or the planet as a whole. It also matters whether "time" means now, tomorrow, or the indefinite future. Boulding goes on to argue that the sense of long-term future connection is a critical determinant of the historical success of societies. "There is a great deal of historical evidence to suggest that a society which loses its identity with posterity and which loses its positive image of the future loses also its capacity to deal with present problems, and soon falls apart."[53] Thus, just as consumption requires "consumer confidence," conservation requires confidence that others will conserve as well, that future generations will receive the benefits of one's care and restraint. Only a collectively held positive image of the future will prevent the foreclosure of future options in a frenzy of now or never—one last big station wagon before we are all on bicycles.

An environmental perspective thus contains a negative corollary to the desire for a more sustainable society—a revulsion toward waste. In particular, environmentalists reject any waste of energy and/or materials. The image of massive barges heading out to sea filled with tons of garbage, of mountains of buried refuse near every human settlement, is repugnant to environmentalists. Since World War II, more and more manufactured items have been designed deliberately to be nonrepairable and "disposable." Environmentalists are revolted by throwaway razors, nonrefillable cigarette lighters, one-way food and beverage containers, excessive packaging, and shoddy toys, shoes, appliances, and furniture. What an incredible waste—an endless stream of junk, much of it peddled in the name of fashion and style.

The revulsion with waste leads directly to an enthusiasm for recycling, particularly source-separation recycling, in which individuals take some responsibility for their own refuse. Nontoxic organic matter is returned to the soil, metal is recycled, containers are reused, paper and cardboard become paper and cardboard again. Even plastics can be reused or recycled, though in practice consumer plastics rarely are. All items, especially large ones, environmentalists insist, should be both durable and repairable. They may be more expensive to produce, but—especially if they are energy efficient—their life-cycle costs (the costs of purchase and operation for the full life of the item) will be lower. Even if costs to the consumer were not lower, such changes would make economic sense from a long-term and global point of view. Similarly, even if hauling everything to the dump is cheaper now, recycling ought to be practiced in any case. It creates low-skill jobs for the unemployed—recycling people as well as goods. And even if durability and repairability are not more economical, our present practices are simply immoral.

In an effort to avoid moralizing, one can categorize two versions of the environmentalist response to conspicuous and wasteful consumption as "hippie" and "yuppie." It is hippie to get out of the rat race, go back to the land, get one's clothes secondhand and pick up one's furniture from junkyards and garage sales. Yuppie environmentalist consumption is less "pure" but still better than the style of 1959. Fashion in these circles emphasizes oriental rugs, for example, goods that last literally for centuries and that are worth more fifty years after purchase than when new. Also yuppie are high-quality arts and crafts that embody much skilled labor and little material and energy per dollar. Automobiles made to last for decades are popular (although alas they are often not very fuel efficient).

Yuppies often prefer classically designed clothes in natural materials—expensive, but used year after year. Finally, instead of heading out from suburbia for a long Sunday ride in the family station wagon with their three children, yuppies go jogging, take a shower, and visit a restaurant near the gentrified townhouse for brunch, with or without their only child. Many such people might view environmentalism as a bit strident or even utterly boring. But, perhaps without ever thinking about it, these style-conscious yuppies have been affected by environmentalism right in the materialist center of their day-to-day lives.

The concern with waste reduction is central to environmentalism. Its roots can be traced back to the 1960s and the popular sociology of Vance Packard's *The Waste Makers*.[54] But even in the 1920s and 1930s links were made between pesticides and product durability. In 1927 Stuart Chase and F. J. Schlink wrote *Your Money's Worth*, a popular expose of the advertising industry's outrageous claims about everything from automobiles, refrigerators, and furniture to toothpaste and mouthwash. Chase and Schlink advocated consumer organization and independent scientific testing of consumer products. They did not, they asserted, advocate "revolutionary change." On the contrary, their claims "imply no drastic change in our system of law or of property. They are practical in the sense that they are already in use in some isolated instances. We shall plead for an extension of the principle of buying goods according to impartial scientific test, rather than according to the fanfare of trumpets of the higher salesmanship. This is all."[55] This book served as the basis for the consumers' movement and its publications.[56] Schlink, with Arthur Kallett, went on in the 1930s to champion the dangers of lead arsenate pesticide sprays (see chapter 2).

This first campaign for product testing and against waste may have been an effort even more central to the meaning of environmentalism than discussion of pesticides, if seemingly less direct. Chase and Schlink decried the obsolescence caused by model changes and fashions and the waste of money associated with the envies, fears, and phobias induced by the advertising industry. They also examined product durability and efficiency:

The Bureau of Standards recently analyzed the wood entering into furniture. It found that 9 per cent of such wood made for "very durable" furniture; 35 per cent made for "durable;" while 56 per cent was dubious or definitely "non-durable." Thus families with low incomes are buying furniture—often on the installment plan—which by virtue of its flimsiness is in the long run the most expensive. It is difficult to name a commercial article of wide and important use in which less research and standardization have been done than household refrigerators. Nor one which needs them more. . . . An extra inch of corkboard insulation, adding $20 to the selling price of a 100 pound capacity box, will save over six pounds of ice per day, or 18 per cent on the investment if the box is used but six months out of the year.[57]

If one changes "ice" to "electricity" and allows for inflation one has a statement that might have come, virtually word for word, from *Soft Energy Notes* more than a half-century later. Sensitivity to waste is a value that a century of advertising has rekindled and doubtless stirred to anger on numerous occasions.

Efficient management of resources is a principal means to sustainability with minimal ecological disruption. Environmentalism also embodies a strong inclination to simple restraint in consumption—perhaps this is even more primary than efficient production and careful use. This view separates environmentalism most from the traditional political left, particularly the trade union movement. Brooks and McMullen see it as the distinguishing characteristic of contemporary environmentalism: "What the previous three phases shared was their emphasis on industrial use of resources, in other words, on the supply side of the demand/supply equation. The fourth environmental movement made a significant break from the past when it put a 'why' to demand. For the first time in modern history, the goal of ever-increasing consumption was being challenged."[58]

Not only does waste appear as gluttony in the face of global need, it is purchased at the price of damage to the global biosphere and probably to human health; and it hastens exhaustion of nonrenewable resources. Environmentalists believe developed economies, if not the global economy itself, have probably reached a limit to material and energy throughputs. In this view most nonessential economic output is waste.

Environmentalism, as we have seen, incorporates a sophisticated literature on steady-state economics and a less sophisticated literature on voluntary simplicity.[59] Environmentalists and nonenvironmentalists alike see economics increasingly as a zero-sum game: what one person uses is unavailable to another, however urgently it is needed. A family cruising North America in a Winnebago could be assuring that someone else will soon be unable to heat his or her home. With an emphasis on this perspective, environmentalism might restore the cutting edge to socialism, restoring a sense of the absolute to perceptions of deprivation. Alas, however, for those who favor such a perspective, hypothetical future lack does not make a revolution. Nevertheless, in environmentalists' anger at the wasteful organization of capitalist political economy, there may be some potential for socialist-environmentalist agreement.

I hasten to add that an archetypical socialist/unionist has a view of waste and need very different from that of an archetypical environmentalist/intellectual. One person's waste is another's profoundest pleasure, or even a basic need: public transportation, for example, is more energy efficient, but it also tends to be a particular hardship for the disabled. The elderly are uncomfortable at household temperatures to which younger people can adapt. And neither group would greet the 1970s environmentalist nirvana of woodchopping with great enthusiasm. The desirability of nuclear power changes according to whether one sees a nuclear plant supplying the most necessary or the most trivial 5 percent of electrical demand. Environmentalists tend to see nuclear electricity in terms of electric toothbrushes and hedgetrimmers.[60] Nuclear engineers and Marxists alike see the same electricity lighting dark staircases, baking cherry pies, and/or keeping the wheels of industry turning. The question of what is wasteful and what is not is not simple to answer. This is the point in practice where environmentalists and socialists frequently diverge.

In the late 1970s, the idea of voluntary reduction in earning and spending—called variously voluntary simplicity, elegant frugality, and conspicuous poverty—enjoyed a brief popularity. It faded once the economic difficulties of the early 1980s became apparent. Advocacy of voluntary poverty, however "elegant," seemed inappropriate in the face of involuntary poverty caused by high unemployment and inflation. Nonetheless, numerous public opinion surveys and analyses indicate that many younger people are participating in what may be the beginning of a revolution in the value structure of most, if not all, Western societies. In 1981, Ronald Inglehart concluded from a review of more than one hundred national opinion surveys that "Materialist" values are increasingly being replaced by something he identifies as "Post-Materialist." "A decade ago it was hypothesized that the basic value priorities of Western publics had been shifting from a Materialist emphasis toward a Post-Materialist one—from giving top priority to physical sustenance and safety, toward heavier emphasis on belonging, self-expression and the quality of life."[61] Evidence of this shift, rooted in the economic security of the postwar era, is apparent in the United States, Canada, Australia, Japan, and fifteen Western European nations.[62] Such studies are important empirical measures of the widening acceptance of this important environmental value.

The tenth environmental value in our list, a love of simplicity, is connected with the revulsion toward waste. Environmentalists assert that there is more pleasure in walking or skiing through the woods as in snowmobiling along the same path. Furthermore, walking neither disrupts the pleasure or peace of others nor denies future people access to nonrenewable fuel resources. Neither capitalist nor socialist ideologies share this inherent discomfort with snowmobiles.

In the same spirit a complete environmental ethic carries a preference for painstaking production over hasty consumption. The political left tends to welcome enhanced productivity accompanied by advances in labor's share of consumption. Environmental values, in contrast, emphasize deep respect for craftmanship and many environmentalists aspire to emulate these precepts in everyday living.[63] Distinctiveness, functionality, design, and durability are highly regarded in part because they make possible decreased material throughput. Self-production is taken to be a superior pleasure. Gardening, preparing and preserving foods, and sharing leisurely meals are raised to the level of virtue. Not only do such activities often substitute for those that might damage the environment, they are inherently better. Such concerns are not central to the traditional ideologies, although they have been very important to anarchists and anarchosocialists throughout history.[64]

The love of simple things is also found in the writings of the early conservationists Henry David Thoreau, John Muir, and Aldo Leopold. Here too is where environmentalists might part company with many yuppies. Simplicity, a dimension of the rejection of materialism, in many cases takes on a religious or quasi-religious character. Life in a medieval monastery, or in some modern fishing and farming communities, is not without fundamental appeal—hard work, modest but sufficient material means, simplicity, proximity to the beauty of nature and, especially in the monastery, a great deal of time in which to be thankful. The love of simplicity can also carry political implications. It is important, for example, not only to environmentalists but to some neoconservatives as well. It can be associated with rejection of the complexities of political life, including bureaucracy and the tax system. If carried to the extreme, simplicity can also ominously imply disinclination to the complexities of democratic politics. There is nothing simpler, after all, than trusting one's leaders. Comfort with simplicity, therefore, is not always an enlightened instinct.

Osborn, Ordway, Mumford, and Mishan are more or less appropriate exemplars of the mood associated with simplicity. So too are the goals of many with whom one might disagree about means. For example, many conservatives seek decency, honesty, and old-fashioned morality in what they see as a corrupt, unduly complicated contemporary world. Much of the politics of the 1970s and 1980s, from the Moral Majority to Ronald Reagan's tax simplification plans to environmentalism, can be linked to an urge toward greater simplicity. But this urge is often twisted to its opposite in a politics of denial. The problem is not seen as tax loopholes for various special interests but taxes themselves, not environmental pollution but those who are always talking about it. The problem is not with one's own attitudes toward, for example, economic inequity and war and peace, but with others who meddle in matters that are none of their business. Ophuls wrote about such a politics well before the contemporary neoconservative and fundamentalist upsurge: the "first response to threatening doubts is to redouble effort and belief in support of the current paradigm, which is after all a kind of civil religion. Thus our tendency, already very apparent, will be to react to the challenges of ecological scarcity with policies of denial and with more and more desperate efforts to stave off the inevitable changes."[65] Thus the same instinct that fuels environmentalism can also fuel its rejection in political practice.

There is within environmentalism another manifestation of the need for greater simplicity. Energy conservation and diverse, renewable sources of energy supply are, Lovins stresses, far easier to understand than are the technologies that underlie most energy megaprojects. Lovins himself is aware of the economic and political importance of this aspect of an SEP. Energy can be supplied without ten-year financing schemes; capital can be turned around more quickly so that less is needed. Nor are SEP project organizers easily "held to ransom" by unions, as on nuclear plant or pipeline projects.[66] Politically, the public can participate in energy decisions only if it understands the technologies involved.[67] A soft energy path is less complex, more naturally part of a simpler, easier world. Lovins likens SEP technologies to that of the hand-held calculator—very sophisticated, but elegant in its ease and simplicity of operation.

Another environmentalist value can be readily related to several we have just considered: preference for natural materials. An environmentalist aesthetic is also highly sensitive to season, climate, and setting. Some environmentalists reject out of hand high-rise office towers and much of the contemporary plastic world. Plastic is often ugly, of course, and the term has come to connote artificiality and limited durability. Plastic does have appropriate uses, however. Plastic auto parts reduce vehicle weight so that the oil feedstock used to produce the plastic is more than replaced in fuel saved. Plastic pipes do not readily corrode and in some cases can be produced using less oil and energy than metal pipes.[68] The question of when to use natural materials can become quite complex. What would be the ecological effect, for example, of replacing synthetic fibers with wool and cotton?[69]

A natural aesthetic is perhaps the least political of environmentalist tenets. But even this value can have political implications. Witness the opposition to the seal hunt or Lady Bird Johnson's attempt at highway beautification in the United States.[70] This value also stands at the center of a potential future division among environmentalists. Renewable energy can threaten scenic vistas if, for example, coastlines or mountain valleys are used for wind generation; the dangers of nuclear power, while more severe, are largely invisible.[71]

This aesthetic can also have significant economic effects. It may lead to greater appreciation of durability and "natural" character. Thus old houses with visible wood interiors and/or stone exteriors might become more valuable with time. If they are not torn down in the name of progress such structures can last for a millennium or more. Antique furniture could also be preferred to new furniture. A culture that respected durability would imbue certain purchases with a real investment value. Old, durable goods thus would become more economically desirable than new, fashionable, disposable goods. This aesthetic would boost some businesses and hurt others, and in the process it would encourage considerable reduction in per capita energy and material consumption.

However, matters aesthetic we cannot anticipate with undue certainty. Environmentalist designers or architects would not likely come to advocate one style as "the" environmental design. Both a "country" look and a more modern "minimalist" look might be appropriate. Interiors that were very fashionable in the 1970s often stressed bare brick walls, wood, antiques, and plants—"natural" materials, mostly reused, renovated, and recycled. In the mid–1980s minimalism took hold, also environmentally appropriate—classic design, durable goods, a minimum of clutter, fewer "things" altogether. Either appearance can reflect an environmental aesthetic. Another appropriate "look" is catch-as-catch-can eclecticism—low-cost indifference, garage-sale design, or I'm-not-home-much-anyway.

The twelfth value in our list follows from those that precede it, but it is worthy of separate identification and brief comment. A movement that questions the need for increased economic output says something about our society's basis for esteem. Material measures of personal success, environmentalists would have it, are overemphasized within our culture. Success should be measured in terms of less tangible attributes such as skill, achievement, taste, or integrity. Or at least those material symbols of success that are employed should be judged on their quality, using environmentally guided standards, rather than by quantitative measures.

Environmentalists place greater emphasis on production than on consumption, and they emphasize qualitative over quantitative production. The restoration of old and beautiful buildings is highly valued. So too is writing a symphony or learning a language. Driving a big car or owning several homes is simply not an important measure of one's worth. Two economic implications of this perspective are that quality in terms of beauty and durability is worth paying for, and that advances in productivity should be translated as much into reduced work time as into increased production. These two implications will prove central to any future attempt to link distributive to environmental politics. (The meaning of *work* in this statement is taken up in chapter 9.)

This value too can have a spiritual or religious dimension. Both environmentalists and sincere practitioners of most of the world's religions see virtue and personal growth as more important than material gain.[72] Inglehart defines Post-Materialism as a greater emphasis on self-expression and the quality of life. Being becomes more important than having, quality more important than quantity, both in one's own life and in one's assessments of others. E. F. Schumacher's term "Buddhist economics" captures the essence of this value: "Buddhist economics must be very different from the economics of modern materialism, since the Buddhist sees the essence of civilization not in a multiplication of wants but in the purification of human character. Character, at the same time, is formed primarily by a man's work. And work, properly conducted in conditions of human dignity and freedom, pleases those who do it and equally their products."[73] Consumption is less important than creative activity, and conspicuous consumption is openly offensive. The notion of taste, a basis for judging oneself and others, is bound up more and more with personal dignity, restraint, and real personal achievement. Grandiosity and price are no longer a measure of uniqueness and beauty. Decency, integrity, and creativity are more real measures of worth than "things" of any kind.

These twelve basic values of environmentalism are all goals, ends in themselves, individually and collectively. In general they are compatible, but in some circumstances they conflict, bringing difficult choices both to day-to-day living and to public policy decisions. The final value is both an end in itself and a means to the achievement and integration of all the others. Political democracy maximizes openness and participation in political and administrative decision-making. (In later chapters I develop in greater detail both an empirical and a theoretical association between democracy and environmentalism.)

Empirically, to choose North American examples by way of illustration, nearly every piece of important environmental legislation in the United States has contained provisions for the expansion of openness and participation. Needless to say full success has not been achieved. But democracy, as many social theorists of the 1960s demonstrated to the new "empirical" school of political science, is never a fact, but always a goal. That all citizens are not "perfect" democratic citizens all of the time is not a basis for revising the theory of democracy, they argued.[74] Likewise, here the important point is not the imperfect performance of environmental legislation but the fact that the National Environmental Protection Act and many others that followed sought to enhance the democratic and participatory character of economic and environmental decision-making.[75] The enhancement of openness and participation has been a central part of such other major pieces of legislation as the Toxic Substances Control Act, the Occupational Health and Safety Act, and the Resources Conservation and Recovery Act, as well as important wilderness preservation legislation and the toxic substances bill known as superfund.[76]

In fact, some analysts distinguish the U.S. environmental movement from the conservation movement largely on the strong distrust environmentalists express toward the relatively closed process of decision-making common to conservation bureaucracies.[77] Too often agencies established to protect and conserve end up indistinguishable in outlook from the interests they are established to regulate. Environmentalists consistently seek to bring administration into the open and allow—even perhaps force—the public to be the protector of the public interest.

Public hearings and public discussion and involvement are characteristic goals of environmental organizations. In Canada, where parliamentary sovereignty and a British tradition of closed administration inhibit the development of open and participatory environmental administration, there has been extensive use of "special" public hearings.[78] Outside the "normal" administrative channels, these commissions of inquiry, both provincial and federal, have been used on numerous occasions regarding environmental matters. This technique generally allows a role for the public and promotes openness in process and deliberation.[79] The Berger Commission, concerned with Northern pipeline megaprojects, broke new ground in both regards. Its deliberations were often televised; the inquiry traveled to the tiny and remote Northern settings; and the Commission's Final Report, *Northern Frontier/Northern Homeland*, would have been on the all-time Government of Canada best seller list if there were such a thing.[80] Other such inquiries have also broken new ground, funding participation by public interest groups. And some Canadian environmental legislation has carried a participatory component similar to that found in American legislation. Occupational health legislation in Ontario, for example, went beyond the American equivalent in seeking to mobilize union members and others in the defense of the workplace environment.[81]

On a more theoretical level, Barnet argues for the necessity of involving the public in the solution of many kinds of environmental problems. And Richard Andrews writes, "in closed or low-visibility arenas the power of highly organized private interests is maximized."[82] Andrews speaks of interests opposed to environmental protection and argues that environmentalists strongly advocate opening the arenas of environmental decision-making. Schrecker's important recent work for the Law Reform Commission of Canada has a similar theme—secret environmental decision-making in Canada has turned out badly.[83] As an environmentalist, Schrecker strongly advocates reforms to open up the process, thus expressing a fundamental value of environmentalism.

seven

Environmentalism and the
Ideological Spectrum

Environmentalism is a
perspective based in part on findings in the natural and social sciences, especially the sciences of ecology, toxicology, epidemiology, and the assessment of energy supply and demand. Environmentalism is also based in a set of values about life, health, the world, the human future, and human activities, societies, and economies. This chapter examines environmentalism as a new ideology in relation to the history of ideology. All ideologies blend concepts, values, and science into an integrated perspective from which spring ideas about how best to alter political and economic patterns and processes. Ideologies are sometimes an overly rigid base for political action. From this weakness environmentalism is not wholly exempt. But environmentalism may be in some ways more adaptable than most ideologies that have preceded it.

Seeing environmentalism as an ideology can alter our understanding of the ideological spectrum that has emerged over several centuries. For environmentalism is inherently neither left nor right.[1] Some of its dimensions fall on the left side of the spectrum, others seem more conservative. Some noted environmentalists identify with the political left; others are just as clearly more comfortable on the right. The German Greens, on entering the Bundestag, insisted that they be seated in the center, rather than to the left of the Democratic Socialists. But the political center also inadequately represents the politics of environmentalism. Seeing environmentalism as an ideology urges us to rethink what we mean by left, right, and ideology. When one draws a distinction between the "distributive" politics of the traditional political spectrum and environmental politics a two-dimensional (rather than a one-dimensional) ideological map is suggested.

The Evolution of the Classical Ideologies

The "age of ideology" is often taken to have begun in earnest with the events leading up to the beginnings of modern liberal democracy, particularly in Britain, France, and the United States. But let us go back a bit earlier to look at the means and myths by which predemocratic, monarchic, and aristocratic societies sustained their political structures. Such power structures endured only in part through the use and threat of force. Why, as Max Weber might have asked, did most people obey those with authority? In his phrase, this was an age of "traditional" authority, the authority of the "eternal yesterday."[2] Ask a citizen, "How do you know who is the ruler?" and he or she would probably answer, "the ruler is the ruler because he and his forebears have always been the rulers." God might come into the matter, but no one would answer by referring to characteristics of the ruler, or by describing the selection process, or by means of any complex reasoning. And if the question were not asked, the citizen probably would not ever think about it.

Almost no one thought in terms of a complex rationale for rule until Thomas Hobbes said that without a single unified authority, recognized by all, life would be miserable. Without a "visible power," a leviathan, to keep men "in awe" there would be "no place for industry; because the fruit thereof is uncertain: and consequently no culture of the earth; no navigation, nor use of the commodities that may be imported by sea; no commodious building; no instruments of moving, and removing, such things as require much force; no knowledge of the face of the earth; no account of time; no arts; no letters; no society; and which is worst of all, continual fear, and danger of violent death; and the life of man solitary, poor, nasty, brutish, and short."[3]

A cautious man, ever fearful of political disruption, Hobbes claimed that it was not important whether the authority rested in a monarch or in a parliament—what was important was that the leviathan be hegemonious and altogether clearly so to everyone. Hobbes's argument is obviously a very conservative one, a justification of centralized power and perhaps centralized wealth as well. But it is less conservative than that which went before it, unquestioned traditional authority. Hobbes had established a basis for the age of ideology.

In the age of ideology people came to expect some explanation of, some justification for, concentrations of power and wealth, and they were stirred to action by arguments against such concentrations. They began to ask whether the regime provided their families, peers, communities, or nations with what was needed most. Some even asked whether their economic or political system was a good one and whether a better one might be possible. These questions and the various answers that came forward are the essence of the age of ideology.

First used to stir people to challenge established political authority were liberal ideas widespread during and after the brief revolutionary period in Britain in the mid-seventeenth century, and especially in eighteenth-century France or America. John Lilburne and Richard Overton, soldiers in Cromwell's Army, first put forward their liberal, even socialist ideas in the 1640s. Lilburne's 1646 pamphlet stressed that all men were children of Adam and thus "by nature equal and alike in power, dignity, authority and majesty."[4] This stood in sharp contrast to the prevailing belief in divinely ordained hierarchy. Lilburne was a spokesman for a small group referred to as Levellers, who argued that civil authority should be exercised only by mutual agreement and consent. All men had innate and inalienable rights; legal and political institutions existed only to protect those rights.

Lilburne was a liberal democrat. But a group that called itself True Levellers or Diggers soon went well beyond radical democracy and liberal notions of legal and political rights. In 1649, they seized some unenclosed common land and grew food which they distributed free to the poor. (Their actions were, needless to say, suppressed in short order.)

In 1652, the leader of the True Levellers, Gerrard Winstanley, produced a ringing cry to radical action entitled *The Law of Freedom*. This tract took private property as the root of all social injustice and corruption: "You Pharaohs, you have rich clothing and full bellies, you have honors and your ease; but know the day of judgement is begun and that it will reach you ere long. The poor people you oppress shall be the saviors of the land. If you find mercy, let Israel go free; break to pieces the bands of property."[5] Winstanley envisioned a utopia in which "there shall be no buying and selling of the earth, nor the fruits thereof. . . . If any man or family want corn or other provisions, he may go to the storehouse and fetch without money. . . . As every one works to advance the common stock, so everyone shall have free use of any commodity in the storehouse."[6] The arguments of liberalism and socialism were thus fashioned as spurs to popular political action. At times such words were as effective as the wealth, armies, churches, and arguments of the established authorities.

As the seventeenth and eighteenth centuries unfolded, the radical claims of socialists were seldom heard, but the arguments and demands of liberals for freedom and democracy became more and more effective. This was an age of dramatic advances in science, art, commerce, and invention. It became the dominant view of the age that people ought to be free—to speak their minds, to publish their thoughts, to assemble and to worship as they pleased, when and where they pleased. There was great excitement among the small but growing urban middle class, which sought freedom and a share in political power. The liberal ideas of Locke and Rousseau, Jefferson and Paine, Montesquieu and Condorcet gained a widespread following.

To these liberal political thinkers men were fundamentally good and fundamentally equal—the notion of "degree" no longer counted for so much. All men—and sometimes even all people—were seen to have basic natural rights. Even if many appeared to lack talent, all were presumed to be educable. The conservatism captured here in Shakespeare's *Troilus and Cressida* was seen to be in error:

The heavens themselves, the planets, this center
Observe degree, priority, and place,
. . . How could communities,

Degrees in schools and brotherhoods in cities,
Peaceful commerce from dividable shores,
The primogeneity and due of birth,
Prerogative of age, crowns, sceptres, laurels,
But by degree, stand in authentic place?
Take but degree away, untune that string,
And hark, what discord follows!⁷

The new liberal thinkers did not demand elimination of degree, but they wanted to limit it. They wanted an elected parliament to be as powerful as the monarch or the aristocracy. They wanted all people with property to have economic opportunities, not just the aristocracy and their retainers, and they wanted educational opportunities for all who might benefit from them.⁸ Discord would not follow, in their view, but rather more musicians than society had ever known.

John Locke assumed that people were by nature peaceful, rational, and free. Governments existed to protect people's natural rights from an errant minority. Such governments should exist at the will of the majority, and the people had the right to overthrow any government that violated their trust. Unlike Hobbes, Locke did not imagine that chaos would ensue from this right. People were reasonable, and the right to rebel would not in itself lead to rebellion; the determining factor would be the quality of government.⁹

Conservatism, too, soon added to its ideological repertoire. Edmund Burke made a far subtler case for conservatism than had Hobbes, a case more appropriate to freer and more prosperous times. Governments and societies were not like machines or houses to be built according to blueprints. Constitutions should evolve; they cannot simply be created by excessively rational, inexperienced liberal thinkers. Societies are organic; like trees that ought to be nurtured and pruned now and again by sensitive and seasoned gardeners. Societies are also like fabrics, woven of numerous fibers, of habits, duties, and obligations. As a cloth woven of traditions, a society cannot simply be taken apart and put back together again. Government ought to be handled gently by men bred for the task, perhaps for generations. Change will come when it must, but radical change disrupts habits and weakens the social fabric.

The evolutionary process of early nineteenth-century England followed Burke's image. Suffrage was extended first to an educated and wealthy minority of propertied men. Universal male suffrage developed gradually from 1832 to 1885. The American Revolution was led by a propertied class, and the U.S. Constitution was written almost exclusively by wealthy men.[10] While the American Declaration of Independence was in the liberal spirit, the Constitution contained compromises between the principles of liberalism and a moderate conservativism. Populist democracy gave way to representative democracy with strong political advantages for the propertied classes and a separation of powers that avoided both tyranny and easy enactment of majoritarian desires. A government that governed least was deemed best.

Liberals of the eighteenth and nineteenth centuries believed that the strength of sociopolitical systems was to be found less in government than in the economic sphere. The economic privileges of the aristocracy, monopolies granted by the crown, private toll bridges, and the like were outrageous impediments to commerce; economic and political freedoms were seen as inseparable. The political struggle was one between the paternalistic conservatism of landed economic privilege and the burgeoning forces of commerce, artisanship, and industry. Both were enthusiastic about property rights, but they stressed different forms of property. In sum, in early nineteenth-century England and the United States, the two forces on the ideological spectrum were balanced. But the balance shifted toward liberalism as time wore on. In continental Europe conservatism held on more tightly and was confronted in due course with more violent and sudden opposition.

With the industrial revolution, fully developed by the mid-nineteenth century in England, the ideological spectrum was altered radically. The rural poor were forced off the land; factories and cities grew rapidly. In the cities there were no effective sewage systems. The horribly crowded tenements were almost always dark, cold, and dirty. In the factories, mines, and mills adults and children worked twelve to fourteen hours a day, seven days a week, and often went hungry nonetheless. These workers' lives deteriorated radically as industrialization "progressed." The early liberals' glowing words about equality of opportunity and political freedom rang false—if they were heard at all by ordinary citizens. Concepts like trade unions and phrases like "property is theft" and "nothing to lose but your chains" made more sense to them. The rise of socialist ideology moved the whole ideological spectrum to the left, bringing about changes in both liberalism and conservatism.[11]

Classical liberalism, which prevailed before the rise of socialism, stressed political, religious, and market (economic) freedom. It developed in the context of markets whose participants numbered in the hundreds, if not thousands, and were of roughly equal size. This world was short-lived. Economic enterprises grew rapidly and many markets soon became oligopolistic. Workers faced lives of ignorance, ill health, and backbreaking labor. Few of them were as concerned as liberals about government interference; they wanted to have, for their labor, a warm home, food, and education—at least for their children, if not for themselves. Liberalism in the late nineteenth century adapted rapidly to a situation in which most men had gained the right to vote and intellectual and political rivalry came from the left as well as the right.

Liberals soon stressed positive freedoms for the majority. The freedom to achieve equality of opportunity became more important than freedom from excessive government. Government became an active protector of public health and a provider of urgent social and economic needs such as education, economic infrastructure, and many varieties of social insurance. The new liberals stressed free secular education, in keeping with their long-standing belief in the educability of the common people. They made it the duty of government to assure at least minimal equality of economic opportunity. Socialists pressed for more—higher wages for industrial workers and higher taxes on factories, land, and wealth. They constantly urged governments to provide more services for all, and progressive liberals accepted many of their demands. The active welfare state expanded its range of services continuously from the late nineteenth century until the 1970s. (Nor is it certain that this pattern of expansion has ended.)

Conservatism too moved to the left—sometimes more successfully than liberalism—from 1850 to 1950. Classical conservatives were not so adverse to state intervention in the economy as were classical liberals—they saw fostering economic growth and national strength as a duty of the state. Many conservative governments have built vast economic infrastructres through governmental rather than private corporations.[12] In reaction to socialist demands, conservatives simply updated their traditional paternalism, that sense of noblesse oblige rooted in real feelings of community. On many occasions they accepted, sometimes even initiated, the principal policies of the modern welfare state. The conservative Bismarck created one of the first nationwide social insurance schemes well before most liberals had turned to progressive economic and social policies.

Each of the classical ideologies has been a living, dynamic set of ideas, and each has evolved in relation to the others. The ideological spectrum has become more and more complex over time. Ideological debates, for the most part, focus on what might be called distributive issues. The left, for example, presses for a greater governmental role in redistributing wealth and power from rich to poor, while the right seeks to protect the expansion of capital and attempts to maintain concentrations of economic and political power. The center seeks a balance, fostering state neutrality toward the market. Environmental concerns have not been utterly ignored by these political thinkers, but only rarely were they seen as important.

The Meaning of Left and Right

By the early part of the twentieth century, the ideological spectrum had evolved in complexity. Socialism was to be found in a thousand varieties but none of these held much power. The sharpest division in the socialist camp, as in the conservative, was that between those who accepted the basic principles and institutions of liberal democracy as they had evolved, and those who did not. This situation endured until the rise of fascism and again for a time after World War II.

The mapping of ideologies along a line does not accommodate the view of some commentators that the extreme poles have much in common. Nor does it depict clearly the deep differences between such "adjacent" views as communism and democratic socialism. (Indeed, democratic socialists and democratic conservatives, especially those of a paternalistic variety, have more in common than many varieties of socialists do with each other.) But the spectrum does capture well the way many people view ideology.

It is not always clear, however, what the line represents. One distinction has it that a position on the spectrum indicates the extent to which an individual or government advocates political intervention in the economic marketplace in the interest of those relatively disadvantaged within the marketplace. A position slightly to the right of center then represents neutrality toward market outcomes.[13] Those further to the right would intervene in the interest of advantaged groups more extensively than they would for disadvantaged groups.

I need to mention several problems with this perspective on the spectrum before I go on to draw a distinction between left-to-right distributive politics and the politics of environmentalism. The first of these problems is noted by the historian Karl Polanyi, who wrote that the existence of a market is itself the product of governmental intervention.[14] The free market is not a "natural" phenomenon; it is created by the deliberate action of government. Economic competition continues to exist only by virtue of governmental intervention. If anything is natural, it is the monopoly to which free markets tend. This granted, our definitions of left and right are still useful if we assume that true "free marketers" indeed seek to minimize intervention but, when they do intervene, they seek to inhibit the tendency to monopoly. In practice most who claim to be free marketers are not—because they seek above all to provide further advantages to advantaged groups, regions, and industries.

This view puts true free marketers nearer to the center than to the right of the spectrum. To the left of this point are those who advocate interventions that aid the less advantaged. They might, for example, provide low-cost public schools. To the right stand those who intervene on behalf of the rich, seeking to grant advantages beyond what the market alone might offer. A classic example of such intervention is the oil depletion allowance—whereby oil companies were freed from taxes that other, often less wealthy corporations and individuals were obliged to pay. Another is the governmental provision of economic infrastructure necessary to particular businesses—roads leading to forests being logged or mines being opened. One might also characterize in this way the new sewers and schools built in the suburbs-to-be when desperate inner-city needs were ignored.

A second problem with the left-to-right spectrum is that one must remain conscious of the distinction between principles and practice, between advocacy and action, and even between assertion and belief. Politicians almost never practice what they preach, and much of the time they do not even believe what they say. Socialism in principle looks different from socialism in practice. Democratic socialists do less than they promise, while revolutionary socialists do things they did not mention on the road to power. Conservatives speak of the interest of the glorious nation but often deliver the goods principally to a very small group of supporters, or they speak of free markets while quietly giving massive subsidies to particular industries or individuals. Progressive liberals' cures can sometimes prove as bad as the disease. An understanding of ideology requires more than taking ideological assertions at face value. This applies to environmentalist ideology as well.

During the late 1950s and early 1960s, a number of observers asserted that the age of ideology was at an end. S. M. Lipset offered the hypothesis in its baldest form. "The differences between left and right in the Western democracies are no longer profound," he wrote in 1960. "This change in Western political life reflects the fact that the fundamental political problems of the industrial revolution have been solved: the workers have achieved industrial and political citizenship; the conservatives have accepted the welfare state; and the democratic left has recognized that an increase in overall state power carries with it more dangers to freedom than solutions for economic problems."[15] The remainder of the decade, of course, brought into question much of this statement, as a global left-wing movement was born which insisted that urgent socioeconomic problems remained and that their solutions would not necessarily dangerously increase state power. In the 1970s and 1980s, conservatives began openly to reject the modern welfare state. Left–right ideology was clearly pronounced dead somewhat prematurely.

Though left–right ideology cannot be dismissed outright, Lipset's view contains some truth. The democratic class struggle had indeed been institutionalized. Union–management relations are a fine-tuned system, and the party and electoral systems of most advanced democracies have pushed politics toward the center. The left, in the Anglo-American democracies, embraced a quiet, moderate blend of progressive liberalism and democratic socialism. The right had become a bland conservatism whose best argument for deserving power rested on its desire to manage government in a more "businesslike" way. There was rarely, in the period 1945–73, much open talk on the right about anything having gone "too far." Few on the left urged and fewer acted to transform the class structure or to alter the structures and principles of economic decision-making. The moderate left seemed to have lost interest in mobilizing opposition to the economic status quo.

Of course, political quietude automatically favors the forces of the status quo, which in turn prefer the absence of mobilizing claims of any kind. In the language of one noted political scientist, capitalist democratic systems carry a considerable "mobilization of bias" against change.[16] Some will see an ideology of quietude as an opportunity to roll back the long, slow pattern of change associated with moderate progressivism. Benign, moderate progressivism is a truly profound social compromise, but it will hold only as long as there is continuing pressure from the left.

The end of ideology rested on the right's willingness to accept growing shares for all, which in turn rested on continuous and substantial economic growth—a foundation of sand. The great compromise was based on a long period of Western economic expansion that depended on dominance of the poor nations and on costs unsustainably imposed on nature.[17] The ideological revival of the 1960s questioned the former basis for growth; that of the 1970s and 1980s, the latter. In the 1960s political questions addressed more than domestic economic distribution. In the 1970s the rise of environmentalism placed on the political agenda a set of issues largely outside distributive politics itself.

The 1980s, however, have brought resurgent conservatism as those on the right reopened supposedly settled questions. This took place for several reasons. First, the energy price shocks of the 1970s

represented the first real threat to the expansion of Western industrial strength in more than a century. Second, traditional economic
power in the Anglo-American democracies was threatened by the
rise of new industrial forces offshore, as well as the lesser irritants
of domestic environmental legislation.[18] Third, the power of the labor
movement was declining as industrial workers were replaced by
rationalization and automation. These changes, combined with the
loss of progressive political momentum, led to the rise of neoconservatism. Moderate progressive politics were in fundamental retreat
for the first time in a century. Perhaps the greatest opportunity to
restore moderate progressivism now lies in the distinction between
"distributive" and "environmental" politics.

Distributive politics is concerned with the distribution and redistribution of the products and other intended benefits of economic
activity. Who should be taxed? How much? On what and for whose
benefit should government spend money? Distributive politics involves property, ownership, transfer payments, tax expenditures,
tax loopholes, social welfare measures, trade union rights, and
budget deficits. The ethical debate is carried out in terms of equity.
Which region or district gets a new dam or road? Which segment
of society has been treated fairly or unfairly?

It is in the context of distributive politics that the fundamental
institutions and processes of liberal democratic institutions have
evolved. They are based on the assumption that everyone has the
right to choose representatives who will stand up for their interests.
Interests are understood to be primarily distributive. Individuals
"naturally" look out for themselves in this regard and the liberal
democratic system effectively integrates and makes compromises
involving the diverse distributive claims made upon it. It is based
on some degree of tolerance between the economically advantaged
and the economically disadvantaged. In addition, virtually all participants assume that economic expansion is both desirable and
inevitable.

Little within the nature of environmental concerns automatically
suggests how their costs ought to be borne. Making the polluter pay
for cleanup, thus forcing the costs of pollution prevention through
to the producers and consumers of potentially dirty products, is only

one way. If the products are useful to society and they can be produced cleanly, it might be just as reasonable to finance such cleanups
out of the public treasury. But pollution is only one aspect of environmental concern—environmental politics competes with the
whole distributional agenda.

Environmentalists take a wide range of positions on distributional
issues. Environmental politics does not merely concern who pays.
More often it asks what changes are necessary, whether they will
be required and, if so, when. Also critical is the question of margin
of safety. Environmental politics thus becomes involved in design
of the production process itself. Environmental politics is about
choosing technologies, about the criteria for such choices, and about
their unintended effects. In environmental politics, distributional
issues take second place to choice of technology, design of technology and use of technology. How ought we to organize our
collective habitat? What are the best communications and transportation systems? What are our principal future energy sources to be?
How much energy will be needed? How large should the population
be in the future? How large should the economy be? Why? None
of these is a distributional issue although they all have distributional
implications. There is thus no necessary relationship between one's
position on environmental issues and one's position on distributional issues.

Those who pollute on a large scale and those who make
money on the rapid depletion of resources tend to hold right-of-
center positions on distributional issues. But these individuals or
corporations can learn to live with selling fewer resources at
higher prices or using public money to adjust their plants and
processes. The forestry industry in Ontario, for example, has
had no difficulty accepting public payment for replanting trees at
a rate comparable to the money they made cutting them down.
Nor do those who produce pollution abatement equipment object to stringent governmental standards and enforcement. These
may not be the best possible policies, but they are policies both
environmentally sound and acceptable to many positions on the
left–right political spectrum.

The contemporary ideological spectrum might now be pictured

FIGURE 1

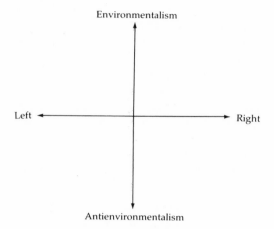

as in figure 1.[19] Two ideological dimensions provide a more satis-
factory means of locating and assessing the ideas of both individuals
and groups, political theorists and political practitioners. It might
also be a better perspective from which to develop tools for assessing
policies. This change is part of the ideological spectrum's continuing
evolution toward greater complexity. Left and right are still relevant,
but they are no longer sufficient.

The Autonomy of Environmental Politics

Crucial to a recreation of the ideological map is a demonstration that
environmental ideas and policies cannot be subsumed easily under
one or another of the traditional ideological headings. In this regard
it is interesting that each major ideological tradition evinced early
sensitivity to environmental concerns. Historically, no particular ideology has had a monopoly on environmental thinking. Environmental values can point in several political directions, and articulate
contemporary environmentalists are found all along the left–right
spectrum.

Benjamin Disraeli, the quintessential conservative prime minister, was environmentally concerned about the character and quality of urban life. He saw country living as healthier than urban living in terms of working and living conditions, air, water, food, and community life. Disraeli, like many other conservatives of his day, was highly sensitive to the evils of industrialization. (At this time conservatism was based in the landed classes, which looked on industry and commerce as undignified, even temporary.) Malthus too gave us a classical conservative perspective on environmental issues: natural passions must be held in check, or misery will result. Those in authority must rule with a firm hand. Quite clearly, many of the concerns of modern environmentalism can be traced back to conservative ideology. The very words *conservation* and *conservatism* have the same root.

Equally important to an environmentalist way of thinking are several aspects of the conservative "mood" so eloquently expressed by Burke and in the contemporary era by Michael Oakeshott. Prudence is fundamental to both conservatism and environmentalism. It is prudent to suggest that technologies and chemicals must be proven safe before they are adopted. Both conservatives and environmentalists are ever mindful of the responsibilities we bear to both past and future generations. An undue emphasis on present gain is short-sighted and greedy, constituting a failure to one's duties.

Liberalism can also claim common origin with environmentalism, particularly if one sets aside its early free-market origins and emphasizes instead the writings of John Stuart Mill. Mill was one of the earliest political thinkers to recognize the advantages to a steady-state economy. In 1857 he wrote, "I cannot . . . regard the stationary state of capital and wealth with the unaffected aversion so generally manifested towards it by political economists of the old school. I am inclined to believe that it would be, on the whole, a very considerable improvement on our present condition."[20] In addition, perhaps the most central theme of classical liberalism—the notion of rights—has become important to environmentalism. Environmentalism can be taken as an extension of liberalism in its claim that the basic human rights established by liberalism belong also to future human generations and to other species. Environmentalists also say, in essence, that all of us have a right to a clean, healthy, and diverse natural environment.

Socialists and Marxists can also trace to their classical thinkers an intellectual basis for environmentalism. Speaking of the early development of capitalism, Karl Marx wrote:

> Nature becomes for the first time simply an object for mankind, purely a matter of utility; it ceases to be recognized as a power in its own right; and the theoretical knowledge of its independent laws appears only as a stratagem designed to subdue it to human requirements. Pursuing this tendency, capital has pushed . . . beyond the deification of nature and the inherited self-sufficient satisfaction of existing needs confined within well-defined bounds, and the reproduction of the traditional way of life.[21]

Marx spoke of capitalism's tendency to reduce all values to monetary values. What better critique might an environmentalist make regarding the destruction of environmental values in contemporary society? As Peter Victor put it, "Marx discerned that capitalism transforms everything of value into commodities to be bought and sold, and this includes people as labor power and nature as resources. . . . Many environmentalists . . . do not presume that solutions are possible without far-reaching socio-economic changes, and this provides them with a common perspective with Marx on the *need* for societal change if not on its *inevitability*."[22] About urbanization's effects on the relationship between humans and the natural world, Marx wrote,

> Capitalist production, by collecting the population in great centres, and causing an ever-increasing preponderance of town population, disturbs the metabolism of man and the earth, i.e. the return to the soil of its elements consumed by man in the form of food and clothing, and therefore, violates the external condition for lasting fertility of the soil. . . . All progress in capitalistic agriculture is a progress in the art, not only of robbing the labourer but of robbing the soil; all progress in increasing

fertility of the soil for a given time is a progress toward ruining the lasting sources of that fertility.[23]

This passage might have come from *Organic Gardening and Farming*. If it contains an error from an environmental perspective, it is perhaps the assumption that urbanization and exploitative agriculture are unique to capitalist societies. The solution to the problems Marx understood so thoroughly may require changes of a sort he could not envision. Such solutions have also escaped most of those who have held political power in his name. Socialists have concentrated on distributive, not environmental, values. They have even put aside redistribution in the name of "catching up with the West." In principle, however, environmentalists and socialists agree that noneconomic values should come to prevail over economic values via the political process.

One might assume from environmentalism's compatibility with the three classical ideologies that practitioners of each ideology potentially respect the environment. But history has proved otherwise. One might also conclude that no single ideology has an exclusive claim on environmental wisdom. Or the evidence may have been selectively assembled. One can almost as easily show that the classical ideologies have all ignored environmental concerns or have contained elements that resulted in harsh treatment for the environment. The extreme free market emphasis of classical liberalism and or neoconservatism, for example, all but guarantees environmental rapacity. So too does the siege mentality associated with isolated socialist regimes, which strive to outperform economically their capitalist enemies. Environmentalism nonetheless has clear links with all the classical ideologies. But to be effective it must also stand alone; it must become an autonomous political ideology in its own right.

Environmentalism Left, Right, and Center

Those rooted in one or another of the classical ideologies take various views of the importance of environmental concerns. Where Marx,

Mill, and Disraeli were sensitive to such issues, others have been oblivious or openly hostile. Likewise, environmentalists have been relatively indifferent to distributive issues—especially in the early years of the movement.[24] But even more significant to an understanding of environmentalism as an ideology is the fact that environmentalists occupy almost every position on the traditional right-to-left ideological spectrum.

On the political right are many of the populationists, including Paul Ehrlich and especially Garrett Hardin. (Ehrlich, however, is difficult to categorize; his more recent writings place him nearer the center, which itself has moved right as Ehrlich has become more sensitive to the concerns of the less advantaged.)[25] Also to the right of center are those radical decentralists who favor breaking up and privatizing publically owned electrical utilities. There is an implicit conservatism too among environmentalists who propose detailed economic restructuring without ever mentioning the institution of private property,[26] and among those who are generally at odds with modern life, who seek a return to a preindustrial past regardless of the effects of such a change on social structures.

Both William Ophuls and Robert Heilbroner, whose personal sympathies are probably left of center, too easily accept a decline in liberal democratic institutions in the face of environmental stress. Such pessimism could inform an argument for an extreme environmental conservatism. Historically, vehement pessimism about the future has almost always been associated with political conservatism. One can reasonably place these arguments on the right side of the spectrum even though those who made them may not belong there.

Left-oriented environmentalists include Barry Commoner, William Leiss, Frances Moore Lappé, Murray Bookchin, David B. Brooks, Peter Victor, Rudolf Bahro, and Richard Barnet. Barry Weisberg, David Dickson Andre Gorz, and Claus Offe are also discussed here. This group represents an astonishing variety of opinion, including Chinese communist sympathizers, even Maoists, moderate social democrats, unorthodox Marxists, and anticapitalist anarchists.[27] Also fascinating is the variety of approaches to environmentalism among those on the nonenvironmental left. Some wish to subsume it, some seem to deny its importance, and some are sensitive to the contradictions between a left-wing orientation and environmentalism.[28]

In the center or the moderate left stand probably the majority of active members of North American environmental organizations.[29] This group also includes such vitally important environmental thinkers as Amory Lovins, Lester R. Brown, E. F. Schumacher, Hazel Henderson, and others whose position on distributive issues is difficult to determine from their writings. The pessimists Ehrlich, Heilbroner, and Ophuls might also prefer to position themselves here.

Lovins in particular seems almost deliberately to avoid any political (left or right) classification. He has written, for example, "There are very strong forces, particularly in this [Reagan] administration, seeking to bail out those technologies which are dying of an incurable attack of market forces, while trying to suppress those succeeding in the marketplace, namely efficiency and renewables. So, until we start to replace the corporate socialists with the real conservatives the transition will be unnecessarily slow and painful."[30] But he has also written with deep caring about the technological displacement of industrial workers and the loss of craftsmanship. Lovins concludes his comments on the decline of craftsmanship, "We defined work as obtaining a commodity (a job) from a vendor (an employer)—so that work itself became a commodity produced, no less, by a process of production, like a brick or a car. We substituted earning for an older ethic of serving and caring as the only legitimate motivation for work. Thus alienation in the place of fulfillment, inner poverty alongside outward affluence, a pathological restless and rootless mobility became the symptoms of a morbid social condition that corroded human values."[31] Elsewhere Lovins seems very much at home as a Jeffersonian liberal. He clearly manages to straddle a good measure of the traditional political spectrum.

The variability among environmentalists' political stances suggests that, in principle, a case for environmentalism can be made to a wide variety of governments in terms they can appreciate and understand. Environmentalists construct policies acceptable, even desirable to a wide range of political actors. Left-oriented environmentalists might propose rapid and total pollution cleanup with all costs to be borne by polluters. If some particularly dirty industries were to collapse under the burden, so much the better. Such a view might alienate some on the traditional left, particularly trade union-ists, but the "polluter pays" principle makes sense to many socialists. In contrast, a conservative environmentalist might be content to raise energy prices with no protection for less advantaged groups and no tax on windfall profits. Neither of these positions is necessarily de-sirable; the point is that environmentalism can adapt to many po-sitions on the left-to-right spectrum.

Environmentalism can be developed to appeal to almost any po-litical persuasion, perhaps excepting two. The extreme ideological left, especially when in power, finds virtually any kind of dissent unacceptable, and there is little reason to think such a government would countenance any attempt to slow the march of economic development seen to be necessary to the achievement of socialism. Also beyond environmentalism's reach is the extreme ideological right, those, for example, who fervently advocate free market eco-nomics while delivering further advantages to those with established economic power. The far right views environmental concerns as false unless "proven" true; when the damage is obvious, it is seen as an unfortunate but altogether necessary cost of progress. Or the right uses a "blame the victim" approach, attributing the problems to misfortune, to negligence on the job, or to smoking (not entirely a matter of free choice) and arguing that victims are always "free" to live or work elsewhere.[32] In contrast, the notion of putting a price on human suffering and death is, to environmentalists, immoral: rather than discounting future costs, we should forgo present eco-nomic benefits. Environmentalists sometimes suggest that we should forgo such benefits to aid other species, even species not economically beneficial to humans. This sort of thinking is too much for the ideologically orthodox far right to contemplate.

It is interesting to compare the environmental performances of such ideologically diverse regimes as those of the United States, the Soviet Union, France, Japan, Brazil, and Malaysia.[33] The differences in their environmental policies are probably more easily attributed to level of development than to ideological disagreements. One could add West Germany, Britain, Canada, and Czechoslovakia without calling this generalization into question. All of these countries are deeply committed to further economic growth. Some are more careful in environmental matters now than they were a decade or two ago, but all remain hesitant to call on their citizenry or significant economic interests to make real sacrifices in the interest of environmental protection.

The West Germans, for example, fail to impose and enforce meaningful speed limits on their highways even though their national forests are threatened through such inaction. One doubts that the Russians intend to add expensive containment buildings to present or future nuclear reactors. Nor does it seem likely that Brazil or Malaysia will soon act to protect their tropical forests, or that the United States will work to reduce acid rain or pollution of the Great Lakes. No matter what ideology they follow, these countries' governments seem incapable of firm action in the defense of the environment.

Let us look more closely at some of the differences between environmental ideas and left–right ideologies, focusing on reasons they have been unable to implement effective environmental policies. I emphasize the left of the spectrum because there lie the greater doubts about the ideological autonomy of environmental ideas.[34]

What are some of the contradictions between socialism and environmentalism? What problems have arisen in the attempt to integrate these ideas? Orthodox Marxists have none: the socialist revolution will eliminate capitalism; capitalists are responsible for environmental damage; case closed. Or—environmental concerns are essentially middle-class concerns; we are a party of the proletariat; we cannot worry about aesthetics and middle-class comforts when there is hunger and oppression in the world. But many socialists are not so glib about environmental issues. Some have merged these two viewpoints at considerable cost to socialist orthodoxy. This has not been an easy process, and it is not by any means been completed.

Socialism is rooted in the beginnings of the industrial revolution, and nearly all socialists have welcomed, indeed celebrated, industrialization and the economic growth it has made possible. Few before the 1960s allowed that any society had yet reached material conditions that could make communism possible.[35] Few conventional Marxists agree, and fewer still consider either the need for or the possibility of an end to economic growth. Nor do many question the view that technological development is, on balance, a benevolent force (its worst ravages are peculiar to capitalism and would not arise under socialism). Under "real" socialism, it is assumed, highways would not be built through prime farmland, automobiles would not pollute, and nuclear power plants would function safely. But there is no evidence that such things are true. In these matters socialism and capitalism seem similar. Environmental destruction is the same whether carried out on behalf of a small number of capitalists or every last one of the masses.

Socialists' claim to solidarity with environmentalism lies in their willingness to intervene in the market to achieve nonmarket values. But traditional socialist intervention has focused on advancing distributive rather than environmental values. When not centered on redistribution, socialist intervention has been used to speed economic growth, not restrain it.[36] But environmental values focus on the unintended negative consequences of industrial production and on the possibility of constraining production. This fundamental difference seems a sufficient basis for asserting that environmentalism belongs neither on the left nor on the right—it is an ideology outside the one-dimensional continuum.

But left-wing environmentalists rarely hesitate to advocate nationalization, long-range governmental economic planning, and even the use of environmental and resource restraints to redistribute wealth.[37] These positions suggest that all socialist tenets need not be sacrificed for environmentalism. But some must. A socialist-environmentalist synthesis would require a revision of socialism as fundamental as the revisions sustained by liberalism in the late nineteenth and early twentieth century in the face of the socialist challenge.

An environmental revision of socialist ideology involves rejecting socialist complicity with centralization of power. As William Leiss put it, "The objective of an alternative social policy would not be to return a larger portion of the population to the harshness of circumstances which have in the past often characterized life in the hinterland, but to disperse the advantages of modern technology—

deliberately sacrificing some of the dubious 'efficiency' of centralized production—over a wider variety of situations."[38]

Perhaps the best-known of socialists who have sought to integrate a decentralist environmentalism with socialist ideology are Andre Gorz and Murray Bookchin. Both are enthusiastic about rural and urban communes and producer and consumer cooperatives. Gorz, Bookchin, and Leiss share a sympathy toward decentralism with such nonsocialists as E. J. Mishan, E. F. Schumacher andd Amory Lovins. But all these, and even such complicating thinkers as Paolo Soleri, only leave one hoping desperately that someone will sort out the economic, political, geographic, and technological dimensions of environmentalism's rejection of centralization. (Some of these issues are considered further in chapter 9.)

Decentralism carries two challenges to socialist orthodoxy. First, it puts at risk that most basic of socialist tenets, comprehensive central planning. Decentralist environmentalism also does not require, as socialism does, the existence of an industrial working class. Technology is not necessarily problematic for environmentalism. Telecommunications, computers, robotics, photovoltaics, and much biotechnology are generally acceptable in environmental terms. But these technologies may imply the end of the industrial working class as we know it. The socialist/environmentalist Andre Gorz, more than any other, has come to grips with the implications of the technological revolution.

Gorz's books *Farewell to the Working Class* and *Paths to Paradise: On the Liberation from Work* celebrate both the demise of the industrial working class and the possibility of transforming the meaning of work. Gorz calculates that the new levels of productivity could reduce work time to twenty thousand hours in the life of an average person (about ten years at forty hours per week). Much work is already unnecessary, nothing but a "useless compulsion" that serves primarily to conceal the possibility of liberation from labor.

The amount of time spent working and the relatively high level of employment have been artificially maintained because of the inextricable confusion which exists between the production of the necessary and superfluous, the useful and the useless,

waste and wealth, pleasures and nuisances, destruction and repair. Whole areas of economic life now have the sole function
of "providing work," or of producing for the sake of keeping
people working. But when a society produces in order to provide work rather than works in order to produce, then work as
a whole has no meaning.[39]

Gorz takes the end of the industrial working class as part of the
development of productive forces that render work itself superfluous. He integrates this view with an explanation of socialism's failure
to attract political support among working people and middle-class
professionals. The failure is rooted in the socialist movement's inability to perceive the central importance of individual autonomy.
Socialists do not emphasize, sometimes do not even recognize, the
deep human fear of collectivism, whether totalitarian or not. "Essentially, the 'freedom' which the majority of the population of the
overdeveloped nations seek to protect from 'collectivism' and the
'totalitarian' threat, is the freedom to create a private niche protecting
one's personal life against all pressures and external social obligations."[40] People create these niches through their family lives, country cottages, gardens, workshops, sports, and hobbies. Gorz neglects
to include the dream of starting one's own business. Some might
thus argue that his socialism is not revisionist enough, although he
is supportive of small-scale entrepreneurship.

Most important is Gorz's blending of the failures of socialism with
the decline of the working class. He proposes a great political effort
toward achieving expansion of the "autonomous sphere of life"
through the "liberation of [working] time." "Imagine that society
were to distribute yearly productivity gains in the following way: a
third in the form of greater purchasing power, and two thirds in
the form of additional free time. . . . A 20-hour week could be
achieved in 20 years, by the year 2001; and, if we take vacations and
public holidays into account, would amount to a yearly total of barely
900 hours."[41] Productivity gains of this sort are upon us. The question is whether they will result in unemployment for some and rising
incomes for others or in greater free time for all who want it. Gorz
proposes allowing people to choose how much they want to work.

He is convinced that a majority will choose to work less, for less money, and he presents considerable survey data to support this view. He also discusses firms and unions that have successfully implemented flexible work time and working patterns, and he suggests many imaginative techniques for introducing variety and complexity into work patterns. "Retirement advances" can be made available in return for an employee's postponing his or her final retirement. "Time savings accounts" would work on a similar principle. Gorz also offers an array of relevant political slogans such as "work less, live more." His position differs radically from capitalism, socialism, and traditional trade unionism.

A related issue for which a clear environmental position has been developed is that of the role of technology in social change. Karl Marx saw technology as a base upon which society and politics ("superstructure") rests. Marx did not emphasize the need for political controls on technological choices. David Dickson, however, argues that the very design of some technologies both results from and supports certain forms of political and social order. Environmentalists argue that new relations of production cannot be established without consciously selecting new means of production as well. This view represents a fundamental challenge to Marxist orthodoxy. Dickson writes:

> Only by realizing the extent to which technology provides an integral part of the ideology of contemporary society, at the same time as forming an essential element of the mechanisms by which the supremacy of existing political systems are maintained, can we see the extent to which the need to develop an alternative technology is both necessary and desirable. To neglect the political dimension of this change is to support an idealistic concept of technology that does not coincide with the social reality of technology as it has been experienced. Yet to imply that the problem involves merely the social relations of production, and not the very nature of the means of production, is to disregard the extent to which our current technology is permeated by the exploitative ideology of advanced industrialized societies, whether nominally capitalist or socialist.[42]

Technology is not politically neutral, nor does it assure a socialist political outcome. Politics must determine technology at least as much as technology determines politics. Socialism and capitalism would probably differ fundamentally from environmentalism in their handling of nuclear power, for example, or in their planning of the output of an automobile industry (they would differ less from each other). And much of socialism's political base in the developed democracies (i.e., the industrial working class) is involved in technologies that do not fit easily into any environmentalist social order. Few people favor, let alone actively struggle for, elimination of the industries in which they gain their livelihoods.[43]

Gorz goes far toward adopting a technological planning aspect of an environmental perspective. In his "Social Ideology of the Motor Car," hed asserts that the automobile is inherently an antisocial luxury. He also argues that nuclear power "irrevocably prescribes a particular kind of society, to the exclusion of all others."[44] These technologies prevent any equitable distribution of use values and political choices and cannot be part of any truly socialist society. This perspective could alienate Gorz's brand of environmentalist socialism from much of socialism's traditional working-class base. He seems to take the "integrated" ideology forever beyond the realm of distributive politics. Gorz's position is well beyond any politics that seeks simply the easy redistribution available within growing economies.[45]

I mention briefly several ideas that follow from Langdon Winner's superb work *Autonomous Technology*. Winner, whose ideology is virtually indeterminate, follows the conservative Jacques Ellul in discussing the loss of social institutions' and individuals' ability to choose ends, to "consider their fundamental commitments." Ellul argues that modern societies develop such an attachment to instruments and techniques that they cannot select outcomes which do not follow from their instrumental (technological) choices. Preserving jobs, providing goods, and achieving economic growth are means, not ends—but both socialists and capitalists can be swept up in the imperatives of autonomous technologies. The means become our masters. Winner assesses Marx's role in the development of a theory of autonomous technology:

Although he [Marx] presents a well-developed conception of technology out of control, in the context of his work as a whole it is merely an interlude in the midst of a much larger argument. For Marx, the alienation of labour and the appearance of a massive, life-draining industrial mechanism cannot be considered independently of the historical class struggle, surplus value in industrial economics, capitalist accumulation, and the social and political domination of the bourgeoisie. Marx introduces the specter of an alien technological force to illustrate how far historical alienation has gone and how little power the worker has over his own daily existence. But Marx makes it clear that mastery over technology has not been really lost. It has simply been removed to a small segment of the social order, the capitalist class.[46]

For Marx a socialist transformation gives mastery over technology into the hands of the majority, leading almost automatically to an elimination of alienation. This is analagous to the view of those who see socialism an automatic solution to the destruction of the natural world. Marx's confidence lingers even among those who would revise socialism fundamentally. Even Dickson, who rejects the notion that technology is politically neutral, expects that producers would soon choose different sorts of machines. And Gorz expects consumers to lose interest in the goods produced by technologically advanced (capitalist) systems. But none of these thinkers can come up with an agent of political transformation to replace the proletariat. Winner ends up suggesting that "we" experiment with "turning off" selected technologies to see what happens. All three accept the necessity of a new process for the political selection of technologies, but none can outline the means to achieve such a process, with or without the advent of socialism. That is the fundamental political question of the balance of this century and beyond.

Another essential element in an environmental revision of socialism is rejection of the inevitability and desirability of economic growth. Gorz writes, "A richer life is not only compatible with the production of fewer goods, it demands it. Nothing—other than the logic of capitalism—prevents us from manufacturing and making available to everyone adequate accommodation, clothing, household equipment, and forms of transportation which are energy-conserving, simple to repair, and long-lasting, while simultaneously increasing the amount of free time and the amount of truly useful products available to the population."[47] Since Kenneth Boulding first used the expression *energy and material throughputs* in constructing his "spaceship earth" analogy, environmentalists have had one eloquent and useful way of characterizing their preferred economy— one that seeks to minimize such throughputs. Others have suggested that environmentalism implies limits on economic growth, but Boulding's phrase seems a more sensible construction of this fundamental tenet of environmentalism. The need for reuse, repair, renewability, and recycling is included in Boulding's conception. In brief, virtually all environmentalists accept that conservation and renewable resources, especially energy resources, should receive great political and technical emphasis. Resource and environmental constraints might imply some restraints on future economic growth. The Boulding formulation allows GNP growth to take place within the limits on resource and energy supplies. But in the end many environmentalists do not see continuing economic growth as desirable, particularly in already prosperous societies.

Boulding's concept stands at the core of an environmentalist ideology as a standard against which new and existing technologies can be judged. Does a given technology, in comparison with its feasible alternatives, use more or fewer nonrenewable resources? Does it endanger or enhance the supply of renewable resources?

Environmentalist and socialist views on economic growth lead to concrete political differences on many key contemporary issues— for example, unemployment. Orthodox socialists and progressive liberals conclude that governmental economic planning should focus on developing new products, production techniques, and markets. In formulating such plans, environmentalists would be far more selective than traditional socialists. But socialists and environmentalists agree that government should further expand (labor-intensive) social, educational, and health services. Some socialists, particularly trade unionists, argue for reduced work time at present annual salary levels. Environmentalists, in contrast, have advocated across-the-board work time reductions with proportional reductions in salary. Hourly wages would remain near to existing levels, but everyone would work fewer hours; the solution leads to a required expansion in hiring. Capitalists, trade unionists, socialists, and most economists would be aghast at such a proposal—indeed, few job-holders would actively support it. "Pure" environmentalism, in this instance, might be a politics without a constituency. Only those with a strongly environmental sense of the meaning of "need" are comfortable with such a proposal.

William Leiss' 1976 book, *The Limits to Satisfaction*, looks at "the negative aspects of the high-intensity market setting" of contemporary Western societies. Escape from high-intensity markets (and excessive material and energy throughputs) could, Leiss hopes, "make possible a rich dimension in genuine satisfaction in both the labour activities and the free time of all individuals."[48] We can come to terms with the excess of goods by placing them in a hierarchy of human needs running from the trivial and artificially induced to those more profound and genuine. This may be the environmental equivalent to the value-laden socialist concept of false consciousness. Some see it as pretentious and antidemocratic.[49] Nonetheless this concept is necessary to environmentalism.

Leiss identifies as a key problem of contemporary society the fact that people often interpret their needs solely as needs for commodities. In a high-intensity market economy, sellers of goods play on the "ambiguous character of human needing."[50] Contemporary child-rearing teaches children to meet every need with a commodity. Other means are rarely even tried. Leiss suggests that Marx, as Bacon and Hobbes before him and William James and many others after him, saw human needs as ultimately insatiable and viewed the natural world largely as a collection of resources to be used for meeting those needs.[51] Marx attributed "an unequivocal, intrinsic quality to the use-value of exchanged goods," thereby underestimating the psychological and/or symbolic dimension of the value of goods. Even food and clothing have symbolic dimensions: "the perception of the usefulness of things related to needs such as food and clothing is . . . conditioned by cultural or symbolic mediations; if this is correct, then no commodity has an unequivocal, objective character that arises simply out of its material attributes alone."[52] Environmentalists' view of human need includes an end to material insatiability, limits on economic growth, and devaluation of the contemporary material nature of fulfillment. This puts environmentalism at odds with the foundations of socialist ideology.

In sum, environmentalism and socialism diverge on at least five fundamental points:

1. Environmentalists more consistently reject political and economic centralization.
2. Environmentalists see technology as a reflection of political and economic power and as a vital subject of political choice within both capitalist and socialist systems.
3. Environmentalists anticipate, even welcome, the decline of the industrial working class.
4. Environmentalists are not particularly enthusiastic about economic growth, and they reject many of its forms outright. Traditional socialists welcome growth; indeed, they see economic growth as the very basis for the historical evolution of socialist possibilities.
5. Environmentalists reject "economic man" as either necessary or desirable. In contrast to socialists, they prefer social, psychological, spiritual, and symbolic fulfillment of human needs to fulfillment via commodities.

These differences between environmentalism and the traditional left suggest why left regimes do not always respond effectively to environmental issues. I do not speak just of the Soviet Union. (Marshall I. Goldman has carefully documented some technical reasons why environmental problems have been handled badly there.)[53] The democratic socialist government of Saskatchewan, in the late 1970s, reached a decision very doubtful in environmental terms when the New Democratic Party (NDP) allowed the expansion of the province's uranium mining industry over environmentalists' strong objections. This decision shook the Saskatchewan NDP deeply, but in the end the party and the government made the choice that yielded the most public revenues. The traditional social democratic emphasis on health care and social programs pushed aside environmental considerations in the decision. Even issues of international morality (Saskatchewan itself had no need whatsoever for uranium) were put aside—by a party founded and led by Christian internationalists.[54] The local environmental costs of that decision are proving as considerable as environmentalists anticipated.[55]

Why have center and right regimes, supposedly more pragmatic, behaved in a similar fashion? Are their judgments not less cluttered by ideological baggage and rigid traditional patterns of behavior? No, of course not. Moderate, centrist regimes depend perhaps on less elaborate intellectual and theoretical underpinnings, but nonetheless they behave predictably, according to their ideological roots. There is not a body of literature that details centrist contradictions with environmentalism, but I consider here several academic analyses of the day-to-day practice of moderate to conservative regimes.

Two fundamental similarities between moderate and conservative governments, on the one hand, and far-left governments, on the other, are that military expenditures make up a large proportion of governmental expenditures and GNP; and that the governments emphasize economic growth as their principal goal. These two features are seen as the important base on which to judge success or failure of administrations and governments. Massive expenditures on and testing of military hardware are environmentally problematic, not only because they represent nonessential energy and material throughputs. But in the United States particularly, moderate progressives rarely hesitate to approve massive military spending, whether in office or in opposition.[56] Similarly, the pursuit of economic growth without consideration of its environmental effects is habitual across the political spectrum. Right-wing governments' enthusiasm for growth is not necessarily greater than that of the left, which assumes economic growth will produce more jobs.

This leads us to the political dimension of market-economic regimes. The environmental effects of highly market-oriented systems are, at best, mixed.[57] A market system, however far it might be from a pure free market system, has profound political consequences as well. As Charles E. Lindblom puts it: "Property is a system of authority established by government, just as what we call government is itself a system of authority. In its preoccupation with problems of authority in government, liberal democratic theory remains insensitive to problems of that authority which is embodied in property rights. . . . In all of the political systems of the world, much of politics is economics, and most of economics is also politics."[58] Lindblom elaborates how independent economic power, in regimes of many types, puts disproportionate political power into the hands of the economic elite.

This observation explains why most moderate to moderate right regimes respond weakly to environmental concerns. Their political power is based predominantly on business, professional, and agricultural entrepreneurs—individuals and institutions whose incomes depend on avoiding government-imposed environmental regulations and limitations. The market itself imposes a few limitations, as in the case of rising energy prices, but usually these are not as prompt or thorough as environmental prudence suggests. In the meantime these groups, even if they constitute a minority, are able to slow, limit, or stop effective and consistent governmental action to protect the environment. Only extensive public outrage induces legislative action, and the wave often crests before sustained enforcement resolves the problem.

Lindblom suggests several ways in which economic dominance of the political system is enhanced. Economically powerful individuals are often highly educated and able to participate in the political process much more than less well-to-do people.[59] Furthermore, they are particularly dominant in the internal politics of center and right parties. The economic elite is particularly effective within the process of day-to-day, nonelectoral, political and administrative decision-making. Their skills and the considerable prestige that our culture grants them are very effective within both closed and open forums. They have at their disposal large, multi-talented corporate staffs and considerable travel and public relations budgets. Their opponents, if any, are usually amateurs working on their own limited time and personal resources. Finally, government requires the cooperation of the economic leadership to carry out its policies.

If this is politics as usual in most developed liberal-democratic societies, it is perhaps a wonder that the environmental movement has made the gains it has. The left gained power against similar odds in part because workers in the trade union movement withheld labor. Within the political process, the left gained only when a clear majority was working hard within the rules of the democratic class struggle to better its own economic situation. Environmentalists have had neither of these sorts of countervailing power. But gains have been made in many countries, particularly between 1969 and 1980. Can we account for this within Lindblom's analysis of moderate democratic regimes?

The 1970s were generally prosperous, particularly the early part of the decade, when the greatest environmental initiatives were won. At that time the economic elite, intelligent humans who eat, drink, breathe, and enjoy nature, were willing to give some ground—particularly because environmental claims were new and thereby gained a considerable boost in the media. Environmentalists also had the political sophistication to push for structural gains, changes in the decision-making process. Particularly in the United States, environmentalists put in place more open and participatory decision-making, which has served well in the very different political context of the 1980s. The OPEC-induced oil price increases of 1973 and 1979 also resulted in a good deal of unintentional environmental protection. Less energy was used and thereby less pollution was incurred; more materials recycling was also induced. Industry, government, and consumers alike became far more efficient in their use of energy and materials than they otherwise might have. Finally, much environmental improvement followed from personal, rather than political, decisions. People changed their behavior voluntarily, motivated by environmental concern.

In the 1980s environmental protection has weakened, and environmentalists have met the firm resolve of resistant power at every turn. Political gains have been few and far between and rollbacks and losses commonplace, particularly in the United States. The uneven distribution of political power within developed market/democratic systems has shown itself to be more than the environmental movement, as presently constituted, can handle. The perspective and methods of the 1970s seem altogether insufficient for the 1980s and beyond.

Related to Lindblom's analysis is the dimension of ordinary politics that Theodore J. Lowi calls *interest group liberalism*. Lowi's analysis focuses on moderate and progressive regimes and can be usefully applied to environmental politics. Interest group liberalism rests on the assumption that all important interests in society are organized, homogeneous, and roughly in balance. Government's task "is one of ensuring access particularly to the most organized, and of ratifying the agreements and adjustments worked out among the competing leaders and their claims."[60]

Interest group liberalism is really a formula for a politics of incrementalism and compromise between *organized* interests. In such a system the less organized and the unorganized lose ground, particularly in hard economic times. The elderly, the poor, the unemployed, and the ill are grossly underrepresented. So too, of course, are future generations and other species. Furthermore, as Lowi notes, interest group liberalism does not allow for moral arguments. Decisions are quantified; disagreements are resolved by splitting the difference. Policies favor the most organized groups, whose members tend to be wealthy and tend to seek concrete, economically self-interested, and immediate gains.

In this context environmental groups often seem foreign to the political decision-making process. Environmental issues are treated as inconvenient, time-consuming add-ons. Environmentalist leaders are "self-appointed," their issues forced into separate environmental departments or ministries, agencies that carry little or no weight in decision-making bodies. Environmental inputs too often come after the fact in such areas as energy, transportation, or industry.

Rethinking Liberalism, edited by Walter Truett Anderson, is a rare liberal attempt to come to intellectual grips with environmentalism. In a chapter entitled "Beyond Environmentalism," Anderson argues, "The negotiating methods of interest-group liberalism and the principles of zero-sum economics don't give us much help in ecological governance, and are in some ways incompatible with it. There is simply no reason to assume that calling the representatives of the major interest groups into a room and getting them to iron out their differences is going to produce an approach to ecosystem management that will be sane, economical, and that will not produce problems for future generations." Anderson also gets to the heart of the problem of interest-group liberalism—and thereby to the heart of most contemporary moderate regimes with his insight that "the whole style of American politics is non-ecological. Ecology is a comprehension of systems, interdependancies, webs of relationship, connections extending over space and time—and the very essence of our politics is to zero in on single causes. . . . Environmental positions are required, by the very rules of the political game, to fix on single issues—save the whale, clean up the air—that allow the real issues to recede into the background."[61]

Moderate solutions are piecemeal, partial, and technical. They rarely address the need for fundamental changes in our production, consumption, and "disposal" habits. Environmentalism itself, then, implies some doubt about the liberal tradition of technocratic management. It suggests that we need to find new means of intervening deeply in the market process—an idea foreign to liberalism and moderate progressivism. Environmentalists need to induce market-based political systems to be at least as responsive to centuries-long concerns as they are to day-to-day concerns. Moderate progressives might ask, "Can we go beyond technical 'add-on' solutions without crippling market-based decision-making?" Perhaps not. But environmentalism emphasizes that add-on solutions are not sufficient.

As Brooks and McMullen put it, environmentalists question the very products and processes of industrial society. They question whether economic rationality is an appropriate principal basis for technological, political, and consumer decision-making. This questioning opens a gulf between environmentalism and liberalism, indeed, between environmentalism and all ordinary, moderate politics. The gap will not easily be bridged. But environmentalists have no choice but to try.

What is at stake here is the meaning of progress. Liberalism, perhaps ideology itself, was born with the notion of progress, and throughout the long history of liberal democracy, progress has driven society both politically and economically. Environmentalism, however, suggests that our idea of progress is too linear, even arrogant. Growth in GNP is not progress. Nor is bigger better. Progress must be redefined as *meeting real needs more efficiently*. Both recently and historically, the market has moved slowly in this direction without intervention.[62] But this process must be accelerated. To worried traditionalists, one can observe that market rationality will remain even if the market is guided politically in broad terms. Indeed, it is the essence of the political compromise of progressivism to leave the market dominant economically but subject it to a variety of social, fiscal, and monetary controls. On one level environmentalists merely seek to add one more form of broad control. On another, however, they seem to be attempting to reverse the objectives of progressivist interventions. The truth, I suspect, lies somewhere between these two interpretations.

Liberalism has always accepted with great enthusiasm, indeed emphasized, a notion of progress rooted in technological development and economic growth, and conservatism soon abandoned its nineteenth-century doubts about this liberal conception of progress. In the twentieth century, conservatives cast away their doubts with a zealousness typical of converts. Even the conservation movement, with the notable exception of John Muir and a few others, remained almost wholly in tune with this technical and growth-oriented notion of progress. As Hays notes, "The new realms of science and technology, appearing to open up unlimited opportunities for human achievement, filled conservation leaders with intense optimism, they emphasized expansion, not retrenchment; possibilities, not limitations."[63]

Environmentalism, in contrast, emphasizes the necessity to forgo some technological possibilities, even some that are economically advantageous. It challenges the business-as-usual outlook of moderate and progressive regimes. Against interest group liberalism, environmentalists actively promote moral argument as a part of political and economic decisions, throwing into question the criteria by which to measure progress.

The politics of moderation was fundamentally rejected in the 1980s. Interest group liberalism and pragmatism were overwhelmed by a resurgence of neoconservative ideology. In the developed Anglo-American democracies, the political styles and techniques dominant for the better part of this century were rejected, while neoconservatives sought to revive the expansionist state, to bury the social compromise called the welfare state, and to achieve an economic recovery based in militarization and deregulation. They decried Keynesian economics and governmental growth while seeking to restart capitalism through deficit-financed military expenditures.

From an environmentalist perspective the danger is not that this strategy may fail, but that it may succeed. Further, whether or not neoconservatism remains dominant in the short-term future, environmentalists suggest that the forces which permitted and promoted its rise will return again. Neoconservatism arises in the absence of "easy" economic growth. Thus far traditional progressives have had little or no effective response to it. Only environmentalists and the peace movement have asked whether there is any limit to what will be sacrificed and risked in the name of economic growth. Contrary to today's seemingly ineffective progressives, environmentalists—like neoconservatives—are willing to raise fundamental questions about the criteria and agendas of contemporary decision-making.

part three

An Environmental Perspective in
Contemporary Politics

eight

Neoconservatism, Environmentalism, and Contemporary Political Realities

This chapter brings a shift in tone. The argument presented here and in the balance of the book is more hypothetical and speculative, concerned not only with what environmentalism has been and is but with what it might become: an important part of a response to neoconservatism, which may be the dominant ideology in the Anglo-American democracies today. I do not provide evidence for this or any other transformation of the contemporary ideological scene. I am more interested in conveying environmentalism's potential for development.

I focus in this chapter and the next principally on the existing and potential relationship between environmentalism and neoconservatism. These ideologies are currently in hostile opposition; thus I begin by mentioning some of their similarities. Both environmentalists and neoconservatives, for example, emphasize decentralization as a goal. Both focus on the restoration of morality and traditional values, although they do not agree what these values are. Finally, both support reductions in government deficits and restraints on consumer spending.[1] On the whole, however, environmentalism and neoconservatism are better understood as alternative and opposing reactions to the same set of problems.

Some environmentalists might fear that this analysis will link environmental ideas too much with what may be a fleeting ideological phenomenon. Some suggest that neoconservatism is peculiar to the United States and Great Britain and successful only because of the personal appeal of President Reagan and Prime Minister

Thatcher. The current "neoconservative mood" may fade soon. Environmental thinking, on the other hand, is oriented toward both the present and the distant future, decades hence, when neoconservatism may no longer be of other than historical interest.

But this view is difficult to sustain unless one assumes that the natural world will act with a vengeance human societies cannot ignore. This may not happen. David Brooks and Alma Norman point out that environmental decisions require human choices. We must establish value hierarchies that place environmental values at a higher priority; if we do not, human individuals and societies are very capable of ignoring these important issues until it is too late to act effectively. Many societies, for example, could be led to accept modest increases in cancer rates as inevitable, especially if the damage were proven after it was too late to correct. A combination of nuclear power, a little easy energy conservation, and a radical increase in use of coal and oil shales and frontier energy supplies may well be adequate for a century, perhaps even a bit more. A majority might be convinced that the consequences—more lakes acidified, a few Chernobyls, huge increases in water pollution in Western North America—are the necessary price of otherwise acceptable lives. Many would appreciate neither that we might have done much better nor that ultimately a fundamental transition must be made. Neoconservatism aids in this deception.

I also speculate in these closing chapters for two other reasons. First, many academics avoid speculation for fear that they will be proved wrong; they tend to confine themselves to ever more precise answers to narrower and easier questions. The collective academic enterprise based in modest individual efforts is noble, important, and necessary. But it may well not be sufficient. Some of the fraternity need to play the fool, to take a chance on exploring riskier, wider, value-laden issues. That, as we have seen, is perhaps the essence of environmentalism and the interdisciplinary outlook it has urged on some in the academic community. Second, and perhaps more important, I am convinced that neoconservatism will be significant in some form for decades to come. It arises from the same transformations in our society and economy that have given birth to environmentalism: the onset of a new age of physical and social limitations on economic expansion. Even if neoconservatives should be swept from power before the close of this decade, their ideas will have become an important part of society's response to this new era. And neoconservatism has already led to several profound political and economic changes. Neoconservative ideas will stay with us, perhaps rising and receding in a cyclical fashion, as postindustrialism and the double energy transition take hold in the decades ahead. Let us now consider the interplay between neoconservatism and environmentalism and examine how the interchange might evolve in the future.

The years 1945–73 were the glory days of the industrial era. Suburbs spread out over endless miles of what was once prime farm land. More automobiles were driven farther than ever by more and more drivers. In North America especially the cars grew so large that drivers of ordinary skill could no longer park them with ease. Streets and roads were widened, lanes were added to highways everywhere; steel, rubber, concrete and oil were the materials of the day. The disposable container was popularized, and people bought products the cost of whose packages exceeded the value of the contents. "Better living through chemistry" was a favorite motto; teenage lives were measured in terms of annual automobile model changes.

This is a familiar story; it has by no means ended. Only since 1973, however, has it been obvious to what extent all this was dependent on declining real energy prices. The postwar boom thrived on the belief that energy would never again be a problem. But since the late 1960s the growing concern with pollution has led to an appreciation that industrial society must be fundamentally altered. Since 1973 many, perhaps even most people have sensed that the industrial system is impermanent in its present form. It has also been widely accepted since the late 1970s that the transition to postindustrialism may be more difficult than originally expected.

But what is postindustrialism? Are we moving into an age of dominant "information" technologies or an age of stringent environmental and resource limitations? Will change primarily involve production technologies or the kinds of products made? Will the new system be added on to, or will it replace, industrial society? How soon will these changes be upon us and how rapidly will they emerge? Will they be primarily technological in nature or primarily sociopolitical? Will the market economic system foster these changes, anticipate them, or hinder them? And, finally, what sort of politics will be associated with the transition?

Postindustrialism involves several simultaneous transitions. Some of its aspects, especially in market-driven systems, seem inexorable. Many of the new computer-controlled production technologies save energy, capital, and labor all at once. Most automation, control systems, and robotics allow round-the-clock production and sharply reduce the need for human labor. There are fewer factories to construct, staff, and heat; and fewer workers, including white collar and maintenance workers, to pay and transport to and from work. Many new products and designs use less material, energy, and labor than products they replace. A compact disc player and lightweight earphones produce better sound than did a stereo unit of ten times the weight only a few years ago. These devices can be produced by a small number of people and many more can be shipped for the same cost. The cost of hand-held calculators and digital watches is approaching zero. Telephones weigh half what they used to and perform more functions. These technological changes characterize both an information age and a conserver society.

On the other side of the coin, there is little doubt that postindustrialism is causing and will continue to cause many significant sociopolitical dislocations. Some traditionally dominant economies have all but lost their position on the cutting edge of technological advance. These socioeconomic dislocations have affected the ideological spectrum, especially in the Anglo-American democracies, which have been particularly hard hit by the transformation.

In the 1970s and early 1980s the world economy made a "down payment" on the price of transition in terms of radically higher energy prices. The social, economic, and political dislocations that followed were considerable. Unemployment, inflation, interest rates, and governmental deficits were for a time clearly out of control, and some governments deliberately induced near-depression conditions in order to "regain control" of their economies. Leaping interest rates crushed numerous small and medium-sized businesses and small-scale investors and caused people to defer home purchases. Even some larger businesses and whole nations avoided economic collapse only because large lenders needed debtors. The economic adjustments were particularly costly to the young people who spent many of their formative and potentially creative years immersed in the frustration and hopelessness of unemployment.

Some of the most difficult and necessary aspects of the transition to an environmentally sound postindustrial economy were begun during the years 1973–85. But some of the more promising aspects of that transition have now been diminished in an undoubtedly temporary return to lower energy prices. Societies are now contending with the economic costs of readjustment to lower prices—some perhaps as severe as those associated with the earlier adjustments to higher prices. This is doubly tragic: it means that many of the costs of the first adjustment were borne in vain, and that, since no one can now anticipate short- or medium-term energy price trends, few, if any, will make significant new investments in future energy efficiency.

There is every reason to think that we will be subjected in the future to a long series of lurches in energy prices and in the rate at which improvements in energy efficiency are made. And every sharp lurch in energy prices, up or down, will carry serious economic, social, and political repercussions. The inexorable dimensions of the postindustrial transition will move forward regardless of energy prices, but the course of the more contingent dimensions, generally those most significant in terms of environmental protection, is far more difficult to predict.

This unpredictability will be compounded by the ideological impacts of the transition. Accompanying the changes so far has been neoconservatism, which has rapidly risen in several wealthy nations, particularly the English-speaking democracies. Neoconservatism's popularity can be explained in part by two factors associated with the postindustrial transition. First, the unionized, industrial working class has been weakened, particularly in the United States. Second, large government budget deficits have frustrated the traditional progressive technique of spending one's way out of recessions.

Before looking more closely at the complexity of the ideological situation let me reiterate that neoconservatism is not likely to be a short-term phenomenon—because it is related to the conserver and/or postindustrial transformations that will be central to our economy and society for at least several decades to come. Neoconservatism will probably remain a deep-seated tendency within most bureaucratic capitalist systems, emerging in any extended period of slow economic growth. This is the central dilemma of environmentalism: while moderate economic growth is quite acceptable in environmental terms, it may contribute to political outcomes hostile to further environmental advance.

Several socioeconomic forces have helped advance neoconservatism in recent years. Since the mid–1970s, three long-standing contradictions of the market economic system have resurfaced, after several decades of relative calm. First, higher energy and capital costs have led to a renewed and intensified quest for lower wage costs. This in turn has speeded the phenomenon of jobless growth; the already rapid expansion of low-wage sectors (i.e., fast food restaurants); and the transfer of many manufacturing operations to other regions such as the Asian Pacific Rim. In addition, some of the new technologies tend to "de-skill" manufacturing jobs.[2] These changes have undercut consumer confidence and threatened the capacity to generate sufficient consumer demand to sustain continuous domestic economic growth.

Second, many corporations and wealthy individuals have managed to reduce their share of the total tax burden even in the face of large public budget deficits. Many North Americans seem to believe that tax concessions to the rich ultimately aid the situation of the poor and the middle class. But so-called "stimulative" tax cuts have not in themselves significantly enhanced employment opportunities. Nor have they often even resulted in increases in capital investment.[3] Even when such investments are made, they often lead to further use of labor-reducing technologies. And government deficits have continued to rise despite real reductions in expenditures on health, education, and social welfare.

The third contradiction—continuing environmental damage and resource depletion—may have been less important to the public at large during the economic turmoil of the early 1980s. The economic troubles seemed to overwhelm environmental concern, and few saw that it is precisely environmental problems—principally but not exclusively excessive dependence on nonrenewable energy sources—that are at the root of many of the economic difficulties of the past twelve years.[4]

Throughout 1945–73 many of the contradictions of market-based political economies were softened by the continuing expansion of public bureaucracies and the occasional use of Keynesian economic techniques. But industrial employment did not expand through this period—indeed, as a proportion of total employment, industrial employment has declined steadily from 1945 to the present. Most new jobs have been created by expanding governments. Figures on government spending (such as those compiled so carefully and pointedly by G. Warren Nutter of the American Enterprise Institute) carry two insights other than the standard neoconservative claim that government growth has been excessive.[5] First, while Nutter makes clear that growth in government spending is common to all Western democracies, government expenditures as a proportion of national income vary considerably, and, contrary to neoconservative theory, there seems to be no clear correlation between government restraint and economic performance. The big spenders include the Scandinavian countries, which have performed well economically, but Japan, another excellent economic performer, is among the low spenders. Lester Thurow points out that Western European countries usually collect a higher proportion of GNP as taxes than does the United States—and this speaks badly of the neoconservative theory that improved economic performance follows from shrinking the public sector.[6]

The reason public sector cutbacks will probably not lead to economic growth is also hidden in Nutter's statistics. Government spending—especially nonmilitary domestic spending—is directly reflected in employment levels. If spending as a proportion of GNP continuously rises so too does public sector employment as a proportion of total employment. The universal growth in government expenditures suggests that the private sector has practiced jobless growth, the nemesis of the 1980s, for several decades now. The manufacturing sector has not provided a net increase in employment in over forty years—even in periods of unparalleled economic growth.

The neoconservative claim that the private sector can now be stimulated to expand employment levels, therefore, requires an extraordinary leap of faith. At the very least one must say that, if many new jobs were created in the private sector, they would not tend to be high-paying, full-time industrial jobs. Nor will management positions likely increase—reductions there have been pervasive and considerable for years. And the technological revolution may soon cut quite deeply into office and clerical employment.[7] In short, without at least some of the items on the environmentalist agenda, it is not at all clear where new jobs will be gained in the future. What expansion there is likely will be low-paying.

The extended period of economic growth from 1945 to 1973, as Alan Wolfe notes, permitted a wide range of errors in economic and social policy.[8] But it also allowed for the full evolution of that distinctive entity, the bureaucratic capitalist state. The initial ideology of bureaucratic capitalism was moderate progressive liberalism. Therein virtually every organized interest was protected, at least to some extent, from the worst economic disbenefits of capitalism. Some interests were, of course, better protected than others: the better organized, the more bureaucratic in structure and style, the better the protection in bad times and concessions in good. Thurow notes that almost everything was indexed to something else. No debts, other than personal debts, were ever repaid. That is, the Keynesianism of deficits was practiced more effectively than the Keynesianism of surpluses.

Competing interests—regional, sectoral, and ethnic—were satisfied by a large and complex public bureaucracy expert at balanced consideration. Even class interests, relatively unorganized as such, were nonetheless considered in terms of trade unionists, pensioners, or middle-income voters. Those least favored with basic economic security were unlikely to be organized or represented. Nonetheless, the administrative state of contemporary bureaucratic capitalism is far more than simply the "governing committee of the ruling class."[9]

The style of this administrative state is bureaucratic, explained as well by Max Weber's political sociology as it is by that of Karl Marx. The process of "balancing interests" tends to be a discreet and largely closed process, hierarchical in structure, expert oriented, cooptative, and to a certain extent responsive and self-corrective. The political harmony of the 1950s, 1960s, and early 1970s was ultimately achieved through economic growth; but it was based as well on the widespread perception that the bureaucratic state was fair. Overall economic growth made relative gains by some groups and regions easier to ignore. The economic growth that made bureaucratic balancing possible was itself sustained by the constant expansion of the state apparatus, by the continuing growth of public and private debt, by a steady decline in the price of energy, and by ignoring the long-term environmental costs of many forms of industrial activity.

The extent to which this ideological pattern and political/administrative process is temporary and contingent is not yet apparent to many. But the rapid rise of neoconservatism suggests that the political and ideological dynamic supportive of advances in social and economic equality has been fragile indeed. The range of political systems in which this new dynamic has arisen suggests that it is rooted in social and economic changes more than in particular political institutions, processes, and cultures.

From an environmentalist perspective, neoconservatism does not represent a long-term solution to the problems that led to its rise. It is more often a means of denying their existence. From the perspective of the left, one might say that neoconservatism substitutes the needs of capital for the needs of society; it is a poor means of achieving economic progress. Environmentalists see neoconservatism as an ideology that is using highly risky means to force unneeded economic growth.

Bureaucratic capitalism, so comfortable in the easy progressivism of the growth era (in the Anglo-American democracies at least) has found itself unable to sustain a humane a face in the 1980s. The culture and ideology of bureaucratic capitalism is undergoing a fundamental change. Just as Horatio Alger and the need for rapid accumulation of capital gave way to the bland commercialism of television in the growth era, that blandness seems at times to have been yielding to Rambo and an endless succession of imitators. Whatever the cultural manifestations, the neoconservative political upsurge is based politically in economic limits and the dislocations of economic adjustment. Until there is a presentable and clear ideological response, neoconservative images may continue to dominate the political culture in the 1980s and 1990s.

Neoconservatism blends five principal elements:

1. A new economic strategy largely within the bounds of supply-side economics, defined by Robert Reich as calling for "government measures that will raise the level of investment (particularly in plant and equipment), reduce the level of consumption, and thus create new capital. To accomplish these goals, a supply-side program would reduce taxes for savers and investors, curtail regulation and anti-trust enforcement, limit the growth rate of public expenditures for social security, health, and welfare, and in general restrict government interference with the workings of the economy."[10]
2. An attack on "big government" coupled with calls for decentralization, procedural simplification of all aspects of government, and budget balancing.
3. Enthusiasm for renewal of the "entrepreneurial spirit."
4. Restoration of traditional moral and religious values.
5. Increased militarism and military spending and renewed hostility to Third World nationalism (especially in the United States).

The combination of high inflation, high unemployment, and high government deficits involves contradictions which are not easily resolved by governments of any persuasion. Any move to resolve one of these problems exacerbates one or both of the others. The neoconservative formula, for example, risks inducing depression— if the government acts on stated neoconservative economic principles. But neoconservatives have not actually sought balanced budgets—they have expanded, not stabilized, military expenditures; they have reduced, not increased, taxes. Such measures, in combination with slowed transfer payments, restrictions on nonmilitary governmental hiring, accelerated business investment (which might well supplant existing jobs at least as fast as it created them), and restraints on consumer spending, might turn inflation into radical and rapid deflation. But in this difficult economic scenario, the contradictions inherent in neoconservative solutions may well be less fundamental than the difficulties suffered by several varieties of moderate progressivism.

Although its focus was often on foreign policy problems, the moderate-progressive Carter government foundered on a combination of low growth, high unemployment, inflation, and rising government deficits. The Trudeau government was also unable to cope with these problems, especially when coupled with high interest rates. And the Thatcher government came to power after an extended period of economic decline in Britain presided over by moderate progressives. The progressives' problem is that, in the face of these economic conditions, the rationale for continued bureaucratic expansion and Keynesian economic strategies collapses. Indeed, that traditional cure for economic stagnation is popularly characterized by neoconservatives as the cause of our current economic problems.

But expansion of government economic activity is still thought to be needed, because economic growth itself has come to depend upon it. The only plausible basis for such expansion, in the United States particularly, has been military necessity and national security. Thus neoconservatives, who came to power claiming their goal was to reduce government spending, have actually accelerated spending levels. This has been necessary because, in a climate of stagnation, business will not invest heavily in the production of consumer goods, and consumer spending itself cannot expand because so many people are out of work or insecure in their positions. Government thus has to gamble on growth and justify the gamble to its constituency. In the face of large budgetary deficits, only a national emergency can justify government expansionism. An ideologically based desire to "get the private sector moving again" is thus necessary. But these initiatives are not new—they are just another means of jump-starting a "weak" economy. From this perspective neoconservatism might be characterized as military Keynesianism, government debt incurred to pump money into the hands of corporations. This effort is accompanied by a wide variety of attempts to suppress attention to one of the ultimate sources of the economic problems: looming and actual resource limits.

In the United States the neoconservative commitment to military spending assures that resource and environmental problems will not be addressed in the near future. Ironically, it was the neoconservatives themselves who developed the idea that government spending tends to move up in a "ratchet" effect; they also noted first that the Keynesianism of stimulative deficit spending is easier to achieve than the Keynesianism of tax increases or spending reductions; and they emphasized that administrative expansion tends to perpetuate itself. But they are silent about the ratchet effect of expanded military spending. Such spending, however, probably perpetuates itself far more effectively than do other forms of government spending. Pressure for further expansion in this case comes not merely from civil servants and the unorganized poor but from an extensive and highly organized network of corporate, government, regional, and ideological forces. The network grows every time military spending advances another notch, and it is now probably far better organized and powerful than the array of interests that support government social programs.

But public opinion still supports government social programs and active government. This is one of the truly remarkable aspects of the rise of neoconservatism in the 1980s. Neoconservatives were elected not because of their programmatic approach, but despite it. This is thoroughly documented by Thomas Ferguson and Joel Rogers, who report that "the percentage (in 1982) favoring 'keeping' outweighed the percentage favoring 'easing' regulations regarding the environment (49–28), industrial safety (66–18), the teenage minimum wage (58–29), auto emission and safety standards (59–29), federal lands (43–27), and offshore oil drilling (46–29). In 1983 the Los Angeles Times again asked about regulatory policy and found that only five percent of Americans considered regulations 'too strict' while 42 percent thought they were 'not strong enough.' "[11]

Nor has there been any increase in support for cuts in domestic spending. There is a slowdown in the "liberalization" of opinion, dating from 1973, but the trend has neither halted nor reversed. "The National Opinion Research Center found in 1980 that only 21 percent of Americans (the average across the different spending areas) thought that 'too much' was being spent on environmental, health, education, welfare, and urban-aid programs—the same percentage holding that belief in 1976, 1977, and 1978."[12] Thus no "ground-swell" of conservative opinion led to the 1980 Reagan landslide.

Most surprising, perhaps, survey data suggests that even on the moral issues so important to many U.S. neoconservatives, public opinion has not moved to the right. "Soon after the [1984] election an ABC News poll found that the share of Americans supporting the relatively radical position that women should have the right to abortion on demand, 'no matter what the reason,' actually increased over Reagan's first term, rising from 40 percent in 1981 to 52 percent in 1985. According to a *Los Angeles Times* poll, only 23 percent of the electorate supported a constitutional amendment prohibiting abortion, and only 32 percent of those who voted for Reagan endorsed his policy on abortion."[13] This last figure is particularly impressive and, astonishingly, typical. The majority of those who voted for Reagan have been consistently opposed to his policies on issue after issue. When Canada's Prime Minister Mulroney attempted to modify federal social transfer payments in a very modest way, he too found that public opinion was decidedly not inclined to neoconservative initiatives on particular social issues. Indeed, his government was unable to fully recover even from the suggestion of cuts. The Thatcher government in Britain and its policies have been unevenly popular—except perhaps its smashing of the coal miners' union or its war with a minor and distant power over the Falkland Islands.

If their policies do not appeal to the electorate, how did neoconservatives come to power and how do they maintain their power? Has there really been a resurgence in conservative opinion? First, those who are enthusiastic about neoconservative ideas are more assertive, more lucid, and more forceful than they once were. Many broad aspects of their case doubtless make sense to the public. For example, the proportion of government spending devoted to debt service has been rising for a long time now, especially since the mid–1970s, and the argument for deficit reduction is widely accepted. Environmentalists agree that it cannot be refuted without remarkable, if not absurd, assumptions about future rates of economic growth. The costs of debt service will soon erode the capacity for all forms of governmental spending. This fact has doubtless been a significant source of neoconservative appeal.

But neoconservatives have been generally unable, or unwilling, to reduce the deficit. In the United States the expansion of military spending has more than absorbed any cuts in domestic social and environmental programs.[14] In Canada, where the deficit is even more out of control, the Mulroney government is painfully aware that it lacks a popular constituency for cutting social programs. But it has continued and sometimes even expanded an extravagant administrative style and has felt politically obliged to expand the support system for large Canadian and multinational corporations.[15] The underlying problem is that any rapid reduction in deficits will likely halt economic growth for several years or more. Neoconservatives, of all politicians, are unable to countenance such a result; thus they are now caught in a deep ideological contradiction. But neoconservatives are adept at avoiding the contradictions in their position; more important, there remains a decided vacuum on their political left.

Both moderate progressivism and democratic socialism have seemed out of date since 1973. In the face of huge deficits, there is little rationale for spending our way back to full employment—at least for spending on anything that can be labeled as an unnecessary luxury. Expanded support for the arts, educational programs, or for national dental insurance sounds fine under ordinary circumstances, but not when government may plummet into bankruptcy at any moment. The public continues to support these programs "in the abstract," but there is little deep commitment for pushing forward now.

Progressivism has lost much of its intensely committed constituency. It is not that none stand to benefit from additional progressive advances, but there is little depth and intensity in the moral and intellectual arguments for further change. Why did Walter Mondale look so lame in the 1984 U.S. elections? It was not simply a question of personality. The fact is that the U.S. Democratic Party for some years has seemed little more than a tired collection of special interests. Prime Minister John Turner, the leader of the Canadian Liberal Party, looked equally ineffective in the elections of 1985. His views seemed both to the right and to the left of Mulroney and the Conservatives. Why is there now a three-party system in Britain? The pattern of failure and division within the forces of moderate progressivism is too broad to be attributed solely to the incapacities of particular individuals. Shallowness of conviction and incoherence of view seem rampant on the moderate left.

To appreciate the cause of this, one might review again the plausible ideological responses to neoconservatism. Some hope that, as in the 1930s, hard times might lead to a rebirth of the traditional left. Perhaps a neo-Marxist critique of both neoconservatism and the bland bureaucratic progressivism that preceded it would be effective. I think not, for several reasons. First, there has never been less interest in an orthodox left critique than there is today—particularly in North America. In part, neoconservatism has promoted anti-left attitudes through its strong ideological power base, especially in the print media. But more important is that socialism has had little useful and new to say about the root of contemporary economic problems: the fundamental physical limits on continued industrial growth.

Against a resurgence of the traditional left there also remains the resistance inherent in the recent expansion of public bureaucracy seemingly beyond government's ability to pay. It is widely assumed that any left-wing solution will entail further expansion of the state. Central economic planning is on the wane even in Communist regimes. But neoconservatives have not been able to dismantle the progressive bureaucratic state, however much they have tried. Some benefits to the elderly, the unemployed, and the poor remain, and these groups still have a great deal more to lose than their chains, even if they have already lost their jobs. Thus even the disadvantaged are not yet likely recruits for the far left. Finally, the industrial working class is in decline—and in North America it never did show much interest in socialism in any case. It seems even less likely that our present mix of civil servants, computer programmers, and hamburger servers will seek the revolution of the industrial working class.

Would the prospects of a highly unorthodox, environmental left be better? Willingness to restructure much of the economy is, after all, essential to environmentalism. Such a political movement would be deeply decentralist, would consider environmental protection a higher priority than economic growth, would promote balanced government budgets, and would be open to limiting wage increases in order to reduce average work time. Obviously some of the traditional left constituencies would strongly object. But some of these constituencies have already been eroded, and it does seem possible that a moderate left perspective could be blended with environmentalism in such a way as to appeal to some within these groups. In North America such a combination could hardly be less appealing than the ideas of the traditional left were in the early 1980s.

Moderate progressivism—despite its present problems, or perhaps because of them—seems a more plausible candidate for fundamental revision. But the U.S. Democratic Party has thus far been unwilling to identify military spending as a principal cause of runaway public debt. Nor can it find a clear way out of either Keynesian economics or the bureaucratic balancing act of interest-group liberalism. Moderate progressives have had little new to say. Many articulate young people believe that the excesses of liberal progressivism are at the root of our contemporary economic dilemmas—and few seem able to articulate a response to such a perspective. Neoconservatism is thus the intellectually dominant ideology of the 1980s largely by default.

Moderate progressivism's failures can be traced to its ideological basis in fundamental sociopolitical compromise. More than the ideologies of the left and the right, it has been implicitly dependent on long-term economic growth, without which the fundamental compromise on which that progressivism rests is difficult to maintain. For decades progressives worked effectively to soften the blows of failure and misfortune common to both the human condition and the market system. For example, almost every developed society (with the notable exception of the United States) now protects its citizens against the economic disaster that can accompany catastrophic illness, and social insurance systems protect the aged against spending their final years as wards of the state. These programs in total, particularly the many varieties of insurance schemes, helped to prevent the economy of the early 1980s from lapsing into the sort of tailspin that took place in 1929. But these social welfare achievements have never significantly altered the distribution of wealth.[16] The proportion of income and wealth in the hands of rich and poor has remained essentially unchanged since the Depression. Moderate progressivism is not a redistributive ideology; instead, it has sought to assure a reasonably equitable distribution of the benefits of economic growth. It does not favor those of modest means— most important programs are truly paid for by everyone; the rich do not pay extra. (On the contrary, since many programs include a cap on maximum contributions and maximum payments, the less advantaged pay proportionately more.) On occasions when progressives sought programs that tended toward redistribution, they were compromised, offset by concessions on other fronts, or rolled back after the next election.

The expansion of government programs and services that the progressives have overseen has kept the overall distribution of income roughly constant. The tax structure has reinforced this situation. But the wealthy have not gained a radically disproportionate share of the expanding pie—and the expanding employment and income opportunities provided by government have allowed the pie to keep expanding. The postwar period, until the rise of neoconservatism, was thus an era of civility and social compromise.

The compromise of moderate progressivism also depended on a vital trade union movement. Much of the industrial working class gained middle-class incomes, if not middle-class working conditions. The trade union movement transformed gains in productivity into higher incomes for workers and provided a principal political support for progressivism. The compromise might not have been possible without an effective and expanding trade union movement. Nor would it have been possible without a Keynesian economic perspective; both were rooted in consensus and compromise. As one observer has put it: "Keynesianism was a method which promised to contain the capitalist tendency to depression without challenging the existence of trade unions and without accepting the necessity of a socialist transformation or a draconian state intervention in the economy."[17] ´

All things considered, then, it is little wonder that without economic growth moderate progressivism seems flat: it is left with nothing new to propose. It is hard to excite the young to defend existing social programs when they are out of work. If they have never found work they are not eligible for unemployment insurance. Even if a solid majority agrees that progressive social programs should not be rolled back, an ideology cannot rest on tired, bland assertions that things should "stay as they are." Our society is so oriented to change, novelty, and excitement that few are interested in merely protecting the victories of the dim past, however hard-won. Few care to protect the smokestack industries whose physical plants are unable to compete or whose output is simply no longer needed: even many who work there would be happy to do something else so long as it provided a comparable level of income and security. Indeed, contrary to popular mythology, many would be delighted to do little or no work, and would remain useful citizens, so long as their incomes were assured.[18]

But moderate progressives have hesitated to propose new solutions to such problems as unemployment. There has been no coherent response to neoconservatives' claim that they can restart economic growth. No one has suggested, for example, that unemployment might be reduced or eliminated without economic growth. Only the militant peace movement has questioned the costs of economic growth through militarism. Even environmentalists, particularly in the United States, have rarely taken strongly antimilitarist positions.[19]

A progressive rebuttal to neoconservatism might have a broader appeal were it to combine a new long-term view on unemployment with a firm opposition to the self-perpetuating expansion of military spending and a rejection of government deficits. It might also propose a new definition of security, one based in world peace, energy transition, domestic employment security, and global protection of the environment.[20] A moderate left with an environmentalist vision could articulate alternative uses for much of the money spent on military projects. It might also object to the absurd levels of wealth present tax laws permit. Such a vision might help restore moderate progressives' courage to speak with the intellectually grounded anger and decisiveness that has been missing from their ranks, particularly in the United States, for nearly two decades now.

A coherent response to neoconservatism is vitally necessary. Although neoconservatives in principle might have embraced aspects of an environmentalist perspective, they have clearly chosen to deny the existence of environmental problems. Environmentalists, however, have been less often raged against than ignored by neoconservatives. In part this is because environmentalists have been politically ineffectual, but it also suggests that refuting environmentalists' claims is not easy. More important, environmentalists have limited themselves. They have not sufficiently appreciated how much they have to say on matters of public policy outside the narrow area of environmental protection.

The transformation of environmentalism from an ideology of limited scope to one of broad scope involves at least five changes. The work of Amory Lovins on alternative energy paths, for example, has helped define an environmental position on employment opportunities. Other environmental ideas could gain such acceptance and might broaden he potential appeal of an environmental ideology. The five changes necessary are:

1. *Integration of the analytic perspectives of the environmental movement and the peace movement* (discussed at the conclusion of this chapter).
2. *Application of an environmental perspective to the policies of traditional moderate progressivism.* As we will see in chapter 9, it may be possible to restore and update the progressive compromise once rooted in Keynesianism.
3. *Clarification of the meaning of decentralization within an environmental perspective* and delineation of an urbanist environmentalism (see chapter 9).

4. *Advocacy of the need to reduce average work time, even when this might involve reduced gains in total wages.* This could be achieved by redirecting some of the gains associated with productivity improvements from wage increases to work-time reductions. Nonetheless, there is little doubt that achieving this goal is the greatest political challenge on the environmental agenda.

5. *Taking seriously the claim that environmentalism is neither left nor right.* In particular environmentalists must examine neoconservative appeal in order to reach some of its constituency without deeply compromising environmental principles. This is not as difficult as it might seem.

I consider only the first of these propositions here, concentrating the balance of this chapter on this vital issue.

Many environmentalists in Western Europe have rejected militarism, the contemporary rationale of bureaucratic capitalism. (Pacifism and disarmament are central tenets of the West German Green Party.) Environmental opposition to nuclear power is based in large part on the association between nuclear power and nuclear weapons. Since environmentalists are not enthralled by economic growth, they are not committed to massive government deficits to drive the economy forward. Environmentalists thus fundamentally reject much neoconservative rationale and practice. But environmentalism could appeal to neoconservatives for whom truly conservative fiscal policies make sense.

Both environmentalism and neoconservatism strongly oppose the notion of large, central bureaucracies. This characteristic, and its openness to market economics, distinguish environmentalism from the traditional left and may allow it to capture some of the political ground now occupied by neoconservatism. For example, there seems to be no environmental basis for opposing such popular neoconservative ideas as tax simplification, economic (as opposed to environmental) deregulation, or greater government efficiency.[21]

The constituency of neoconservatism, especially in the United States and to a lesser extent in Great Britain and Canada, is divided between fiscal conservatives and those committed to military expansionism even at the risk of long-term economic instability. For environmentalists, however, global military budgets represent the only source of capital large enough to address environmental problems, especially the transformation of the energy sources on which our economies are based. Anyone who acknowledges the reality, importance, and scale of these matters must have doubts about any massive government borrowing against rapid future economic growth. Many nonenvironmentalists as well are concerned about leaving to future generations an ever-growing debt that assures declining policy flexibility. Environmentalists may be able to reach these "real" conservatives through their common concern with future generations.

Perhaps North Americans can be made to realize that we can achieve a truly defensive defense using much less money than we are now spending. Stronger domestically based conventional forces, for example, would not automatically provoke the Soviets. Reciprocal reductions in hardware could be accelerated if pressure were brought to bear on both superpowers by third parties. A defensive defense, one which would be perceived as such on all sides, would require radical reductions in expensive high-tech military hardware. (The Strategic Defense Initiative or SDI, for example, is viewed as an offensive weapon by the Soviets.)[22]

Gaining a wider hearing for a peace–environmentalist perspective lies in communicating the fact that defense spending is not necessarily of great economic benefit. Even if one favors economic growth, an economy based on military spending is a mistake. Seymour Melman argues that many of the U.S. economy's present problems are rooted in its excessive military spending over the past thirty to forty years.[23] Economic damage results from the fact that military spending generally involves maximizing rather than minimizing costs. Economic efficiency is defined not in producing for less but in enhancing the costs on which cost-plus military contracts are based. In addition talented engineers and designers have gravitated to the generally higher wages associated with military contract work, and the United States has thereby lost the ability to compete effectively in many consumer markets.[24]

This inability to compete cannot be completely accounted for by international wage differentials or the mysteries of Japanese management. It is a result of corporate inattention to anything but the more lucrative world of military procurement. It also results from the misdirection of public money, away from such things as transportation infrastructure, industrial strategy, nonmilitary research and development, education, and "quality of life" and into military procurement. Military spending creates jobs and profits, but it does not support the economy over the long term as the same money spent in other ways might.

As well as dealing directly with militarism, environmentalists might also urge that the North American economy become less dependent on politically unstable regions of the world. We are already less dependent on foreign sources of some fundamental resources, but these changes will not be permanent without deeper commitment to energy conservation. Greater autonomy in essential resources will ease fear, particularly in the United States, regarding the affairs of the Middle East and other regions. The strategic dimension to energy and materials conservation and self-sufficiency perhaps has been given too little emphasis. Litter is by no means the worst result of North American resource profligacy.

But both progressive and environmental agendas are stymied unless they directly attack militarism and military spending. There is simply no effective way to proceed without reversing the increases in such spending. In the words of an unnamed *Washington Post* analyst quoted by Robert Lekachman, "We are coming into the presence of a new way of thinking about defense, the idea—unfamiliar since World War II—of a national-security commitment so unending and all-consuming as to subdue other economic and social priorities as though we were at war."[25] Unfortunately, the self-perpetuating character of the military-industrial complex will make it extraordinarily difficult to slow the expansion of military spending, even with strong public support for such cutbacks. But public resistance to military spending and to the mentality of deterrence is potentially of considerable political significance in every country in the world. Most sensitive persons under the age of fifty probably remember childhood fears of imminent nuclear war. And those who take the time to think about it often become angry at being subjected to a lifetime of concern. Even if it is not in our minds on a daily basis, the nuclear age issues of war and peace are at the back of our minds, the basis of a deep and universally shared insecurity. Others have feared for their children in the event of war, but ours is the only age to fear for the life of every last human and to fear accidental war. Surely that absurdity must be faced head on before anyone, of any ideological persuasion, can begin to find a way out. It can also serve as the cornerstone of an environmentalist restoration of moderate progressivism.

There are three distinctly environmental solutions to nuclear absurdity. The first is described by Amory and Hunter Lovins in *Brittle Power*, which puts forward a military/strategic argument for a soft energy path,[26] emphasizing the vulnerability of an energy system dependent on a few large, complex production units. The Lovinses contrast this to the resilience of an SEP, with its many diverse and dispersed generation units. They discuss in detail the vulnerability of integrated electric grids based on centralized facilities that are easy targets for military or terrorist action. Nuclear power, of course, is particularly vulnerable; but Arctic pipelines, liquid natural gas tanker terminals, and oil refineries are as well. In winter, many people's very lives are dependent on such networks, as is virtually our whole economic system. Much less than a full-scale nuclear war would be required to completely disrupt North American society and economy.

End-use energy efficiency results in more resilience per dollar. A superefficient house could function for weeks or even months on reserve energy (propane, oil, or wood) stored within its walls. It would not need to rely on an Alaskan pipeline's pumping virtually every moment of every winter's day. A more energy-efficient agricultural system, one whose machinery ran on alcohol produced locally from agricultural wastes, could also function regardless of disruptions in the overall energy system. In the event of disaster short of nuclear war, such a society might not be able to supply Coca-Cola or frozen T.V. dinners, but food would be available. A resilient energy system would result in an economic system flexible in the face of international turmoil, natural calamity, economic dislocation, or domestic or international terrorism. And if we felt more secure, North Americans might not feel the need to beef up our military capacity to the point of dangerous absurdity.

Furthermore, such resilience could be achieved with far less than a complete SEP. If planned for, it could even be achieved well before the midpoint. Such resilience could have significant psychological effects. Part of the need for vast technological defense systems is based in the vulnerability of our complex and overly interdependent socioeconomic systems. Some such systems—for example, the public and automobile transportation systems of New York City, or nuclear power plants anywhere—only barely function even without external disruptions. This complexity and fragility may escape the conscious attention of most people, but it lives in our dreams and in our art, and it is closely related to our need for the expensive illusion of security through deterrence. More resilient energy systems would not in and of themselves lead to disarmament. But they could play an important part in leading more nations toward nonmilitary means of enhancing their sense of security.

The second environmental comment on the threat of war concerns dependence on "strategic" materials of all kinds. Lower world oil prices are leading to renewed North American dependence on the energy resources of the unstable Middle East. Our efforts toward energy self-sufficiency are collapsing on almost every front.[27] In its advertising the auto industry has replaced fuel efficiency with an emphasis on the "pinch" growing families may feel in small cars. The drilling rigs in Texas and Alberta have gone into mothballs, and many other energy supply initiatives have fallen apart. Many of these projects are environmentally doubtful, but progress toward an SEP is equally vulnerable to lower oil prices. And all efforts toward energy self-sufficiency help ease the military anxiety to which so many nations are so prone.

Environmentalists could stress that these dilemmas can be solved by establishing steady oil price increases, set in periodically negotiated settlements between producers and consumers or in an evolving system of contingent agreements.[28] In such a context long-term investments in energy conservation would be more secure. The environmental impacts of hard path energy projects could also be softened, because such projects could be planned and developed with greater care. (Without a stable regime of price increases energy projects are alternately economically hopeless or conceived and executed within a crisis mentality.) Most important perhaps, a deliberate and gradual increase in oil prices might help the world feel more secure. Presently the world as a whole is often forced to be as unsettled as its most unstable region. If a new pricing regime assured prices even marginally in excess of those the market might deliver, there would be a considerable pressure on OPEC nations to remain within the system.

No other material or commodity is remotely as important strategically as oil. The one exception might be food, and here again, environmentalists have argued the importance of widespread self-sufficiency. Massive monocultures producing specialty foods for export tend to be ecologically unsound, more dependent on chemicals to control diseases and pests and often part of energy-inefficient food systems. Extensive external supplies of energy for agriculture will not last long—particularly in countries that will not be able to afford the next leap in world oil prices.

Most other materials, beyond a few relatively rare metals, are less significant in strategic terms.[29] Steel, aluminum, and silicon are in good supply, and wood pulp, at least in principle, is completely renewable. Furthermore, all of these can be recycled. The strategic environmental perspective, therefore, makes its most important contributions in terms of energy and food.

The third environmentalist answer to the nuclear threat involves applying several environmental values to the problem of military and strategic tensions. The obvious value of relevance is reverence for life in all its forms. Deep love for the earth and its beauty makes militarism all the more repellant. But once that is said, it is said; and all one can do is work towards a world where more people appreciate this value and act upon it.

Environmentalists' revulsion for waste and sense of resource limits, as well as for the economic costs associated with the environmental agenda, can also lead toward a new perspective on militarism. Only sustainable forms of economic growth are desirable, all else (including military spending) is a tragic waste. Karl Marx once claimed that he had turned the Hegelian understanding of the world on its head: ideas were not the basis for guiding human economic and technological evolution; rather, the latter determined the former. In this same sense environmentalism can "turn on its head" society's sense of the need for and purpose of economic activity, and even its understanding of work. This reversal is at the core of environmentalism's transformation from "single-issue" political involvement to a broad ideological perspective. Without this new perspective military expenditures are seen at least in part as a means to economic development, rather than as a waste of limited resources. In the old perspective, people not working in a missile plant might have nothing to do; capital not used to produce nuclear weapons might not be used at all. This perspective seems absurd, but it is commonplace in our society.

Much activity in our society is justified in terms of its ability to create jobs, as if jobs were a physical entity of tremendous inherent value and as if all jobs in and of themselves provided great pleasure. We have not yet realized that performing the activity we call work makes sense only if at least one of three conditions is met. First, there must be little or no direct or indirect environmental damage. Second, the product of the work must have some use value. Third, the work must be enjoyable or a means of significant self-improvement, as enjoyable or as significant as whatever else might have been done in the same time by the same person. The further elaboration of this point will take me well beyond a reply to the logic of neoconservative militarism.

nine

Environmentalism and the Restoration
of Progressive Politics

I seek in this chapter to answer one question: aside from the difficult questions associated with excessive military spending, how might environmentalism play a role in the restoration of moderate progressive political ideas? As we have seen, this is not the only position on the left–right ideological spectrum to which environmentalism might be adapted. But because of the intensity of neoconservative anti-environmental efforts, especially in North America, and the unfortunate history of splinter parties, it may be the most plausible position available for environmentalists now.

My emphasis is to some extent on the present but principally on the medium- to long-term future. I do not examine contemporary policy issues in detail. Rather, I concentrate on broad issues that will endure over the next several decades. I hope that linking environmentalist and progressive ideas at this level will produce an integrated whole somewhat larger than the sum of its parts, and I attempt to construct an ideological and political program potentially of broad appeal. Since the exercise is hypothetical and speculative, we cannot yet measure the potential appeal of this construct in terms of public opinion surveys. Majority appeal, however, is a goal of my attempt, and my programmatic proposals are thus moderate in character. A moderate program appeals to my personal politics, but there are several more objective reasons to focus on a politics of moderation.

First, the political systems with which we are dealing, especially those of the United States, are in essence majoritarian (two-party) systems.[1] Except for the innovative role of the New Democratic Party in Canada, the impact of minority (third) parties in these nations has been minimal.[2] Even in Britain the third party has had rough sledding during most of this century. Second, neoconservatism, an ideology openly hostile even to the modest and explicit environmental measures of the 1970s, at the least has majority potential in the 1990s and beyond, whether or not a majority supports its stance on environmental issues. And we must remember that even if the neoconservatives lose their majority support, the ideology is likely to remain important far into the future.

There is really only one politically effective response to majority power in a majoritarian system. While environmentalists once made considerable gains as special interest groups and via many negative single-issue organizations, this approach has been less effective in the 1980s. With hostile regimes in power, most recent contests have been defensive and many campaigns have been lost. It has been nearly a decade since environmentalists gained ground by political means. Neoconservatives have not had a decisive majority with them in every environmental case, but they have prevailed most of the time.

Finally, an environmental perspective ought to be more than a concern with pollution and resource problems of an immediate sort. But broader environmental goals require far-reaching sociopolitical and economic changes. If solutions to environmental problems are socioeconomic in nature as well as technological; if the socioeconomic changes involved are likely to be deep-seated, requiring more than the type of legislation that can be administered by environmental ministries or departments; then environmentalists cannot be politically effective outside the bounds of everyday political discourse. They must find means of relating their ideas to the issues of principal concern to those actively involved in the political world. It is my objective to make these connections.

Let us begin by taking up from chapter 6 the discussion of decentralization as a core value of environmentalism. Recall that any unselective emphasis on political or geographic decentralization

carries considerable problems. Focusing on geographic decentralization, I discuss here the difficult relationship between environmentalism and an appreciation of urban life. This is an issue of
considerable political importance, since the overwhelming majority
of North Americans and Britons are urban dwellers. Any set of
political ideas purporting to appeal to a majority in these countries
must address urban concerns. Beyond this, however, I suggest that
environmentalists' anti-urbanism is not only politically risky, but
environmentally unsound.

Environmentalism's focus is already far more urban than that of
the conservation movement, which emphasized wilderness protection, efficient use of renewable resources (especially forests), development of hydroelectricity, maintenance of soil quality, and
protection of habitats. Indeed, some early conservationists' love of
wilderness included deep-seated doubts about urban life, even industrialization itself.[3] Environmentalism, in contrast, has quite consistently focused more on human settlement, stressing air and water
pollution, population, energy use, resource depletion, occupational
health, hazardous waste management, and recycling. All imply predominantly an urban orientation.

In their vision of an ideal society, however, environmentalists
have at times asserted a preference for geographic decentralization;
and some have advanced a vision that can only be called bucolic.
Aspects of this vision of the future include, for example, the eco-
anarchism of Murray Bookchin, the soft energy path planning of
Amory Lovins, E. F. Schumacher's motto "small is beautiful," and
even the "telecommuting society" of what might be called high-tech
environmentalism. In contrast, few within the environmental movement envision a future more urban than the present. (One exception
is the somewhat enigmatic Paolo Soleri.)[4]

Few environmentalists have considered the place of cities in an
environmental future; few have appreciated how compatible with
environmentalist values are the views of such urban writers as Lewis
Mumford or Jane Jacobs. Indeed it might be useful to understand
the "new urbanism" as environmentalism in an urban setting. The
development of an explicitly urban dimension to environmentalists'
image of the future directly opposes the decentralism of such classic

environmental works as *The Limits to Growth*, William Ophuls' *Ecology and the Politics of Scarcity*, or Theodore Roszak's comments on deurbanization in *Where the Wasteland Ends*. "To call for the deurbanization of the world," Roszak writes, "is only to recognize the historical truth that city life has never suited more than a strict minority of mankind—mainly merchants and intellectuals."[5] Roszak grants cities value but does not see them as dominant in his environmentally sound future. Likewise, Howard T. Odum and Elizabeth C. Odum include in a long description of a moderate-energy steady-state economy (which includes the demise of capitalism and most advertising) the view that "urban construction will be replaced by separate and smaller buildings separately constructed and maintained."[6] But this vision makes little sense in terms of the goals to which these authors aspire.

These are not isolated examples. Lovins, too, emphasizes the decentralized and relatively nonportable character of many renewable energy sources. It seems that many environmentalists so appreciated the opportunities SEP planning afforded that they did not look closely at the long-term implications of decentralism as a societal goal. Much of the planning for an SEP strongly reinforces the bucolic mythology of the conservationist/environmentalist perspective. Thus it has only rarely been articulated—by Nash and Soleri, for example—that perhaps the only way to assure wilderness preservation on a planet soon to be populated by ten billion humans is to accept and even welcome increases in both urban density and the proportion of population resident in urban areas.[7] A full environmental appreciation of the essential nature of cities would lead to more open promotion of a future celebrating both great cities and pristine wilderness. It would be wary indeed of perspectives that envision mass dispersal of population.

Reflecting on the environmental advantages and disadvantages of urban living, one is left wondering why so many environmentalists embrace decentralism. Perhaps it is based on the same need that allows advertisers to promote automobiles and cigarettes as if they were at one with nature, wilderness, and fresh air. In an increasingly urbanized and mechanized world, people really need to feel as if they are a part of the natural world. This need is so strong that it capitulates to the illusions created by the advertisers. Environmentalism itself is also based in part in the intellectual and emotional reaction to modern society's obsession with technology, industry, and nonorganic products—the essentials of urban existence. Environmental protection, it is assumed, would be enhanced if people could only feel closer to the natural world. Environmentalism is equated with escape from the plastic artificiality and congestion of modern urban living. Most contemporary urban dwellers constantly need to "get away from it all." The "all," it seems, has something to do with the pace and setting of life in the city.

But apart from advertisers' nature imagery and the discomforts of urban living, well-managed high-density cities could make good sense from an environmental perspective. People's need to return physically to nature might be addressed by altering work patterns to allow more people to spend extended periods of their lives in rural areas or wilderness. These issues are addressed in the central theme of this chapter: environmentalism's view of the concepts of work and play. First, however, I list the principal environmental advantages of high-density urban living.

1. Given the high cost of urban land and the generally inflated value of urban housing, average residential space per person is inevitably lower in downtown urban areas. It follows that city homes use less energy than rural or suburban homes. Fewer other materials are needed as well—home furnishings, for example. Fewer people own and use cars in core urban areas; the cars that are in use tend to be smaller. Shared appliances (e.g., in laundromats) are also more common. All these things mean fewer material and energy throughputs per capita.

2. The multiple dwelling units more common in urban settings can be heated and cooled using less energy per unit of area, because there are fewer exterior walls per unit of floor space. Studies have shown that individual electric meters in multiple dwelling units would reduce demand more than 30 percent.[8] (Without such metering many urban areas lose part of their natural energy efficiency.) Even without these potential savings, in 1982 the average single-family detached dwelling in the United States used 127 million BTUs of nontransportation energy; the average household in a building

with five or more units used only 77 million BTUs.[9] This difference cannot be accounted for wholly by income discrepancies, which may not be a factor at all.[10]

3. Birth rates in urban areas across many cultures are measurably lower than they are in rural areas. Children's labor is not needed in nonagricultural settings. In urban settings, women's educational and employment opportunities are enhanced, residential space costs more, and birth control aids and medical care are more easily available.

4. In dense urban areas more energy-efficient modes of transportation, such as rail and bus are in greater use. These forms of transportation also require less land per passenger mile than automobiles. The land saved would often be agricultural land.[11]

5. Even more important energy gains are made because distances traveled in dense cities are reduced. This can be achieved without compromising quality of life, if the city is designed intelligently. Urban areas that mix residential, commercial, cultural, and industrial uses should achieve significant reduction in travel—precisely the sort of city that such "new urbanist" thinkers as Jane Jacobs advocated largely prior to the advent of environmentalism. Urban design with an eye to reducing transportation needs could be the most significant characteristic of an environmental urbanism. Such cities would be not only environmentally sound but, as Jacobs has so lucidly argued, socially and humanly preferable.

6. Carless cities can be designed. This vision may seem at first glance utopian or just plain wrong. It goes well beyond the fifty-year goals of most SEP studies.[12] But several noted environmentalists—for example, Mishan and Gorz—have eloquently pleaded for limiting automobiles. The case for reduced dependence on automobiles was made in urbanist terms by Lewis Mumford in 1958 and earlier.[13] Carlessness is a meaningful option in well-designed, multiple-use urban cores or throughout cities with excellent public transportation systems. It is also a viable choice in moderate-sized and moderate-climate cities where most daily needs are accessible on foot or by bicycle. A third possibility is less pleasant to contemplate but perhaps more commonplace: urban settings so dense and/or so badly designed that automobile ownership is more trouble

than it is worth. In Manhattan, lack of parking, high maintenance costs, and stringent street regulations tend to discourage all but the most determined, prosperous, or auto-addicted individuals. In contrast, nonurban carlessness is difficult indeed.

7. Recycling, reuse, and repair—the core of a conserver society—are far less costly in urban settings because collection costs are not prohibitive. And the high cost of landfill sites, in combination with those of transportation, make recycling an economically sensible option in urban areas. Finally, the environmental risks associated with both landfills and incinerators are generally of greater concern to dense populations.[14] (Returning organic wastes to the soil, however, is more easily achieved in nonurban settings.)

8. Environmentalists have preferred rural settings as models for the future in part because of the higher levels of pollution, especially air pollution, associated with urban areas. Dispersing a population commuting into the city in cars would not reduce air pollution. Only when people imagined that "the solution to pollution is dilution" did such a perspective make any sense. But now the most urgent pollution problems are acid rain and the greenhouse effect. No improvement will be achieved in these problems by population dispersion; indeed, it may be counterproductive. More effective would be reducing travel needs and using more and better pollution abatement devices.

9. Even hazardous waste treatment facilities may be more appropriate in relatively urban settings. Despite public resistance, properly designed and sited facilities are superior to such means of disposal as deep-well injection or landfilling relatively untreated liquid wastes.[15] If facilities are located in urban areas, untreated wastes do not have to be transported so far. Only treated and solidified wastes need be shipped to long-term storage sites, if these are separate from treatment facilities. The Ontario Waste Management Corporation, after perhaps the most exhaustive and careful siting procedure used anywhere in the world, chose a near-urban location for its facility. Urban areas are also better suited to reuse and recycling of toxic substances.[16] Relatively dispersed industrial systems would find recycling and reuse of hazardous materials less economical.

10. Finally, one must recall that wilderness and agricultural pro-

ductivity in many nations will be put at risk if urban populations are not contained. Wilderness should not be "loved to death" in an orgy of convenient access and multiple use.[17] And to protect agricultural lands, farms and defined communities must predominate over strip development.

To achieve these environmental advantages, humans must continue to dwell primarily in urban areas. The new urbanist perspective of Mumford, Jacobs, Soleri, and others, in combination with an environmental sensibility, suggests moving toward living spaces neither bucolic, nor overcrowded, nor suburban "energy sinks." Many informed people might prefer environmentally sound cities in any case. Jane Jacobs' *The Life and Death of Great American Cities* makes the now classic case that complex, high-density cities can be safe, comfortable, and exciting. Successful urban neighborhoods, Jacobs argues, combine housing, commerce, employment, culture, and recreation within one small area. Streets, parks and stores are ideally busy most of the time. Old buildings mingle with new buildings, high rent with low rent. In this way sociocultural and commercial diversity are maximized. Pedestrians move freely and easily from one function to another. Blocks are short with something different and interesting around every corner. Street life is based in commerce and culture and is always vital and interesting.

Jacobs' city stands opposed to the bulldozer urban renewal vision of the 1950s and the sprawling suburbia of that era and ours. These types of urban design separate housing from both commerce and employment. Meeting almost any need requires transportation, usually by car. One works in a factory district, shops in a shopping mall, and lives away from all that "congestion." But that very congestion results largely from the separation of functions. This regrettable pattern Jacobs attributed primarily to Ebenezer Howard, the British town planner: "Howard set spinning powerful city-destroying ideas: he conceived that the way to deal with the city's functions was to sort out and sift each of these in relative self-containment."[18] As Lewis Mumford put it some years earlier, "But if we are to make walking attractive, we must not only provide trees and wide pavements and benches, beds of flowers and outdoor cafes, as they do in Rotterdam: we must also scrap the monotonous uniformities of American zoning practice, which turns vast areas, too spread out for pedestrian movement, into single-district zones, for commerce, industry, or residential purposes."[19]

Since Jacobs and Mumford wrote, some North American cities have adapted very well, especially at their gentrified cores. More high-quality downtown residences mean that more people live a walk or a subway ride from jobs, shopping, classes, restaurants, schools, and theaters. A good life, and one that is relatively benign environmentally, is more than possible in such settings. An urban environmentalism makes much more sense than commuting many miles every day in order to "get back to the land." It also has far greater political promise. Free of their ruralist past, contemporary environmentalists in alliance with more traditional progressive forces might emphasize such urgent public policy issues as low-cost urban transportation, city-core building conversion and renovation, support for the arts, and intelligent handling of municipal wastes. They might also stress that cities ought to be places from which people do not feel a need to flee.

Critics of environmentalism emphasize its association with voluntary asceticism. But environmentalists do not need to call for economic stringency. Environmental positions on economic growth are complex and not fully agreed upon. Herman Daly, for example, insists that societies cannot move ever closer to "angelized GNP." He seems to believe that growth in GNP is near to its desirable endpoint. E. J. Mishan is likewise convinced that further growth within highly developed economies will probably do more harm than good. Lovins, however, argues that economic growth and energy growth do not march in lockstep. He implies that further economic growth is both possible and desirable so long as it occurs within the bounds of an SEP. Barry Commoner is open to further economic growth so long as more effective technological choices are made along the way. These positions seem disparate. But we might say that no environmentalist sees economic growth as an appropriate overriding focus for a complex society. Societies must first assure that none of their economic activities harm the environment and must recognize that such activities may be constrained by limits inherent in the need for long-term sustainability.

But most environmentalists would agree that it is very difficult to ascertain what level of economic activity can be achieved within the strictest adherence to environmental limits. Environmentalists are agnostic about economic growth more than they are opposed— particularly economic growth measured in monetary (GNP) terms. If GNP growth can be achieved without additional material and energy demand, it is welcome. Environmentalists would not object, for example, to the development of systems that could provide most homes or neighborhoods in the world electronic access to all the world's information, literature, film, and music. Such a prospect would obviously involve, in monetary terms, immense amounts of economic activity.

The point is that environmentalists are open to a wide range of possible economic and technological futures. Lovins is correct: a splendid range of possibilities is open within the reasonable bounds environmentalism suggests. Those futures might even include freedom from hunger and virtual freedom from work, as well as wealth based in concentrated and low-material forms, in information and culture, and in anything that does not require vast amounts of environmentally costly and/or nonrenewable energy. The environmental future might also include a world without war or the threat of war. The size of the GNP, however, is beyond prediction, because one cannot anticipate how many "real" dollars people will pay for these possible things.

We might conclude that things which cannot be sustained in the long term, or which damage the environment, are less important than sustainable things. It is useful in this regard to glance at what might be the most politically difficult of environmental sacrifices— automobile use in the North American, or even Western European, pattern. It is already clear that this pattern could not be sustained on a global basis for very long. Nor can it likely persist for more than a century or two, even where it has already established itself, without considerable environmental costs.[20] What might follow politically from such a radical conclusion?

First, there is no reason to place heavy emphasis on the most speculative and depressing aspects of an environmental view of the distant future. A present-day North American majority would not likely vote for a party that emphasized all the possible dimensions of a long-term environmental future. Greater political effectiveness lies with the Lovinses' perspective, which accentuates the positive and focuses on the medium term. Environmentalists can stress, for example, breakthroughs in fuel efficiency and such relatively benign and sustainable technologies as biomass fuels. Combined with greater use of existing technological possibilities, these would certainly buy time and move us toward, though perhaps not to, energy sustainability. Over time, improved urban design and communications might decrease the felt need for automobiles. A century of careful energy management might lead gradually and naturally to a pattern of automobile use appropriate to the post-oil age. There is thus no real political issue here. The changes implied by an environmental perspective are not massive when translated into short-term policies focusing on continued improvements in automotive efficiency, research funds for renewable liquid energy, better urban designs and public transportation, and fewer tax subsidies for oil companies. These are the environmental issues of today; we need not shock people with our images of the twenty-first century.

Although most environmentalists imagine that in the long term limits on particular economic activities will be necessary, these limits do not necessarily diminish present economic prospects. Indeed, recently many environmentalists have argued that emphasis on environmental protection and sustainability is the best long-term economic course.[21] Every economy ultimately depends on the biological cycles of the earth; thus, especially in the long term and from a global perspective, the best environmental choices will also be the best economic choices. Of course, this may not apply to particular decisions, firms or economies, especially in the short term. Environmental protection involves economic costs, and societies must choose who will bear those costs and when. In the long run, however, choices that assure environmental protection and enhance sustainability will pay economic dividends on a global basis.

Environmentalists can also make clear that periods of economic stability or even occasional modest contractions are not the worst possible scenarios. Few governments, however intensely committed to growth, have bettered this since 1973. Growth is limited by things other than stringent environmental protection, which need not restrain growth; anticipated restraint is easier to bear than forced growth that fails unexpectedly. If we do not protect the environment, however, we will bear massive costs, both human and economic— additional cancers (which increase medical costs) and rising prices for fresh water, energy, fiber, and food. Many such costs are being borne all over the world, especially in developing countries. Furthermore, without greater energy and materials efficiency and expanded use of renewable energy, all economies are vulnerable in the long term. Environmentalists cannot avoid this perspective. They cannot reasonably claim that environmentalism is a new route to astonishing economic advances. But environmentalism is far from merely an inclination to asceticism.

The objective of environmentalism is an economy and environment that are productive over the long term. It is impossible to predict whether such sustainability will involve a limit on GNP. But we need to acknowledge the uncertainties of the global economy. Only by refusing to deny the risks and problems can we avoid the worst possible outcomes. Even politically opportunist environmentalists cannot blithely assure that sustained and dramatic growth in GNP is possible. But environmentalists can be optimistic about the future, making clear that further economic growth in some forms is both desirable and probable. They can also emphasize—perhaps in alliance with progressives—that dramatic distributional and quality-of-life improvements do not require further growth in GNP. We might, for example, make significant advances in economic security, in labor and energy productivity, and in the equitable distribution of employment opportunities.

Just as it is important for environmentalists to have a more urban vision and to avoid being characterized as ascetics, they should make clear that they welcome many forms of technology. A few environmentalists have been cranky toward much of modern living, but most are comfortable with many of the principal technologies that are now increasingly at the forefront. In particular, most high-technology electronics is compatible with environmental protection: computers, telecommunications, measurement and control devices, robotics, and most of the hardware and software of the information revolution. These sectors use little energy and material per dollar of output. Furthermore, this technology is useful for environmental monitoring and for environmental and energy controls. And advances in this area might lead to substitution of information and communications for transportation, goods and even materials.[22] Also promising for environmentalists are biotechnologies that might replace risky chemical controls and supplements heavily used in agriculture and forestry.

But perhaps even more important environmentally is that these technologies can replace much human labor. This characteristic of electronic technologies, now widely feared, will force societies to rethink their socioeconomic structures and principles. This process may enhance opportunities for integrating environmental and progressive politics.

An environmental perspective, as we have seen, suffers from apparent economic pessimism. Environmentalists cannot hold out the prospect of dramatic economic growth. Their position is not utterly negative, but it is qualified and complex. In this context it is interesting that a plausible resolution of the sociopolitical problem posed by new technologies could add considerable political appeal to environmentalism. The problem of structural unemployment on a global scale can be solved by radically reducing average work time. In such a future economy, energy and materials demand would decline slowly, environmental impacts would be gradually lessened, total output (in GNP terms) would probably appreciate slowly and free time would be significantly increased. The last can add an element of excitement otherwise lacking in the environmentalist portrait of the economic future. Such a situation could appeal to those who seek enhanced economic security for all and to those who are materially comfortable and/or who find their work lives unrewarding.

Without the issue of reduced work time, environmentalism lacks

an exciting economic agenda. Without work time reductions, however, the very technologies that provide this opportunity may enhance many contemporary threats to the environment: increasing
productivity without reducing work time will lead to not only high
unemployment but also the environmental dangers inherent in
sharply increased industrial output, which usually increases energy
and materials demand even if the means of production are efficient
and clean. Even clean, energy-efficient, automated factories require
materials from not-so-clean mines and smelters, and the increased
output of such factories might be products that themselves demand
energy.

Many people do not see this as a problem. We cannot assume,
however, that present levels of environmental damage are acceptable, and we must be wary of increasing production faster than we
improve energy efficiency or reduce pollution per unit of output.
Furthermore, damage per unit of energy demand will likely increase
as present energy sources are depleted. Thus the environmental
issue of work time reduction has both a positive and a negative side.

There is another dimension to the connection between work time
reduction and environmentalism. Putting environmental considerations aside, traditional progressives might continue to press for a
return to trade union-based wage gains and expanded social expenditures by government. This perspective seems unrealistic at
present. Given high unemployment levels and declining member-
ships and resources, trade unions have been hard pressed in recent
years even to maintain wages in real terms. Progressive politicians
have been left with the hollow task of defending the social programs
of the past. They need to break with traditional approaches and
traditional constituencies.[23]

It is difficult to imagine a new progressive approach that would
not insist on both limits to military expenditures and a more equitable
distribution of employment. These issues lend themselves to pro-
gressive/environmentalist cooperation, based broadly on environmental protection, social, educational, and cultural support, and an
evolution toward liberation from the drudgery of wage labor. Government budgets would be brought nearer to balance through reduced military expenditures, fewer tax subsidies, and caps on public

sector wages. Work time reductions would be paid for by applying the savings associated with productivity improvements to something other than higher wages and profits. Clearly this perspective cuts across traditional political boundaries. But it may not be as unpopular as it might seem at first glance.

There are several less obvious points of potential agreement between environmentalism and progressivism. A fruitful combination of the two perspectives would likely require environmentalists to eschew ascetic, anti-urban, and anti-technological stances (the last, of course, is more a perception than reality). But technological selectivity must remain central to an environmental perspective, as must a somewhat lower priority for economic growth and the expansion of individual incomes.[24] Progressives might have some difficulty accepting that modest rates of economic growth are likely to be the best that can be achieved for the foreseeable future. In the United States many progressives may hesitate to explicitly reject militarism. But broadly speaking, such adaptations might lead to a new common outlook for both perspectives and a plausible ideological response to neoconservatism.

Liberation from work can be made the centerpiece of this new approach. To appreciate the importance of this issue, let us consider for a moment the need to introduce into our language a clear distinction between *work* and *wage labor*.[25] *Work* can be defined as productive activities one might do even if they did not provide income. They require physical and/or mental effort and result in products or services of use to oneself, one's family, or one's society. In this perspective the line between work and play is a subtle one. We can now, for the first time, begin to imagine a future in which this distinction becomes more subtle and wage labor becomes a less significant part of people's lives. Indeed, in some ways this new world seems already upon us: the highest wages (although not the highest incomes) are paid to a small number of professional athletes, musicians, and media personalities—superb "players" all. In addition to remuneration these individuals receive much recognition and prestige.

Bearing in mind the distinction between work and wage labor, one wonders at a society, polity, and economy whose central goal is the creation of jobs. It also seems remarkable that most people cannot imagine being engaged in wage labor for fewer than forty years at less than forty hours per week.[26] Why have we not yet sought imaginative ways to reduce this "term"? One argument is that reducing the proportion of lives devoted to wage labor would weaken the underlying logic of current support for military spending. But this interpretation attributes too much foresight and coherence to the bureaucratic capitalist system. Gorz points to capitalists' need to maintain social discipline—insufficiently emphasizing that this seems an even more urgent need for socialist societies.

An interesting, although perhaps extreme, extension of the logic of time off for enhanced productivity would involve linking reductions in work time to product durability. Here the threat to the logic of the capitalist workplace is most apparent. Products deliberately designed, within the bounds of production costs, for durability and/or repairability would drastically cut into profits. Despite its compelling environmental logic, therefore, this proposal may be beyond the system's capability for adaptation. A related issue is how full employment achieved through work time reductions might affect hiring in occupationally hazardous production facilities. Here is another potential threat to the logic of the market system. If labor costs in hazardous sectors rose disproportionately due to fuller employment, reduced work time would threaten powerful economic interests.

Nonetheless, the need for a gradual but significant separation of income and wage labor seems inescapable. There simply are not enough jobs—industrial jobs in particular are obviously in a long-term decline. Of course changes of this magnitude will be achieved, both economically and psychologically, only in several generations. But an infinite variety of techniques can be applied to the task. The logic of an environmental approach suggests transferring productivity gains to reductions in work time rather than to increases in wages or profits, or to expanded domestic public spending. There will always be questions of balance, but work time reductions should be a significant factor in the complex equation.

Gorz breaks from a conventional Marxist approach to working-class politics based on a calculation regarding productivity and work time reductions. If we assume that the productivity gains of the recent past will continue and we translate two-thirds of those gains to work time reductions, "the length of the working week would fall from 40 to 35 hours over a period of four years. After four more years it would stand at no more than 30 1/2 hours. . . . A 20-hour week could be achieved in 20 years . . . and, if we take vacations and public holidays into account, would amount to a yearly total of barely 900 hours." This means an average lifetime work obligation of some twenty thousand hours, or ten full-time years. The prospect of such a scenario, Gorz concludes, justifies a fundamental break from the traditional left's orientation toward the industrial working class.

> For workers, it is no longer a question of freeing themselves *within* work, putting themselves in control of work, or seizing power within the framework of their work. The point now is to free oneself *from* work by rejecting its nature, content, necessity and modalities. But to reject work is also to reject the traditional strategy and organizational forms of the working-class movement. It is no longer a question of winning power as a worker, but of winning the power no longer to function as a worker.[27]

Given the radical implications of this perspective for our social fabric, and recalling the wisdom of Edmund Burke, many will assume that only over the long term could work time be radically reduced. Nonetheless, now is the time to begin. Unemployment rates in recent years have averaged well over 10 percent in many advanced economies. Of course, environmentalists have suggested a wide variety of means to contribute to full employment (see chapter 4); in the long term all these proposals and radically reducing wage labor may be possible, for four reasons. (1) New production technologies should continue to improve labor productivity. (2) Many current products may prove unsustainable as energy prices increase. (3) Even public sector jobs may soon be lost to automation and/or may be unnecessary.[28] (4) And at present trade unions and some employers are struggling to avoid or delay reducing the demand for labor. What if society actively sought to reduce or even eliminate unnecessary wage labor?

To balance this view, recall that an environmental energy policy, one emphasizing energy conservation and renewable energy sources, would require more labor than any other energy strategy. This principle carries over into other areas of the economy as well. Refillable container legislation creates jobs; recycling is labor intensive, so is pollution abatement. Increased public transportation, particularly buses and trains, generates jobs. Reforestation and an agriculture less dependent on chemicals would also involve more jobs and/or opportunities for meaningful work (as opposed to wage labor).

Another environmental claim regarding unemployment is that social expenditures such as those on health, education, and welfare do not damage the environment or use many resources, but they do create a large number of jobs. That is, a GNP dominated by human services rather than manufacture of goods (particularly primary goods) is less likely to be environmentally threatening and less likely to involve high levels of unemployment. This issue and the equitable distribution of wage labor through career-time reductions may be important to the environmentalist restoration of moderate progressivism.

The combined logic of environmentalism and progressivism can be usefully applied to several other domestic political issues. Environmentalists have not yet widely addressed the problem of government deficits. But, given that most environmentalists consider further economic growth harmful, impossible, or of low priority in advanced economies with relatively steady populations, they should find it difficult to understand why any government would risk the fiscal integrity of the whole system in order to force growth on a reluctant economy. An environmentally oriented government in an overdeveloped economy would thus seek to balance budgets by, for example, reducing military spending, restraining public sector wages, increasing taxes, or removing subsidies and incentives to industry, particularly to primary industries and to the transportation and energy sectors. (Obviously, such measures would need to be applied gradually, to avoid precipitous decline.) Current deficits could be recovered by combining such measures with a reduction in the costs to government associated with unemployment and the lower interest rates which balanced budgets would likely engender. (Difficulties would arise, of course, if the economy contracted in such a way as to reduce the income of government.) Environmentalists, then, are comfortable with slow reductions in deficits, and they have a plan to accomplish it. This is a more realistic view than most progressives' and much more humane than current neoconservative efforts.

Environmentalists have also said some interesting things about inflation. Amory Lovins argues that inflation is largely a result of total dependence on nonrenewable and declining sources of energy. As supplies of nonrenewable energy decline, prices rise. As the energy conveniently extracted from easily accessible locations is depleted, prices rise again. Energy prices force up most other prices. Even renewable supplies, if mismanaged, contribute to inflation: overcutting wood and failing effectively to restore cut forests will lead to higher prices for wood and paper products. Likewise, removing prime agricultural land from agricultural use leads to lower productivity, higher energy demand per unit of food produced, and significant increases in food prices. And lack of emphasis on recycling means we must extract minerals from ever less rich and less available ore bodies—again, higher energy use per unit extracted will raise prices of metals and metal products. Thus recycling, energy conservation, the use of renewable energy sources, reforestation, and careful resource management tend to help curb inflation. Given a conservative (i.e., non-Keynesian) fiscal policy and an acceptance of limited wage gains to combat unemployment, an environmentally inclined regime would tend toward deflation rather than inflation.

Inflation is tied to interest rates, and here we can note that energy megaprojects, in contrast to soft energy, tie up large amounts of capital for a decade or more before interest can be paid from the sale of energy. Capital for equivalent energy conservation improvements can be reused two, three, or more times in a decade, thereby placing less pressure on capital markets. Lower interest rates thus generated lead directly to lower government deficits, since interest payments are becoming a major proportion of government expenditures. Higher interest rates may also contribute to inflation.[29]

Environmentalists have always prominently asserted a bias toward future generations, a concern that they not be charged for the comforts of the present. It is thus consistent with environmental views to avoid deferring present costs. Both deficits and inflation have this result. A *real* fiscal conservatism (not what neoconservatives have practiced) is therefore in keeping with an environmental perspective and might also be acceptable to those progressives capable of thinking in the long term—although it must be balanced against progressives' preference for human services expenditures and full employment.

To recapitulate, environmentalism not only includes a response to neoconservatism on the question of military spending; it also contains a distinctive view of fiscal and economic policy, one that sets it apart from both the traditional left and the traditional right. Environmentalists prefer full employment even when it leads to lower wages—many jobs in insulation retrofitting are better than a few high-paying jobs in nuclear plant construction. Environmentalists might advocate sabbaticals in industry as well as in the academic world, perhaps at less than full salaries. A firm intention to reduce government deficits, and several means to help achieve this goal are part of the environmental agenda. These measures, along with stress on renewable sources of energy and on resource sustainability, will help achieve deflationary rather than inflationary tendencies. Deflation might offset the commitment to a slow, continuous increase in oil prices.

Is this an ideological position neither left nor right? Clearly it is quite distinct from neoconservative claims and in some ways radically contrary to neoconservative practice. But it has dimensions in common with some neoconservative promises—particularly those regarding downward pressure on wage costs and government deficits. Environmentalism also shares positions with progressivism, more than suggest themselves immediately. I outline here some of these areas of potential agreement between the perspectives, as well as some tensions that might be anticipated. We seek something more than a bland compromise.

Political compromise and caution is inevitable with regard to trading time for money. Much experience has already been gained in environmentally induced attempts to move away from a small number of high-paying jobs particularly doubtful from an environmental perspective—for example, in highway and power plant construction and in response to container deposit legislation. Productive discussions of such issues have been going on between North American trade unionists and environmentalists for fifteen years now.[30] But Claus Offe offers a caution in his analysis of the German Greens:

> The dilemma of such a politics is that, while the Greens cannot afford to join the bandwagon of the arms race, industrial growth and the bureaucratic politics of alienation, they cannot pull the emergency brake either, because that would injure actual and potential supporters. . . . Concretely, this means that an ecologically oriented politics of limited growth must show that the sacrifices implied by such a project are bearable, and that their social distribution is acceptable.[31]

Short of violence (unacceptable on principle), environmentalists find ways to achieve broad political support without the blessing of those earning high incomes in military and ecologically destructive industries. Environmentalists' position must appeal to industrial workers, public servants, and those employed in health, education, and the arts. Environmentalists might find a constituency among those employed in the (generally cleaner) high technology and information industries, as well as among women, the aged, the young, and other progressive-minded people. A coherent plan to cope with unemployment, deficits, and inflation is important but insufficient. Environmental protection and antimilitarism also have considerable appeal in and of themselves, but there must be something more.

The something more might be an environmental revitalization of some of the traditional elements of progressivism. Although these suggestions might alienate some sectors of a broad constituency when it is explained who must pay and how, I believe that environmentalism can bring a deeper logic to many traditional progressive ideas and policies. Let us consider here several important examples: aid to the aged, including health insurance; government support for the arts and education; foreign aid; and women's rights.

A flexible retirement policy that encouraged more people to opt for at least partial retirement is one way to let off pressure for maintaining employment opportunities. Lowering the mandatory retirement age might be the easiest way out, but this clashes with the progressive tradition and is problematic demographically as the largest population cohort moves toward retirement age. The only viable prospect is a flexibility that provides more economic security to everyone at a slowly declining age. The underlying goal is to induce voluntary, full or partial, early retirement. Less lifetime wage labor, perhaps accompanied by some employment beyond the present age of retirement, would make sense to many people if social insurance and pension provisions were strengthened.

This leads environmentalists to consider the quality and cost of private and public health insurance, since few will opt for retirement without a sense of security regarding health care. In the moderate growth economy favored by environmentalists, a variety of measures will be necessary to bring down insanely high medical costs.[32]

This flexible approach to retirement age rests on the general assumption that our society already produces enough goods. As these goods are produced by fewer and fewer workers (because of technology and productivity improvements), there are four possible grounds for altering retirement patterns. (1) Given excess labor capacity, some people must stop drawing a wage for the mass production of goods. (2) Shorter work weeks might make longer working careers possible for some people. (3) Many people with twenty to thirty years' experience at an occupation find themselves without work due to technological transformation. Retirement or semiretirement might seem desirable to them. (4) As the economy continues to move from emphasizing goods to emphasizing services, from mass production to information production and transfer, retirement at the arbitrary age of sixty-five or seventy makes less sense. Few eighty-year-olds make good coal miners, but many make good part-time teachers, health care professionals, or librarians.

Both temporary and partial retirement should be made possible. With an energy-efficient home, some food self-sufficiency, and low-cost public transportation, supporting oneself will not be difficult, so perhaps such an option should be open to people of any age willing to accept an income marginally below the minimum wage. (Some environmentalists find the guaranteed annual income an intriguing possibility.)[33] The cost of such programs might be considerably less than expected—especially if unemployment insurance payments were no longer necessary, nor the costs (i.e., in incentives to industry) of inducing jobs in the private sector.[34]

Two other aspects of traditional progressivism—public support for the arts and education—also make sense from an environmental perspective. In both areas, a high proportion of expenditures go directly for wages; the material and energy costs of such expenditures are often well below 10 percent of the total. Wages typically account for more than 80 percent of such expenditures, and they rarely involve many very high salaries. Many jobs are thereby provided at low energy and materials costs. Furthermore, the physical plants in many of these institutions should, from an environmental perspective, be used more intensively—lowering nonwage costs even more.

Where would additional revenue for expanded educational and cultural institutions come from? One obvious source, particularly in the United States, would be money now spent on military hardware. Money might also come internally from early and/or partial retirement schemes. Academic salaries in particular favor those with long-established careers—three energetic young faculty members can be hired for the cost of one aging tenured professor. Overall teaching might actually improve as savings are made despite the fact that some people do get wiser, even if a bit less energetic, as they get older.[35]

In addition, in the arts and education, monies come from both market sources as well as from institutional and governmental sources. Educational and cultural expenditures could continue to grow even without further aid from government. Courses, degrees, computer programs, evenings at a neighborhood theater, and radio broadcast concerts are commodities with little or no material or energy content that are increasingly favored over second cars, domestic gadgets, or the various frills our society offers. The higher energy prices rise, and the higher overall education levels are, the truer this will become. Finally, though this is less automatic in the long run, the higher the average income level the higher the proportion that is spent on education and the arts. Thus it is not outside the realm of possibility that GNP could ultimately come quite near to Daly's "angelized" state. If this were the case GNP could grow indefinitely.

Another expenditure championed by moderate progressives, particularly since 1945, has been foreign aid to less developed nations. There is a large and thoughtful literature on environmentally appropriate development opportunities, but rather than examine this literature in detail, I merely offer the generalization that a more secure world cannot evolve without a more equitable North–South economic balance.[36] Beyond this, environmentalists assert that development aid should not be used principally to foster growth in the North American economy, as it is now.[37] This view is compatible with a progressive perspective on foreign aid expenditures. Environmentalists also see real opportunities in many countries to encourage the use of foreign aid in environmentally sound ways to promote domestic autonomy in the production of food and shelter. Exciting examples of environmentally appropriate development include Thailand's successful birth control program; Brazil's willingness to develop an alcohol-based transportation sector; Kenya's reforestation efforts; Nicaragua's conscious rejection of heavy pesticide use in agriculture; and the remarkable economic gains in the East Asian Pacific rim. Some less developed countries might even leap over the age of nonrenewable energy. Finally, conservationists emphasize that money should be used globally to protect all truly unique natural environments.

Another issue of increasing importance to progressives that is deepened by an environmental perspective is feminism and women's rights.[38] Several important points need to be made here. First, it is clear that in both highly developed and less developed economies, enhanced educational and employment opportunities for women lead to smaller families, without further intervention. Such opportunities are particularly effective in delaying women's first pregnancies—not only a means of slowing population growth but also a health benefit to both mothers and children.[39] Women's rights, including equal pay for work of equal value, are more than simply rights as they might be seen from a progressive viewpoint; assuring them also potentially contributes to global population stability.

Radically reduced work time for all carries great potential for furthering the efforts of the women's movement. A shortened work week would bring more opportunities for those entering or re-entering the labor force. Benefits for those in female-dominated part-time jobs could be improved if work time for most workers were more comparable. But even more important, if both men and women devoted less time to wage labor, they could spend more time on domestic duties and childrearing. Greater career planning flexibility would be possible for both parents if lifetime work approached Gorz's twenty-thousand-hour target.

Some potential tensions between feminists and environmentalists could prove beneficial to an evolving environmentalism. The women's movement, for example, will check male environmentalists' tendency to propose coercive population programs. Not all points of potential disagreement can be easily resolved, of course. What would feminists say to a program of quality daycare whose fees increased for the second or third child of the same parents? Environmentally sound, perhaps, but doubtful from a progressive feminist perspective. Likewise, environmentalists might see the "wages for housework" proposal supported by some feminists as providing financial incentives for larger families (on the other hand, such a program would lower demand for other jobs).[40] The best solution might be to pay a guaranteed annual income (negative income tax) be paid to everyone, male or female, whether or not they spent their time doing housework or bearing children.

A consistent environmental view clashes with such progressive programs as Canada's family allowance plan, under which Canadian mothers receive several hundred dollars per child per year. Over this issue, environmentalists might find themselves comfortably in alliance with neoconservatives and opposed to most women's organizations. This reinforces my point about environmentalism's adaptability. An environmentalist-progressive alliance is not automatic; it will require effort—but a link with progressive feminism is most worthwhile.

Environmentalists and feminists agree that women should not be cast in support roles for male producers. If women's self-definition is achieved only through others, the only role they are left is that of effective consumer. It is too easy, in an undervalued role in a culture dominated by advertising, to see oneself almost solely in terms of the status level of one's purchases. Such lives, however materially rich, are hollow. The contemporary women's movement was born in the affluent suburbs of North America, out of the sheer boredom of empty and unappreciated lives. Feminism is also based in women's inferior educational and economic opportunities. But both feminists and environmentalists see the pointlessness of trying to fill an empty life with an ever-changing variety of goods and services of limited value.

Finally, there are links between feminism and environmentalism at a more philosophical level—the literature of ecofeminism is currently burgeoning. On an everyday level men in decision-making positions have easily undervalued the organic nurturing dimension so central to environmentalism and there seems to be something "male" about a narrow "engineering" mentality. Engineering has been the slowest of the professions to move toward sexual balance, and this is not because of explicit barriers to women. Engineering is often linear and aggressive and sometimes insensitive to ecological or sociocultural concerns. Perhaps women (for whatever reason) are less often foolish in these ways. In contrast, there is a "feminine" cast to many environmentalist concepts ("soft" energy paths) and organizations (which see themselves as caretakers of the earth, of other species, and of future generations). The psychological/philosophical character of this association should not be pressed too far, but it is real.

An alliance between feminists and environmentalists has a great deal of potential. Robert Mitchell found (in 1980), for example, that 80 percent of members of environmental groups also supported the women's movement, the peace movement, and civil rights activism.[41] A progressivism revitalized by these two perspectives, and committed to growing freedom from both wage labor and militarism, might look very different from the tired, bland, confused response to neoconservatism that is so familiar to North Americans in recent years. Such a progressivism could also avoid lapsing into unpopular ultra-leftism. The alliance might even develop in such a way as to avoid alienating progressives from much of their traditional blue-collar, ethnic, and urban constituencies. Environmentalists support most social programs, education, and the arts. Full employment is high on the agenda; the restoration of quality urban life is clearly an urgent priority. The alliance between women and progressives can continue to grow.[42] But it may be more important for progressives to restore their depth of commitment and a sense of humane urgency than to protect any particular set of constituencies. The preceding analysis suggests that an environmental program can help this process without proposing measures that would automatically alienate many traditional progressive supporters. I conclude this chapter with a brief summary statement of the specifics of such a program.

A Contemporary Program for Environmentalist Progressives

First, I might stress that one could almost as easily construct a list of priorities to appeal to both environmentalists and moderate conservatives. Both lists would emphasize deficit reduction, but the latter might focus on wage restraint and publicly funded environmental protection rather than on limits to work time and a more flexible approach toward pollution abatement costs. Given the hostility to environmental protection in some conservative and business circles, it seems unlikely that an environmental alliance is possible there. But this potential flexibility within environmentalism should not be forgotten. Some aspects of neoconservatism have deeply democratic roots, and there is no reason for environmentalist progressives to avoid programs that incorporate this middle ground. Selective efforts toward political and administrative decentralization, deficit reduction, simplification of taxes and regulations, and restraints on public sector salaries would all be consistent with the populist appeal of neoconservatism. All could be carried out in a manner appropriate to both environmentalism and, if you will, neoprogressivism.

The core priorities of a contemporary environmental progressivism might include:

1. *A commitment to seek long-term international agreements that would allow for a gradual, continuous real increase in oil prices.* Periodic limited adjustments to account for economic realities might be built into such agreements. Other government interventions in the energy sector might be limited to, for example, partial subsidies to low-income families or senior citizens for energy-efficient upgrades, and adopting efficiency standards for appliances.[43]

2. *A long-term emphasis on productivity-enhancing technologies coupled with a commitment to full employment.* New employment would be based in enhanced environmental protection (broadly conceived), in improved educational and human services, and ultimately in reductions in average work time (time in which persons are engaged in wage labor). Increased employment opportunities might also be based in urban restoration (item 6), though these might be offset by the effects of deficit reduction measures (item 7).

3. *The development of materials policies to promote durable and repairable products and recycling.* Such a program might include bottle-return bills, more municipally based source separation recycling, and repairability standards for both domestic and imported products. Such a policy should not increase government costs; the new employment involved might reduce the costs of such income transfer programs as unemployment insurance.

4. *The strengthening of environmental protection policies, including those regarding toxic substances and acid rain.* Again, enhanced protection need not increase government costs. For example, community-based environmental organizations (which pay notoriously low wages) might be engaged to monitor compliance and assess environmental impacts.

5. *The elimination of gender-based economic and educational disincentives,* including establishing equal pay for work of equal value in both the public and private sectors.

6. *An emphasis on the restoration and enhancement of urban cores and urban transportation systems.* In cities with good climates, low-cost improvements in bicycle routes and pedestrian flow might be undertaken. Residential/commercial restoration could be achieved principally through modest tax incentives (e.g., waivers on property tax increases for urban core renovators in selected locations) or programs involving "sweat-equity" in abandoned buildings.[44] There is no reason renovations should lead to massive new public expenditures, except perhaps where transportation systems have radically deteriorated. In those cases cities may need to transfer money from highway construction, for example.

7. *A commitment to deficit reduction.* Measures would include (1) reduced military spending, (2) reduced subsidies and tax expenditures, especially for primary industries, including energy industries, and for the transportation sector, (3) lower costs associated with unemployment, and (4) limits on public sector wages and on grand displays of government opulence (e.g., large automobiles and near-empty aircraft).

8. *The expansion of voluntary aid to less developed nations through matching-fund incentives.* Such programs should focus first on environmental protection, particularly on maintaining ecological systems and the renewable resources base. There should be additional support for development projects and programs likely to contribute to population stability—including medical aid, aid for domestic food production, literacy aid, enhancement of education and economic opportunities for women, and widespread provision of birth control knowledge and devices.

9. *The improvement and enforcement of occupational health standards.* Trade unions and employee associations should be recruited to help set and enforce standards. In many cases protecting workers in occupational settings will also help

protect the environment against toxic substances. In addition, government might support health education in the workplace, providing or encouraging stop smoking programs and exercise, nutrition, weight control, and alcohol abuse programs.

10. *The movement of domestic agriculture and forestry toward more ecological and sustainable approaches.* This would include measures to protect prime agricultural land, to preserve and enhance soil quality, to reduce the use of chemical pesticides and fossil fuel-derived fertilizers, to diversify crops (including forest crops), and to assure replanting of forested areas.

Many of these proposals assume that reducing centralized bureaucratic power is compatible with enhanced environmental protection. This might be true even with increased regulation of occupational and environmental health. Citizens, industry, and unions can help carry out such regulations. Such an approach would keep costs down and would help educate the public. It is also in keeping with the radical democratic, anti-bureaucratic emphasis within environmental values. I consider this and further implications of an emphasis on participatory, decentralized environmental administration in the concluding chapter.

ten

Environmentalism and the
Politics of the Future

Environmentalism as an ideology is now at a stage of development comparable to that of socialism a century ago. Environmentalism may never obtain a mass base similar to that of conservatism, liberalism, or socialism, but it has already transformed the way many people understand the political world. Environmentalists have produced a sociological, political, economic, and philosophical literature of remarkable breadth, depth, and variety that has significantly affected the political and administrative agendas of most nations of the world.

Seeing environmentalism as an ideology may also alter our understanding of the concept of ideology itself. Environmentalism is the first ideology to be deeply rooted in the natural sciences (Marxist claims notwithstanding). Scientific findings do not of themselves lead to a particular set of political conclusions, but they are essential to this ideology in a way that they are not to any other. Furthermore, environmentalism cannot be easily located on a left–right ideological spectrum. Ideology, it now appears, is something more than a matter of the economic self-interest of the poor, the rich, or the middle classes, and ideological categories understood exclusively in distributional terms can no longer account for the whole ideological world. Prior to the rise of environmentalism, this might have been suspected. Now the suspicion is confirmed.

Nevertheless, we cannot ignore distributive issues. Some early environmentalists suffered from the popular perception that those who advocated wilderness protection were elitist. Only the rich could afford the time and money to "use" the wilderness, the argument went; but less wealthy people enjoy redwood decks and picnic tables, and workers need employment in the woods and sawmills. Although this sort of argument has usually come from those in investment or managerial positions in primary industries, it has also appealed to conservative editorial writers not inclined to the needs of the working class. Once environmentalists began to question the growth ethic and such things as energy megaprojects, they quickly alienated some in construction unions and even at times certain leaders of disadvantaged minorities. Any potential alliance of environmentalism with progressivism is, of course, threatened by such perceptions.

Fortunately these perceptions can be rebutted with the arguments implicit in the jobs/environment literature. They can also be defused through cooperative action and explicit environmental/progressive policy initiatives. For example, energy conservation or recycling programs provide good employment opportunities for the hard-core unemployed. Energy conservation also aids the poor, a disproportionate share of whose income is spent on energy (34 percent for the lowest decile as against 2 percent for the highest). But conservation programs must provide the skills and time the poor often lack and the capital they always lack. In general, environmentalists need to remind themselves that economic growth has never disproportionately aided the poor. Distributive politics are unavoidable, and environmental protection can alter distributional outcomes, either intentionally or unintentionally. Environmentalism is neither left nor right in the sense that environmental policy tools can have a left, right, or centrist character.

Policy analysis is not, as some would have it, simply a matter of evaluating available sets of policy options. Policy analysis must be a more creative process than that; it must be at least as much an art as a science and must incorporate consideration of the evolution of ideas; reflections on the values that are, or might someday be, held by the citizenry at large; and careful consideration of feasibility, prudence, likelihood, and desirability. Most policy analysts reasonably distinguish themselves from those who quickly leap from the "is" to the "ought," or vice versa. But it does not follow that policy analysis should or can avoid normative matters. Both natural and social scientists are frequently overtrained and overcautious on this point. Some researchers should feel an obligation to consider the practical and policy implications of their research. Contrary to the view of many academics this can be done without lapsing into tedious polemics. Thus there is much reason to hope that environmentalism in its various academic guises can open the door to improvements in policy studies generally.

Environmentalists, whether academics or not, who would prefer to develop links to socioeconomic progressives should take care to avoid neither-left-nor-rightism. Political neutrality will leave in place not only the present relative distribution of economic benefits but also the present distribution of political power, assuring a more inequitable economic distribution in whatever difficult economic times lie ahead. The 1980s have shown all too clearly how this can happen. Even the environmentalists' remedial measures might exacerbate distributional inequities—reduced work time, for example, could lead to gender discrimination with regard to work hours. Academic environmentalists clearly have a responsibility to point out such inequitable forms of economic rationalization and environmental activists should actively resist them.

Many corporate decision-makers doubtless find distributionally centrist forms of environmentalism indistinguishable from any other "impractical leftist radicalism." Since this perception is common and likely ineradicable in some circles, environmentalists must also be careful to avoid being perceived by the less advantaged as competitors for scarce governmental resources. Environmentalism is much more than a middle-class luxury, but not enough people perceive all its important dimensions. Again, political action requires either self-deception or conscious adoption of some left, center, or right position. Economically comfortable environmentalists can find an appropriate left/right position on a moral basis (to achieve, if you will, spiritual comfort), an intellectual basis (to achieve consistency), or a tactical basis (to achieve political gains). My view is that the moderate left of center makes sense on all these grounds.

Outside the United States this position might be represented either by democratic socialist parties or by progressive elements within the traditional parties of the center (for example, the Liberal Party in Canada or the Social Democratic Alliance in Britain). In the United States the Democratic Party is the only choice. Crucial to this political conclusion are two inescapable facts. First, neoconservatism has been consistently and deeply hostile to environmental protection in every country in which it has emerged. To the extent that conservative parties have retained any sympathy for environmental protection, they yet carry within them a significant contingent of what in Canada are called "red Tories." In the United States pro-environmental views have long since lost any real influence within the Republican Party (if they ever had any). Second, the less advantaged sectors of society, polls suggest, *are* concerned about environmental issues, and might become more so if their most pressing economic needs were met, especially the need for an assured source of income. Environmentalism can be creatively associated with the process of achieving social and economic security for such individuals and communities. I make this point prominently here because I do not want the arguments in this book to be taken as part of an easy accommodation of the nonenvironmental status quo.

Let us consider one argument that is open to such an interpretation. Environmentalism as an ideology and as practical politics can adopt an eclectic and pragmatic view of policy tools. Contrary to those firmly wedded to a particular left or right tradition, environmentalists can take advantage of the full range of policy options. They can work within nationalization *and* privatization, entrepreneurship *and* government expenditures to expand education, health protection, social welfare, and the arts; they can seek both economic deregulation (as distinct from health and safety deregulation) *and* significant reductions in military spending. As we have seen, environmental protection does not depend on huge government deficits—some environmentally sound policies might even reduce deficits. But such a policy pattern is one with which neither traditional progressives nor neoconservatives can be fully comfortable.

Environmentalists can distinguish themselves from neoconservatives in at least six ways. Environmentalists would (1) enhance rather than inhibit environmental regulation and enforcement; (2) oppose expansions of military spending; (3) not make rapid economic growth a high policy priority; (4) tend, whenever possible, to increase expenditures on education, social welfare, the arts, and health; (5) systematically increase government revenue in selective ways; and (6) not treat the market economy as an inviolate sacred cow. In addition, environmentalists are much more likely to support enhanced opportunities for women and ethnic minorities than neoconservatives are. Finally, environmentalists might be more comfortable than neoconservatives with *actually* reducing governmental deficits.

One can also list ways in which environmentalists might distinguish themselves from traditional progressives. Environmentalists would (1) promote environmental protection even at the risk of alienating some traditional progressive constituencies; (2) more consistently oppose excessive military spending; (3) promote the technological transformations associated with automation and communications and the demise of smokestack industries; (4) promote reduction of government deficits; (5) be more inclined to political decentralization; (6) promote small and medium-scale entrepreneurship; and (7) flexibly encourage reduced work time as a means of achieving full employment.

Environmentalists' openness to selected parts of the contemporary appeal of neoconservatism could broaden the potential political constituency of an environmentally informed progressivism—at the risk of some losses on the left. But careful policy development or straightforward and open compromise could help to avoid significant losses within traditional progressive constituencies. North Americans, after all, have always been more politically instinctive than politically ideological; and many within traditional progressive constituencies have in recent years voted with the neoconservatives at least temporarily. Whether these losses would be compounded or ameliorated by the addition of a strong environmental sensibility to progressive politics is unknown. But if I were as sure of the hostility of trade unionists as are some environmentalists, I would not have written this book. Similarly, I am one of many environmentalists who think the current public hostility to trade unions is ill founded. All one can say in the end is that opinion polls suggest that environmental issues remain important to large numbers of people and that support for stronger action has an appeal across class, regional, and ethnic lines.[1]

Thus it is important for environmentalists to be receptive to the cross-class appeal of neoconservative ideas. We should not be afraid to look for elements within neoconservatism that might be both compatible with environmental progress and not incompatible with distributive progress. Increased military spending and a too-cautious approach to environmental regulation should be rejected whatever the political risks. But what of a gradual return to fiscal responsibility accompanied by an enthusiasm about creative entrepreneurial initiatives? The latter applies well to recycling, renewable energy, and energy conservation and aids in replacing employment lost to automation and rationalization within the corporate and public sectors. Thus environmentalists need not automatically be hostile to such sociotechnological developments, and enthusiasm about the future is also part of the neoconservative appeal. Of note, too, is neoconservative's willingness at least temporarily to restrain consumer spending in the interest of long-term economic stability. Environmentalists could give this goal a character very different from that asserted within neoconservative circles, channeling the savings and new capital investment achieved into pollution abatement, urban improvement, education, the arts, energy conservation, and full employment rather than exclusively into such projects as nuclear power plants, corporate jets, office towers, military research, and the array of so-called "paper" manipulations.

Two final points of a political nature can be noted more briefly. Environmentalism has always attached central importance to the development of innovative and participatory administrative and political institutions. This concern is at the core of the strong environmental emphasis on decentralization. An orientation to an environmentally and economically sustainable future requires considerable social mobilization to achieve necessary, albeit often modest adjustments in the habits of day-to-day living. These sorts of changes simply cannot be imposed from above; they require enthusiastic public participation. Such willingness in turn requires an understanding of the costs associated with avoiding change, which can only develop within a process of extensive, real public participation in environmental and economic decision-making.

Through decentralization and creative evolution the process of environmental impact assessment could become more effective than it has been. Public participation in decisions about hazardous chemicals could be significantly enhanced in many jurisdictions (as they were in 1986 in California, New York, and New Jersey) with the help of state and municipal right-to-know ordinances. It would not be difficult to enhance the funding base of public-interest organizations while simultaneously enhancing their autonomy. For example, utility-related public-interest advocates could be partially funded through a small surcharge on monthly utility bills, or individual contributions to public-interest organizations could result in tax reductions. Public-interest organizations can then play a greater role in monitoring regulatory compliance—and can probably do so at least as cost effectively as government or the private sector.

There are many ways of expanding participation in environmental decision-making and many ways in which environmental issues can be brought into the political, particularly the electoral, process. In North America, however, establishing autonomous "green" parties is unlikely to be fruitful, since our electoral systems are comprised almost exclusively of single-member plurality constituencies, and the media and the electorate of the United States especially simply do not think in multi-party terms. Much more promising for environmentalists is selective involvement in the electoral process in support of particularly proenvironmental candidates or in opposition to singularly antienvironmental incumbents (as in the biannual selection of a congressional "dirty dozen"). Carefully chosen referenda campaigns can also be effective. In Canada, as in Britain, one is faced with the luxury (and the complication) of two (of three) major parties that are at least sometimes open to proenvironmental policies.[2]

If my thesis is correct—if there really is a potential ideological fit between environmentalism and traditional progressivism—there is every reason to think that existing political parties can be recycled or restored. The best way to do that is to encourage environmentalists to run for public office. My sense of the potential political mood of the late 1980s and the 1990s leads me to suggest that many people with years or decades of involvement in the politics of environmental protection are eminently suited to carry their ideas directly into the electoral arena. They will of course need to talk about issues other than environmental, while forging links with the peace movement on international issues, with feminists, and with labor and community organizations. If they do so, they may find a considerable body of public opinion quite open to supporting their quest for nomination and election at local, regional, and national levels.

Environmentalism is becoming increasingly relevant politically, and environmentalists in many countries are showing ever-greater political maturity and sophistication. Canadian public opinion polls published in early 1987 reported that environmental issues are of greater concern than unemployment, trade, and inflation.[3] In the United States opinion polls are not quite so dramatic, but the 1986 midterm elections showed strong proenvironmental voting patterns.[4] In Britain, "green" demands have increasingly been added to the platforms of both the Labour Party and the Social Democratic Alliance, although the British electorate still appears to lag behind the courageous disarmament stance taken by the Labour Party. In the 1987 West German elections, the Greens significantly increased their total vote to 8.6 percent.

Underlying these changes are other indications that environmental ideas matured significantly during the economic turmoil of the late 1970s and early 1980s. While the media and the public turned from environmental issues to economic issues, many environmentalists sought to understand the connections between these two sets of issues. Many of the authors discussed in this book have contributed to this process, opening the way to political cooperation between environmentalists, traditional progressives, feminists, the peace movement, and some trade unionists. Lester R. Brown and others at the Worldwatch Institute developed an emphasis on such issues as women's rights, government deficits, international debt, and the need for an environmentally informed understanding of national security. Equally important is the recent work of Andre Gorz and Seymour Melman.

Most striking, however, have been the policy ideas jointly developed by leaders of a variety of U.S. environmental and conservation organizations and the stunning report of the World Commission on Environment and Development. *An Environmental Agenda for the Future* goes beyond narrowly defined environmental and conservation concerns and represents a very important beginning.[5] Although it is a politically cautious document, *Agenda* includes intelligent examinations of occupational health and safety, the need for urban-core restoration and urban mass-transit improvements, global debt, nuclear weapons, and foreign aid. *Agenda* mentions only in passing poverty, social equity issues, and government deficits and ignores women's rights, despite the chance to discuss them in relation to its extensive treatment of population. *Agenda* could also be said to underplay the issue of military spending aside from its specific concern with nuclear weaponry. But overall this document is clear evidence of a significant advance in the political sophistication of the U.S. environmental movement.

Perhaps even more exciting is *Our Common Future*, the report of the World Commission on Environment and Development, chaired by Gro Harlem Brundtland of Norway. This report, initiated under United Nations auspices, not only brings together the most current global scientific and political thinking on the relationship between environmental protection and development, it also goes directly to the heart of the central issues in several ways. First, the report is based throughout on the need for sustainable global development and is accordingly explicit and direct regarding future global energy supplies, agricultural and forestry practices, and population control. The report also addresses a range of urban environmental issues in an intelligent and effective way, placing environmental concerns in an urban framework. Finally, and most important, it courageously lays bare the links between environmental protection and the arms race.

The absence of war is not peace; nor does it necessarily provide the conditions for sustainable development. Competitive arms races breed insecurity among nations through spirals of reciprocal fears. Nations need to muster resources to combat environmental degradation and mass poverty. By misdirecting scarce resources, arms races contribute further to insecurity. . . . Global military spending in 1985 was well in excess of $900 billion. This was more than the total income of the poorest half of humanity. It represents the equivalent of almost $1,000 for every one of the world's 1 billion poorest. . . . The true cost of the arms race is the loss of what could have been produced instead with scarce capital, labor skills, and raw materials.[6]

This perspective—linking economic equity, peace, and environmental protection—is potentially politically formidable, especially if pursued globally in terms of ideological moderation and tactical pragmatism. Environmentalists in several nations have recently shown that they can be both effective moderate progressives and highly pragmatic political activists. The West German Greens, despite some links to the traditional left, have explicitly eschewed revolution for evolution, while maintaining a sharp distinctiveness and an urgent moral commitment utterly uncharacteristic of "normal" contemporary politics. The Greens have become tactically pragmatic and centrist, but they remain adamant about their broad range of "green" issues. Yet despite the Greens' obvious successes in West Germany, little money and effort has been lost on attempts to launch green parties in North America. Instead, U.S. environmental activists have worked successfully for specific proenvironmental candidates, most (but not all) of them Democrats. In the 1980s environmentalists' understanding of what is appropriate in various electoral and party systems has been impressive, a far cry from the antipolitical and/or extremist tone of much of 1970s environmentalism. If neoconservatism in North America is now temporarily on the wane, there is every reason to hope that in the 1990s another wave of significant environmental legislation will be adopted. Then perhaps we will begin to treat causes as well as symptoms. It is a long way from personal solutions, survivalism, doom-saying, and back-to-the-land urges to an everyday political activism and an inclination to pragmatic incrementalism, which in the end is the only real possibility. But there should be little hesitation about such a transition.

The only caution I offer is that the environmental movement must remain conscious of its roots in a value-laden appreciation of the human condition. Technical administration (and science itself), when left without moral and political guidance, is at the root of many of the problems discussed throughout this book. In the world of everyday democratic politics it is often easy to lose sight of the long-term future in favor of the immediate concerns of one's constituencies and the electoral and administrative urgency of the moment. Environmentalists should not leave unspoken their fundamental beliefs in the interest of winning a few more seats *this* time. The costs of compromise do not include a lapse into pure tolerance, the universally feared bureaucratic mentality. One can develop and maintain in one's mind utopian visions without suffering the illusion that utopia will actually arrive.

Albert Camus suggests in *The Plague* that in the face of what seems overwhelming one must simply learn to be guided by a sense that "one does what one can." Though doing less is morally unacceptable, one is not morally obliged to do more. For Camus the plague was a symbolic representation of the Nazi domination of Western Europe and North Africa, but its lesson for the 1980s and 1990s could not be more apt, even if brutal repression is on the wane. Appreciating the scale of social and economic changes likely in the next fifty or one hundred years, one can easily be overwhelmed by the magnitude of the task. It is easy to fall into apolitical cynicism, to lose oneself in visions of apocalyptic collapse, or to seek political alliance with those who imagine that everything must be transformed in order for anything to change. A vital alternative is to accept Camus' simple moral vision—one does what one can, no more and no less—and one trusts that enough of one's fellow humans will do the same.

Notes

Introduction

1. See "Flood of Industry Spending Drowns D.C. Bottle Bill," *The Returnable Times* (Fall 1987): 1, 11–12. Available from Environmental Action Foundation, Washington, D.C. For a detailed case in favor of going in the opposite direction on this issue, see Cynthia Pollack, *Mining Urban Wastes: The Potential for Recycling* (Washington, D.C.: Worldwatch Institute, 1987).

2. These terms are used with great effect by Rudolf Bahro in *From Red to Green: Interviews with New Left Review* (London: Verso Editions, 1984).

chapter two

1. John Henry Wadland, *Ernest Thompson Seton: Man and Nature in the Progressive Era, 1880–1915* (New York: Arno Press, 1978), 10, 12.

2. Cited in Roderick Nash, *Wilderness and the American Mind* (New Haven: Yale University Press, 1967), 84, 97.

3. Important figures in these movements in the United States include Francis Parkman, Jr., Horace Greeley, George Perkins Marsh, John Muir, Gifford Pinchot, and Aldo Leopold; active in Canada were Clifford Sifton, Elihu Stewart, Judson Clark, and particularly Bernhard Fernow, who also figured in U.S. conservation history. Some of the key organizations of the U.S. conservation movement have been the Sierra Club, the Audubon Society, the National Wildlife Federation, and the Isaak Walton League; in Canada the Commission of Conservation (a government agency), the naturalist and wildlife federations, the Canadian Nature Federation, and the National and Provincial Parks Association have played important roles. The history of the conservation movement has been analyzed by many authors. Perhaps the best of these analyses are Nash, *Wilderness and the American*

Mind; Samuel P. Hays, *Conservation and the Gospel of Efficiency: The Progressive Conservation Movement, 1890–1920* (Cambridge: Harvard University Press; 1959), and Donald Worster, *Nature's Economy: A History of Ecological Ideas* (Cambridge: Cambridge University Press, 1985). Worster's masterful work, originally published in 1977, roots ecological thinking in eighteenth-century Arcadian thought. Also very useful is the collection of early conservation writings edited by Donald Worster under the title *American Environmentalism: The Formative Period, 1860–1915* (New York: John Wiley & Sons, 1973).

4. The following is indebted to Nash, Worster, and Hays, cited above, nn. 2–3.

5. Franklin Russell, "The Vermont Prophet: George Perkins Marsh," *Horizon* 10 (1968): 17.

6. George Perkins Marsh, *Man and Nature: Physical Geography as Modified by Human Action* (Cambridge: Harvard University Press, 1965).

7. Ibid., 465.

8. Ibid.

9. Stephen Fox, *John Muir and his Legacy* (Boston: Little, Brown, 1981), 5.

10. Nash, *Wilderness and the American Mind,* 131.

11. See Fox, *John Muir,* chap. 10.

12. John Muir, *The Wilderness World of John Muir,* ed. Edwin Way Teale (Boston: Houghton Mifflin, 1954), 117.

13. Fox, *John Muir,* 359. On this same general point see the classic essay by Lynn White Jr., "The Historic Roots of our Ecologic Crisis," *Science* 155 (1967): 1203–07.

14. Both quotes in Nash, *Wilderness and the American Mind,* 182.

15. Muir quoted ibid., 194.

16. J. I. Nicol, "The National Parks Movement in Canada," in J. G. Nelson and R. C. Scace, eds., *Canadian Parks in Perspective* (Montreal: Harvest House, 1969), 3.

17. Robert Craig Brown, "The Doctrine of Usefulness: Natural Resource and National Park Policy in Canada, 1887–1914," in Nelson and Scace, eds., *Canadian Parks,* esp. 49–50.

18. H. V. Nelles, *The Politics of Development: Forests, Mines, and Hydroelectric Power in Ontario, 1849–1941* (Toronto: Macmillan of Canada, 1974), 182, 203.

19. Both quotes Wadland, *Ernest Thompson Seton,* 4.

20. Rachel Carson, *Silent Spring* (Boston: Houghton Mifflin, 1962). *Silent Spring* first appeared in *The New Yorker* in 1960. See also Frank Graham, Jr., *Since Silent Spring* (Boston: Houghton Mifflin, 1970).

21. Allan Schnaiberg, *The Environment from Surplus to Scarcity* (New York: Oxford University Press, 1980), 369–70.

22. Frederick Engels, *The Conditions of the Working Class in England* (Oxford: Basil Blackwell, 1958), 109–10.

23. Benjamin Disraeli, *Sybil* (London: Oxford University Press, 1964);

Thom Braun, *Disraeli the Novelist* (London: Allen & Unwin, 1981); and Elizabeth Gaskell, *North and South* (London: Dent, 1963).

24. Quoted in Louis Klein, *River Pollution*, vol. 2 (London: Butterworths, 1962).

25. John Evelyn, *The Smoake of London* (Elmsford, N.Y.: Maxwell Reprint Co., 1969).

26. See preface to ibid. See also T. C. Sinclair, "Environmentalism," in H. S. D. Cole, et al., *Thinking About the Future* (London: Chatto & Windus, 1973), 175–91.

27. Klein, *River Pollution*, 1.

28. Ibid., 4.

29. Joseph K. Wagoner, "Occupational Carcinogenesis: The Two Hundred Years Since Percivall Pott," in Umberto Saffiotti and Joseph K. Wagoner, eds., *Occupational Carcinogenesis* (New York: New York Academy of Sciences, 1976), 1.

30. See, for example, Samuel S. Epstein, *The Politics of Cancer* (San Francisco: Sierra Club Books, 1978); Lloyd Tataryn, *Dying for a Living* (Montreal: Deneau & Greenberg, 1979); and Robert Paehlke, "Occupational Health Policy in Canada," in William Leiss, ed., *Ecology vs. Politics in Canada* (Toronto: University of Toronto Press, 1979). For a fascinating case study of science, cancer, and policy see Edwin Levy, "The Swedish Studies of Pesticide Exposure and Cancer," *Alternatives: Perspectives on Society, Technology, and Environment* 15 (April/May 1988): 48–64.

31. Wagoner, "Occupational Carcinogenesis," 1.

32. James Whorton, *Before Silent Spring: Pesticides and Public Health in Pre-DDT America* (Princeton: Princeton University Press, 1974), 67.

33. Ibid., 68–69.

34. Ibid., 176–77.

35. Arthur Kallett and F. J. Schlink, *One Hundred Million Guinea Pigs* (1933; rpt. Salem, N.H.: Ayer, 1976); Ruth D. Lamb, *American Chamber of Horrors* (1936; rpt. Salem, N.H.: Ayer, 1976).

36. Alice Hamilton, *Exploring the Dangerous Trades* (Boston: Little, Brown, 1943), 187.

37. See especially the classic text by Alice Hamilton and Harriet L. Hardy, *Industrial Toxicology* (1934; rpt. New York: Paul B. Hoeber, 1949).

38. Hamilton, *Exploring the Dangerous Trades*, 198–99.

39. One lively account of the early history of uranium production is Earle Gray, *The Great Uranium Cartel* (Toronto: McClelland & Stewart, 1982), esp. chaps. 2–3.

40. The production of synthetic pesticides in the United States increased fivefold between 1947 and 1960 (Carson, *Silent Spring*, 25).

41. Graham, *Since Silent Spring*.

42. What follows is developed from my article "Carcinogens: Guilty Until Proven Innocent," *Nature Canada* 9 (April/June 1980): 18–23.

43. Wagoner, "Occupational Carcinogenesis," 3.

44. Barry Commoner, *Science and Survival* (New York: Viking Press, 1963), 9, 10.

45. Ibid., 12–13.

46. Ibid., 128–29, 131.

47. Barry Commoner, "Workplace Burden," *Environment* 15 (July/August 1973): 15–33.

48. During the election campaign a truck carrying a PCB-laden transformer leaked over an extended section of the Trans-Canada Highway in Ontario. Several motorists, including at least one pregnant woman, were extensively exposed to the chemical. The Minister of the Environment reacted with some indifference and later found himself among the defeated Conservative candidates.

49. See Epstein, *Politics of Cancer*, and especially Ted Schrecker, *The Pitfalls of Standards* (Hamilton, Ontario: Canadian Centre for Occupational Health and Safety, 1986).

50. I. J. Selikoff, J. Chung, and E. C. Hammond, "Asbestos Exposure and Neoplasia," *Journal of the American Medical Association* 188 (1964): 22–26.

51. Studies have shown this to be the case in, for example, St. Louis, New York, Washington, D.C., and Hamilton, Ontario. See Jeffrey M. Zupan, *The Distribution of Air Quality in the New York Region* (Baltimore: Johns Hopkins University Press, 1973); Virginia Brodine, "A Special Burden," *Environment* 13 (March 1971): 22–24, 29–33; Famida Handy, "The Distribution of Air Pollution in Hamilton, Ontario," *Alternatives* 6 (Spring 1977): 18–24; and Virginia Brodine, "Point of Damage," *Environment* 14 (May 1972): 2–15.

52. See especially Richard Kazis and Richard L. Grossman, *Fear at Work: Job Blackmail, Labor and the Environment* (New York: Pilgrim Press, 1982).

53. Interaction between these two groups has been surprisingly extensive. See, for example, Robert Paehlke, "Environementalisme et syndicalisme au Canada anglais et aux États-Unis," *Sociologie et Sociétés* 13 (April 1981): 161–79. Recently labor in Canada has been taking several new environmental initiatives. See, for example, Michelle Walsh, "Safety and Health: Cleaning up our Act," *Canadian Labour* 33 (Spring 1988): 28–29, 32.

54. These unions have worked hard to educate their members about environmentalism and have led the trade union movement as a whole toward greater acceptance of environmentalist positions. See Franklin Wallick, *The American Worker: An Endangered Species* (New York: Ballantine Books, 1973), and especially his "Factory Pollution: It Doesn't Go Up the Chimney," *Environmental Action* (January 4, 1972): 3–5.

55. See, for example, Mary Louise Adams, "Right to Know: A Summary," *Alternatives: Perspectives on Society and Environment* 11 (Summer/Fall 1983): 29–36. See also Albert R. Matheny and Bruce A. Williams, "Right-to-know, Democracy, and the Workplace: Lessons for Social Regulation in the United

States," paper presented at Western Political Science Association, San Francisco, March 1988.

56. Jeanne Stellman and Susan Daum, *Work Is Dangerous to Your Health* (New York: Random House, 1973).

57. The chemicals in the Love Canal dump are identified in Michael Brown, *Laying Waste: The Poisoning of America by Toxic Chemicals* (New York: Washington Square Press, 1979).

58. Michael Brown was instrumental in this process. For an academic appreciation of some of the issues involved see, for example, John A. Worthley and Richard Torkelson, "Managing the Toxic Waste Problem: Lessons from the Love Canal," *Administration and Society* 13/2 (1981): 145–60; and Robert M. O'Brien et al., "Open and Closed Systems of Decision Making: The Case of Toxic Waste Management," *Public Administration Review* 44/4 (1984): 334–40. See also Adeline Gordon Levine, *Love Canal: Science, Politics and People* (Lexington, Mass.: D.C. Heath, 1982).

59. In 1983, Cong. James Florio estimated the costs at $40 billion; see his foreward to Bruce Piasecki, ed., *Beyond Dumping: New Strategies for Controlling Toxic Contamination* (Westport, Conn.: Quorum Books, 1984).

60. Samuel S. Epstein, Lester O. Brown, and Carl Pope, *Hazardous Waste in America* (San Francisco: Sierra Club Books, 1982).

61. See esp. Michael McClosky's pamphlet, *Labor and Environmentalism: Two Movements That Should Work Together* (San Francisco: Sierra Club, 1973).

chapter three

1. Donella H. Meadows, et al., *The Limits to Growth* (New York: Universe Books, 1972).

2. Paul R. Ehrlich, *The Population Bomb* (Rivercity, Mass.: Rivercity Press, 1975).

3. Gertrude Himmelfarb in her introduction to Thomas Robert Malthus, *On Population* (New York: Random House Modern Library, 1960), xxv.

4. Malthus, ibid., 476, 477.

5. W. Stanley Jevons, *The Coal Question* (1865; rpt. New York: Augustus M. Kelley, 1965), 164.

6. Ibid., 184.

7. Ibid., 183.

8. Ibid., 185, 187.

9. Ibid., 271, 274–75.

10. Ibid., 460, 461.

11. Fairfield Osborn, *The Limits of the Earth* (Boston: Little, Brown, 1953), 224, 226.

12. Fairfield Osborn, *Our Plundered Planet* (Boston: Little, Brown, 1948), 201.

13. Samuel H. Ordway, Jr., *Resources and the American Dream* (New York: Ronald Press, 1953), v, vi.

14. Ibid., 31–32.

15. Ibid., 39–40.

16. The argument against the automobile was taken up again with great effect by Ivan Illich in *Tools for Conviviality* (New York: Harper and Row, 1973).

17. Ordway, *Resources and the American Dream*, 40.

18. Ibid., 48, 50.

19. Bernard James, *The Death of Progress* (New York: Alfred A. Knopf, 1973), 144.

20. Harrison Brown, *The Challenge of Man's Future* (New York: Viking Press, 1954), 250.

21. Ibid., 256.

22. Ibid., 265.

23. One of the more thorough early critiques of *Limits* was H. S. D. Cole, et al., *Thinking About the Future* (London: Chatto and Windus, 1973). Though *Limits* was often quantitatively inaccurate, it popularized the notion that there are upper bounds on both population growth and resource use.

24. Meadows, *Limits to Growth*, 88.

25. Ibid., 140.

26. Ibid., 145.

27. David B. Brooks, *Minerals: An Expanding or a Dwindling Resource?* (Ottawa: Mineral Resources Branch, Department of Energy, Mines, and Resources, 1973), 4.

28. Meadows, *Limits to Growth*, 91–92.

29. On the Sahara, see J. T. Thompson, "The Politics of Desertification in Marginal Environments: The Sahelian Case," in J. Leonard, ed., *Divesting Nature's Capital* (New York: Holmes and Meier, 1985), 227–62. On the Great Lakes, see several articles in Thomas Whillans, ed., *Alternatives: Perspectives on Society, Technology and Environment* 13 (September/October 1986 (special issue on the Great Lakes); and the continuing publications of the Canada-United States International Joint Commission (IJC). On acid rain and forests, see Sandra Postel, "Protecting Forests," in Lester R. Brown, ed., *State of the World 1986* (New York: W. W. Norton, 1986), 74–94. On forests, see also Norman Myers, *The Primary Source: Tropical Forests and Our Future* (New York: W. W. Norton, 1984); and T. C. Whitmore, *Tropical Rain Forests of the Far East* (Oxford: Clarendon Press, 1984). On fish stocks, consult Lester R. Brown, *Building a Sustainable Society* (New York: W. W. Norton, 1981), 40–44.

30. This is clearly the case with minerals—see Brooks, *Minerals*. Food will not prove a limiting resource if population growth slows by the early twenty-first century.

31. David B. Brooks and Alma Norman, "A Question of Choice," *Alternatives: Perspectives on Society and Environment* 3 (Winter 1974): 4–12.

32. Hardin and Ehrlich raised such concerns, as did Georg Borgstrom, *The Hungry Planet* (New York: Collier, 1967), and *Too Many* (New York: Collier, 1971). The ecological impact of overpopulation was clarified in the work of Lester R. Brown and confirmed in *The Global 2000 Report to the President*, produced by the U.S. Council on Environmental Quality (New York: Pergamon Press, 1980). This important study, which became a best-seller in West Germany (though not in the United States!), noted that its broad conclusions regarding the near-term future were in conformity with those of numerous other studies carried out at about this time. Similar conclusions regarding the increasing ecological impact of human population on soil, forest, climate, water, and other species were drawn in the Brundtland report to the United Nations, completed in 1987. (See chapter 10). All these later works are more level-headed than that of Ehrlich, but he more than anyone else should be credited with bringing overpopulation issues before the public at a relatively early date.

33. Ehrlich, *Population Bomb*, 174.

34. Ibid., 158.

35. Ibid., 166.

36. Ibid., 138.

37. Peter G. Stillman, "The Tragedy of the Commons: A Re-Analysis," *Alternatives: Perspectives on Society and Environment* 4 (Winter 1975): 12.

38. Ibid.

39. Ibid., 13.

40. Barry Commoner, *The Closing Circle* (New York: Bantam Books, 1972), vi–vii.

41. Ibid., 125.

42. Ibid., 291, 294, 296.

43. The debate was published in *Environment* 14 (April 1972).

44. Paul R. Ehrlich and Anne H. Ehrlich, *The End of Affluence: A Blueprint for Your Future* (New York: Ballantine Books, 1974), 257.

45. Ibid., 103.

46. The Ehrlichs did advocate participation in local government up to the county level (ibid., 182), but *The End of Affluence* proceeds largely on the assumption that government will fail, society and economy will collapse and we will all soon be on our own (perhaps with the help of a few neighbors). A better use of one's time than politics is seen as the study of nutrition and the acquisition of self-defense skills.

47. Garrett Hardin, *Exploring New Ethics for Survival* (New York: Viking Press, 1968), 193, 197.

48. Ibid., 198.

49. Ibid., 199.

50. For discussion of natalist policies in Eastern Europe see Alena Heit-linger, "Pro-Natalist Population Policies in Czechoslovakia," *Population Studies* 30 (March 1976): 123–35.

51. But one must contrast the singular political failures associated with crude efforts in India in the 1970s with the apparent recent successes in China.

52. Hardin, *Exploring New Ethics*, 172–73.

53. These were mid–1960s dollars—the astronauts could have brought along Cokes for five cents each (plus the cost of propelling the added weight). The space shuttle might lower costs modestly, but as the shuttle must return to earth, one must assume the additional cost of transporting large numbers of people to the moon at the nearest. This would at least return us to Hardin's cost estimate of getting outside the earth's gravity.

54. The statement by Carlyle was quoted by Gertrude Himmelfarb in her introduction to Malthus' *On Population*.

55. Janet Besecker and Phil Elder, "Lifeboat Ethics: A Reply to Hardin," *Alternatives: Perspectives on Society and Environment* 5 (December 1975): 22–26.

56. Ibid., 23.

57. Ibid., 25.

58. Garrett Hardin, *The Limits to Altruism* (Bloomington: Indiana University Press, 1977).

59 Lester R. Brown, *By Bread Alone* (New York: Praeger Publishers, 1974), 103.

60. Ibid., 113.

61. Frances Moore Lappé and Joseph Collins, *Food First: Beyond the Myth of Scarcity* (New York: Ballantine Books, 1977).

62. The diet suggested in Frances Moore Lappé, *Diet for a Small Planet*, rev. ed. (New York: Ballantine Books, 1975), has since its publi-cation been even more clearly confirmed as healthier than the once nearly universal, still common, North American diet. High-fat diets are now more widely understood to be associated with both heart disease and intestinal cancers.

63. This figure is a 1984 estimate of the World Bank as reported in *The New York Times*.

64. Statistics Canada, *Canada: From Baby-Boom to Baby-Bust* (Ottawa: Queen's Printer, 1984). Ben Wattenberg speaks in similar, if not more alarm-ist, tones in his recent book *The Birth Dearth: What Happens When People in Free Countries Don't Have Enough Babies?* (Washington, D.C.: American En-terprise Institute, 1987).

65. The recent pattern of birth rates at or below replacement rates is broadly true in both the Communist and non-Communist developed world, in those developed countries which have experienced high unemployment and those which have not, in "good" economic years and in "bad." Only

in the past few years has there been any sign of a rebound toward replacement rates, and this is true only in some developed countries.

66. William Ophuls, *Ecology and the Politics of Scarcity* (San Francisco: W. H. Freeman, 1977), 145.

67. Robert L. Heilbroner, *An Inquiry into the Human Prospect* (New York: W. W. Norton, 1974), 161.

68. See Robert L. Heilbroner, "Second Thoughts on the Human Prospect," *An Inquiry into the Human Prospect*, 2d. ed. (New York: Norton, 1975).

69. Richard J. Barnet, *The Lean Years: Politics in the Age of Scarcity* (New York: Simon and Schuster, 1980), 297–98, 302.

70. Ibid., 313.

chapter four

1. The first of Amory B. Lovins' noted works on energy policy was *World Energy Strategies* (Cambridge, Mass.: Ballinger, 1971).

2. On the early history of claims about nuclear power see Douglas Torgerson, "From Dream to Nightmare: The Historical Origins of Canada's Nuclear Electric Future," *Alternatives: Perspectives on Society and Environment* 7 (Fall 1977): 8–17, 30–31.

3. For an overview of some of the environmental problems associated with coal extraction and use see Office of Technology Assessment, *The Direct Use of Coal* (Detroit: Grand River Books, 1980); and Frank R. Anton, *The Canadian Coal Industry* (Calgary: Detselig Enterprises, 1981), esp. chap. 7. Regarding tar sands see, e.g., Gregory Taylor, "Oil Sands Development and Acid Rain in Alberta," *Alternatives* 9 (Winter 1981): 3–10; on oil shale see David F. Prindle, "Shale Oil and the Politics of Ambiguity and Complexity," *Annual Review of Energy* 9 (1984): 351–74.

4. On petrochemicals see, for example, S. Epstein, *The Politics of Cancer* (San Francisco: Sierra Club Books, 1978), 122–49; and George L. Waldbott, *Health Effects of Environmental Pollutants* (St. Louis: C. V. Mosby, 1973). On drilling, see Kenneth W. Kramer, "Institutional Fragmentation and Hazardous Waste Policy: The Case of Texas," in James P. Lester and Ann O'M. Bowman, eds., *The Politics of Hazardous Waste Management* (Durham, N.C.: Duke University Press, 1983). On acid rain, see Ross Howard, *Acid Rain* (New York: McGraw-Hill, 1980), 43.

5. Amory B. Lovins, "Lovins on Soft Paths versus Hard Paths," *Alternatives* 8 (Summer/Fall 1979): 6.

6. Barry Commoner, *The Poverty of Power* (New York: Alfred A. Knopf, 1976).

7. Geothermal energy is unlikely ever to supply more than perhaps 10 percent of energy needs in any developed economy (except for that of Iceland, where it is a major energy source).

8. On high temperatures see Robert Bott, et al., *Life After Oil* (Edmonton: Hurtig, 1983). On liquid fuels see Office of Technology Assessment, *Energy from Biological Processes* (Cambridge, Mass.: Ballinger, 1980). On the new competitiveness of wind energy in selected locations see, for example, *Renewable Energy News* (April 1985). This is significant because wind energy is one of the less economically competitive of renewable sources. Low temperature passive solar energy was highly competitive prior to the 1985/6 drop in world oil prices. Small scale hydroelectricity remains highly competitive in many locations as do considerable expenditures on energy conservation.

9. See Bott, *Life After Oil*, 71. Bott et al. discuss pelletized wood furnaces that use automatic feed. Other developments include wood stoves that burn more fully and thereby pollute the air much less.

10. Lovins, "Lovins on Soft Paths," 7.

11. Toronto gas utilities sought a much higher connection fee from high-efficiency homes.

12. See Christopher Flavin, *Nuclear Power: The Market Test*, Worldwatch Paper 57 (Washington, D.C.: Worldwatch Institute, 1983).

13. See sources cited in Amory B. Lovins, *Soft Energy Paths* (Cambridge, Mass.: Ballinger, 1977), esp. chap. 9; see also the discussion of decentralization in chaps. 6 and 9 below; and Laurence Solomon, *Power at What Cost?* (Scarborough, Ont.: Firefly Books, 1984).

14. Lovins, *Soft Energy Paths*, 39–40.

15. Ken Butti and John Perlin, *A Golden Thread* (Palo Alto: Cheshire Books, 1980), 154–55.

16. Report of the Mid-Century Conference on Resources for the Future, *The Nation Looks at Its Resources* (Washington, D.C.: Resources for the Future, 1954), 221, 224.

17. Ibid., 239.

18. Tiny Bennett and Wade Rowland, *The Pollution Guide* (Toronto: Clarke, Irwin and Company, 1972).

19. See Ward Churchill, "American Indian Lands: The Native Ethic amid Resource Development," *Environment* 28 (July/August 1986): 12–17, 28–34; Sandra E. Bregman, "Uranium Mining on Indian Lands," *Environment* 24 (September 1982): 6–13; and Ralph Torrie, "Uranium Mine Tailings," *Alternatives* 10 (Fall-Winter 1982): 15–26, 31.

20. See Marilynne Robinson, "Bad News from Britain: Dangerous Chemicals, Awful Silence," *Harper's* (February 1985): 65–72; and Mason Willrich and Theodore B. Taylor, *Nuclear Theft: Risks and Safeguards* (Cambridge, Mass.: Ballinger, 1974), 38–41.

21. Fred H. Knelman, *Nuclear Energy: The Unforgiving Technology* (Edmonton: Hurtig, 1976).

22. Amory B. Lovins and John H. Price, *Non-Nuclear Futures: The Case for an Ethical Energy Strategy* (Cambridge, Mass.: Ballinger, 1975), 15–16.

23. Ibid., 21.

24. Ibid., 37, 38.

25. Amory B. Lovins and L. Hunter Lovins, *Energy/War: Breaking the Nuclear Link* (New York: Harper and Row, 1980), 1, 4.

26. Lovins, *Non-Nuclear Futures*, 15.

27. Russell W. Ayres, "Policing Plutonium: The Civil Liberties Fallout," *Harvard Civil Rights/Civil Liberties Law Review* 10 (Spring 1975): 443. Plutonium, of course, would not be delivered to and from individual homes or service stations, but commercial traffic in plutonium might be as extensive as commercial traffic in oil. For some of the dangers see, for example, V. Gilinsky, "Plutonium, Proliferation and the Price of Money," *Foreign Affairs* 374 (Winter 1978–79); and Amory B. Lovins, "Nuclear Weapons and Power-Reactor Plutonium," *Nature* 283 (1980): 817–23.

28. Congressman Craig Hosmer, quoted in R. Leachman and Phillip Althoff, eds., *Preventing Nuclear Theft: Guidelines for Industry and Government* (New York: Praeger Publishers, 1972), 10.

29. Amory B. Lovins, "Electric Utility Investments," *Journal of Business Administration* 12 (Spring 1981). See also Lovins, *Energy/War*, chap. 5, and Flavin, *Nuclear Power*.

30. Lovins, *Energy/War*, 7. For a good discussion of trade unions' attitudes toward nuclear power see Dorothy Nelkin and Rebecca Logan, "Labor and Nuclear Power," *Environment* 22 (March 1980): 6–13, 34.

31. See, for example, Donald C. MacDonald, "Hydro's Nuclear Powerhouse Hums Away Ignoring Debt," *Globe and Mail* (Toronto, February 3, 1984).

32. Lovins, *Energy/War*, 7.

33. Ibid., 113.

34. Ibid., 113.

35. Flavin, *Nuclear Power*.

36. Lovins, *Soft Energy Paths*, chap. 11.

37. Lovins, *Alternatives*, 9. See also *Soft Energy Paths*, 59–60.

38. Amory B. Lovins, L. Hunter Lovins, F. Krause, and W. Bach, *Least-Cost Energy: Solving the CO2 Problem* (Andover, Mass.: Brick House Publishing, 1981).

39. Robert Bott, David Brooks, and John Robinson, *Life After Oil* (Edmonton: Hurtig, 1983), 121.

40. Ibid.

41. Ibid., 120.

42. The latter endorsement came in the forward to Amory B. Lovins and L. Hunter Lovins, *Brittle Power: Energy Strategy for National Security* (Andover, Mass.: Brick House Publishing, 1982).

43. Lovins, et al., *Least-Cost Energy*, 24–25.

44. Ibid., 91.

45. David B. Brooks, *Zero Energy Growth for Canada* (Toronto: McClelland and Stewart, 1981), 43–44.

46. See Lovins, *Non-Nuclear Futures*.

47. See Lovins, *Soft Energy Paths*, 48.

48. Roderick Nash, "Trouble in Paradise," *Environment* 20 (July/August 1979): 25–27, 39–40.

49. Objections, particularly to wind energy projects, have been made in New Hampshire and California, but they were not extensive.

50. See Bott et al., *Life After Oil*, 87–88.

51. Lovins himself granted that nuclear power and a SEP are not technically incompatible. Some limited use of nuclear power would allow a more selective siting of renewable energy sources. Indeed nuclear power plants as a source of hydrogen fuel could be themselves cited at a great distance from population centers. Most environmentalists see nuclear power as anathema, however used.

52. Lovins' warnings came long before Three Mile Island and Chernobyl. For an excellent post-Three Mile Island (pre-Chernobyl) analysis of the risks associated with nuclear power see Charles Perrow, *Normal Accidents: Living with High-Risk Technologies* (New York: Basic Books, 1984).

53. *Globe and Mail* (Toronto, February 19, 1985), B21.

54. These are some of the more important possibilities. The best overall argument for energy conservation and its importance as a part of energy policy is Robert Stobaugh and Daniel Yergin, eds., *Energy Future: Report of the Energy Project at the Harvard Business School* (New York: Random House, 1983). This work, first published in 1979, has presented much of the perspective initiated by Lovins to the business world. It is perhaps the best single book on energy policy written since 1973, surpassed only by Lovins' precedence and breadth of vision. Also very helpful here are John C. Sawhill and Richard Cotton, eds., *Energy Conservation: Successes and Failures* (Washington, D.C.: Brookings Institute, 1986); and Christopher Flavin, Denis Hayes, and Jim Mackenzie, *The Oil Rollercoaster* (Washington, D.C.: Fund for Renewable Energy and the Environment, 1987).

55. Lovins, *Energy/War*, 95.

56. See Bott, *Life After Oil*, 87–88; and Robert Paehlke, "Environmental and Social Impacts of a Soft Energy Path," *Alternatives* 12 (Fall 1984): 21–26.

57. See John Helliwell and Alan Cox, "Wood Wastes as an Energy Source for the B.C. Pulp and Paper Industry," in Peter N. Nemetz, ed., *Energy Policy: The Global Challenge* (Montreal: Institute for Research in Public Policy, 1982).

58. See *Soft Energy Notes* 5 (March/April 1982): 26–27.

59. Lovins, *Energy/War*, 98.

60. Brooks, *Zero Energy Growth*.

61. See Marc H. Ross and Robert H. Williams, "Energy Efficiency: Our Most Underrated Energy Resource," in Robert H. Williams, ed., *Toward a Solar Civilization* (Cambridge: M.I.T. Press, 1980).

62. For a fascinating early history see Robert Engler, *The Brotherhood of Oil* (Chicago: University of Chicago Press, 1977). See also Anthony Sampson, *The Seven Sisters* (London: Cornet, 1980).

63. Unfortunately, the new lower oil prices threaten to reestablish the cycle of price jump, patriotic conservation, reduced imports, price fall, renewed demand, price jump. . . .

64. The following draws upon David B. Brooks and Robert Paehlke, "Canada: A Soft Path in a Hard Country," *Canadian Public Policy* 6 (Summer 1980): 444–53.

65. See Bruce C. Hannon, "Options for Energy Conservation," *Technology Review* 76 (February 1974): 24–32; "Energy Conservation and the Consumer," *Science* (July 11, 1975): 95–102; and "Energy, Labor and the Conserver Society," *Technology Review* 79 (March/April 1977): 47–51.

66. John M. Cogan, Bruce Johnson, and Michael P. Ward, *Energy and Jobs: A Long Run Analysis* (Original Paper 3, International Institute for Economic Research, July 1976).

67. D. J. McCulla, "Minerals in Canadian Economic Development: Recent Quantitative Analysis," in *Proceedings of the Council of Economics of the AIME* (New York: American Institute of Mining, Metallurgical, and Petroleum Engineers, 1976).

68. Mason Gaffney, "Environmental Policies and Full Employment," in George Rohrlich, ed., *Environmental Management* (Cambridge, Mass.: Ballinger, 1976).

69. David B. Brooks, *Economic Impact of Low Energy Growth in Canada* (Ottawa: Economic Council of Canada, December 1978).

70. Richard Grossman and Gail Daneker, *Energy, Jobs and the Economy* (Boston: Alyson Publications, 1979), 53.

71. T. Akarea and T. V. Long, "Energy and Employment: A Time-Series Analysis of the Causal Relationship," *Resources and Energy* 2 (October 1979): 151–62. Roger A. Bezdek and Bruce Hannon, "Energy, Manpower, and the Highway Trust Fund," *Science* 185 (August 23, 1974): 669–75. Charlotte Ford and Bruce Hannon, "Labor and Net Energy Effects of Retrofitting Ceiling Insulation in Single-Family Homes," *Energy Systems and Policy* 4 (1980): 217–37. P.J. Groncki, et al., *Assessing the Employment Implications of Alternative Energy Supply, Conversion and End Use Technological Configurations* (Springfield, Va.: National Technical Information Service, 1978). Edward M. Kennedy, "Energy and Jobs," *Public Power* 37 (November/December 1979): 34–35. The summaries are Grossman and Daneker, *Energy, Jobs and the Economy*; Frederick H. Buttel, Charles C. Geisler, and Irving W. Wiswall, *Labor and the Environment* (Westport, Conn.: Greenwood Press, 1984); and Richard Kazis and Richard Grossman, *Fear At Work: Job Blackmail, Labor, and the Environment* (New York: Pilgrim Press, 1982).

72. On the employment and economic implications of refillables and recycling, see William U. Chandler, *Materials Recycling: The Virtue of Necessity* (Washington: Worldwatch Institute, 1984); D. W. Pearce and I. Walker, *Resource Conservation: Social and Economic Dimensions of Recycling* (New York: New York University Press, 1977); and Charles M. Gudger and Jack C. Bailes, *The Economic Impact of Oregon's Bottle Bill* (Corvellis, Oregon: Oregon

State University Press, 1974). On pollution abatement and employment, see J. MacDonald, ed., *Jobs and the Environment* (Ottawa: Canadian Labour Congress, 1978) and Kazis and Grossman, *Fear at Work*. On transportation, see Bruce Hannon and F. Puleo, *Transferring from Urban Cars to Buses: the Energy and Employment Impacts* (Urbana, Ill.: Center for Advanced Computation, University of Illinois, 1974).

73. See Neil B. Goldstein and Samuel H. Sage, "The Sierra Club's Job Package: An Environmental Works Program," *Nation* 226 (February 11, 1978): 146–48. It is interesting to contrast this beginning with the much more sophisticated statement of several major U.S. environmental groups in *America's Economic Future: Environmentalists Broaden the Industrial Policy Debate* (Washington, D.C.: Natural Resources Defense Council, 1984).

74. Typically 80 percent of all such monies go to salaries.

75. Primary goods production is more energy intensive, causes more pollution, and creates less employment than manufacturing, which in turn is less desirable in these dimensions than human services.

76. See, for example, David Martin, "Time for the 20-Hour Job?" *Canadian Forum* 64 (January 1984): 24–25.

77. This has not been widely perceived. Lovins has noted that tasks which inevitably need electricity—appliances, lighting, electric motors, computers, automatic equipment, and telecommunications—account for less than 8 percent of energy demand in a typical developed economy. The advancing use of such technologies is compatible with diminished overall energy use. See especially William Walker, "Information Technology and the Use of Energy," *Energy Policy* (October 1985): 458–76.

78. The new electronic industries are not utterly benign environmentally. See, for example, Joseph La Dou, "The Not-so-clean Business of Making Chips," *Technology Review* 87 (May/June 1984): 22–36. But per dollar of output this industry is probably far cleaner than most others. And at point of use (except for some possible problems associated with video display terminals and microwaves), there seem to be no environmental or health impacts.

79. But not all uses of recombinant DNA are appropriate as Perrow, *Normal Accidents*, makes clear. See also Howard Eddy, *Regulation of Recombinant DNA Research: A Trinational Study* (Ottawa: Science Council of Canada, 1983).

80. Denton Morrison, "The Soft Cutting Edge of Environmentalism: Why and How the Appropriate Technology Notion Is Changing the Movement," *Natural Resources Journal* 20 (April 1980): 280, 281, 285.

chapter five

1. Here see, for example, Julian L. Simon and Herman Kahn, *The Resourceful Earth: A Response to Global 2000* (Oxford: Basil Blackwell, 1984).

2. See, in particular, F. Engels, *The Dialectics of Nature* (New York: International Publishers, 1940), and his *Herr Eugen Duhring's Revolution in Science* (New York: International Publishers, 1939). Marx was less misguided on this subject than Engels.

3. C. P. Snow, *The Two Cultures and A Second Look* (London: Cambridge University Press, 1964), 4. First published 1959.

4. See Stephen Cotgrove and Andrew Duff, "Environmentalism, Middle-Class Radicalism and Politics," *Sociological Review* 28 (1980): 333–51.

5. See Frank Graham, Jr., *Since Silent Spring* (Boston: Houghton Mifflin, 1970).

6. Snow, *Two Cultures*, 5.

7. Ibid., 25–26.

8. In the nineteenth century it was perfectly clear that early industrial workers and their families often had been better off in the country—especially children who worked in mines and textile factories.

9. The notion of applying discount rates to the value of human lives came into vogue during the Reagan Administration. For a review of the notion of risk assessment and its limits and biases see J. Conrad, ed., *Society, Technology and Risk Assessment* (New York: Academic Press, 1980); and T. F. Schrecker, "The Hidden Agendas of Risk Management," *Alternatives* 11 (Summer/Fall 1983): 9–18. Many of the uses to which risk assessment have thus far been put fall near the pro-development pole. It is doubtful whether all that has been done in the name of risk assessment has indeed been scientific in the sense that the conclusions drawn were not rooted in already-made assumptions. On the other hand, a reasonable case can be made for attempting to quantify risk. See, for example, Lester B. Lave, *Quantitative Risk Assessment* (Washington, D.C.: Brookings Institute, 1982); Lester B. Lave and Arthur C. Upton, eds., *Toxic Chemicals, Health, and the Environment* (Baltimore: Johns Hopkins University Press, 1987); and the Conservation Foundation's *Toxics in the Air: Reassessing the Regulatory Framework* (Washington, D.C.: The Conservation Foundation, 1987). For arguments against some of the objections to quantitative risk analysis, see M. Douglas and A. Wildavsky, *Risk and Culture* (Berkeley: University of California Press, 1982). Although some of the general points made by these authors—that human society cannot be risk-free and that the understanding of risk is culturally determined—are probably valid, their case is overstated. But Douglas and Wildavsky provide one of the best reasoned rebuttals to an extreme environmentalist perspective.

10. Thomas S. Kuhn, *The Structure of Scientific Revolutions* (Chicago: University of Chicago Press, 1962). See especially Paul P. Sears, "Ecology—A Subversive Subject," *BioScience* 14 (July 1964); and Fritjof Capra, *The Tao of Physics* (New York: Bantam Books, 1977). See also Donald Worster, *Nature's Economy: A History of Ecological Ideas* (Cambridge: Cambridge University Press, 1985) esp. xii, 21–25, 339–48.

11. For clear and balanced overviews of the relationship among science, environment, and politics see Walter A. Rosenbaum, *Environmental Politics and Policy* (Washington, D.C.: Congressional Quarterly, 1985), chap. 3, and Samuel P. Hays, *Beauty, Health, and Permanence: Environmental Politics in the United States, 1955–1985* (New York: Cambridge University Press, 1987), chap. 10.

12. William R. Catton, Jr., *Overshoot: The Ecological Basis of Revolutionary Change* (Urbana, Ill.: University of Illinois Press, 1980), 216.

13. Ibid., 213.

14. Ibid., 45.

15. Ibid., 266.

16. Catton mentions Lovins briefly (p. 244) but seems not to appreciate fully the significance of his claims and does not respond in detail to Lovins' ideas. (Catton was probably well along with his writing by the time Lovins' argument gained wide attention.)

17. Recall the 25 percent decline in oil use in several nations in the early 1980s. And in the early 1960s North Americans lived comfortably on less than one-half of the present per capita energy use.

18. Of course, SEP analysts are sometimes guilty of excessive optimism about the potential of renewable sources to meet contemporary demand levels without environmental damage. Overshoot remains a useful concept, shorn of its hopeless pessimism.

19. The term was popularized by Herman E. Daly in several articles, in his edited collection, *Toward a Steady State Economy* (San Francisco: W. H. Freeman, 1973), and in *Steady State Economics* (San Francisco: W. H. Freeman, 1977).

20. E. J. Mishan, quoted in *The Ecologist's Blueprint for Survival* (London: Penguin Books, 1972).

21. See, for example, the recent work of Allen V. Kneese of Resources for the Future, or Michael G. Royston, *Pollution Prevention Pays* (Oxford: Pergamon Press, 1979).

22. Mishan, *The Costs of Economic Growth* (London: Staples Press, 1967), ix, xx.

23. Ibid., 8.

24. Ibid., 13.

25. Ibid., 35.

26. The Reagan administration deliberately put a temporary lid on economic growth by means of high interest rates. The motivations for such an action were undoubtedly complex, but one effect—undoubtedly unintentional—was to dampen environmentalist enthusiasm for an SSE. In the 1980s environmentalists have expended a good deal of effort explaining how their perspective can result in more economic and employment opportunities.

27. Mishan, *Costs of Economic Growth*, 93.

28. This was in 1967; one can only imagine what he would think now.

29. Charles Taylor, "The Politics of the Steady State," in Abraham Rotstein, ed., *Beyond Industrial Growth* (Toronto: University of Toronto Press, 1976), 48, 49, 50.

30. Boulding in Daly, *Toward a Steady State Economics*, 127.

31. In some cases more durable, better quality products require a greater labor input, but this is by no means always the case—robots can often produce higher quality products than human workers. If products were durable and there were no endless increase in demand, work time would decline. This is discussed in later chapters.

32. *Ecologist*, 37.

33. Ibid., 37–40.

34. In 1986, the U.S. forest industry sought relief against Canadian lumber imports, arguing that the Canadian government gives away trees without charging sufficiently for replanting. For a look at subsidies to primary industries in Canada see, for example, Martin Robin, *The Rush for Spoils: The Company Province, 1871–1933* (Toronto: McClelland and Stewart, 1972).

35. Daly, *Steady State Economics*, 17, 18.

36. Ibid., 118.

37. *Ecologist*, 16–17.

38. Gideon Rosenbluth, *Economists and the Growth Controversy* (Discussion Paper no. 75–15, Vancouver: Department of Economics, University of British Columbia, 1975), 3.

39. Heilbroner, *An Inquiry into the Human Prospect* (New York: W. W. Norton, 1974), chap. 3, 84–86.

40. Ibid., 94.

41. Paul Hawken, *The Next Economy* (New York: Ballantine Books, 1983), 8.

42. Science Council of Canada, *Canada as a Conserver Society* (Ottawa: Supply and Services Canada, 1977), 14.

43. Ibid.

44. This is different from centrist in a left-right sense, although the *Conserver Society* is also remarkably cautious in this sense as well.

45. Jeff Passmore and Ray Jackson, *Renewable Energy: Innovation in Action* (Ottawa: Science Council of Canada, 1984).

46. *Canada as a Conserver Society*, 52, 6.

47. Ted Schrecker, *The Conserver Society Revisited* (Ottawa: Science Council of Canada, 1983). See, for example, p. 6, where Schrecker argues that conserver ideas are not antigrowth; rather, the usual indicators of growth, such as GNP, measure the wrong things.

48. Ibid., 43.

49. Ibid., 44. See Nikolai Kondratieff, *Long Wave Cycle* (New York: Richardson and Snyder, 1984) for the original statement of the theory.

50. Peter Drucker, "The Changed World Economy," *Foreign Affairs* 64 (Spring 1986): 768–91.

51. Lester R. Brown, *Building a Sustainable Society* (New York: W. W. Norton, 1981). The quote is on the front cover.

52. Robert D. Hamrin, *A Renewable Resource Economy* (New York: Praeger Publishers, 1983), 7.

53. Ibid., 67.

chapter six

1. Samuel P. Hays, "From Conservation to Environment: Environmental Politics in the United States Since World War Two," *Environmental Review* 6 (Fall 1982): 20.

2. For clear expressions of this important dimension of environmentalism see Duane Elgin, *Voluntary Simplicity* (New York: William Morrow, 1981); and The Simple Living Collective, American Friends Service Committee, *Taking Charge* (New York: Bantam Books, 1977).

3. I cannot resist recalling that Eugene Debs, the noted American socialist, once wrote in some seriousness to John D. Rockefeller suggesting that he give away his money.

4. This succinct definition was coined by David Easton in *The Political System* (New York: A.A. Knopf, Inc., 1953).

5. This material is developed from my article "Communicating Environmental Values," in Paul F. Wilkinson and Miriam Wyman, eds., *Environmental Challenges: Learning for Tomorrow's World* (London, Ontario: Althouse Press, 1986). Environmentalist values of the sort set out here have been studied empirically: see especially the special issue of *The American Behavioral Scientist* 24 (1980) edited by Riley E. Dunlap; Riley E. Dunlap and K. Van Liere, "The New Environmental Paradigm," *The Journal of Environmental Education* 9 (1978): 10–19; and Riley E. Dunlap, "Polls, Pollution and Politics Revisited: Public Opinion on the Environment in the Reagan Era," *Environment* 29 (August 1987): 6–11, 32–37.

6. See Samuel P. Hays, *Conservation and the Gospel of Efficiency: The Progressive Conservation Movement, 1890–1920* (Cambridge: Harvard University Press, 1959). Conservationist Aldo Leopold should not be included within this generalization. Leopold explicitly argued against a wholly economic conservation system. Most of nature—wildflowers and songbirds, for example—has no economic use, but the economic parts require the uneconomic parts to endure in health. See Robert V. Bartlett, "Ecological Rationality: Reason and Environmental Policy," *Environmental Ethics* 8 (Fall 1986): 221–39.

7. David Brooks and Doris McMullen, "The Trade-Off," *Nature Canada* (Spring 1980): 36.

8. John Livingston, *One Cosmic Instant: A Natural History of Human Ar-*

rogance (Toronto: McClelland and Stewart, 1973), 21, 228. In this matter Paul Taylor observes that human self-realization is highly dependent on maximum diversity in nature, which human activity in turn threatens. See Paul W. Taylor, *Respect for Nature* (Princeton: Princeton University Press, 1986).

9. White, "The Historic Roots of Our Ecologic Crisis," *Science* 155 (1967): 1203–07. See also Ian G. Barbour, ed., *Western Man and Environmental Ethics* (Reading, Mass.: Addison-Wesley, 1973). Rejecting the myth carries radical implications: see the article by George Sessions, "Ecophilosophy, Utopias, and Education," *Journal of Environmental Education* 15 (Fall 1983): 27–42, and the very important works of the "deep ecology" movement especially Arne Naess, "A Defense of the Deep Ecology Movement," *Environmental Ethics* 6 (1984): 265–70; William Devall and George Sessions, *Deep Ecology: Living as if Nature Mattered* (Salt Lake City: Peregrine Smith Books, 1985); and A. K. Salleh, "Deeper than Deep Ecology," *Environmental Ethics* 6 (1984): 239–45.

10. William Leiss, *The Domination of Nature* (Boston: Beacon Press, 1974), 178–79, 49.

11. Christopher D. Stone, *Should Trees Have Standing?* (Los Altos, Calif.: W. Kaufman, 1974).

12. Livingston, *One Cosmic Instant*, 23.

13. H. V. Nelles, *The Politics of Development* (Toronto: Macmillan of Canada, 1975), 218–19.

14. Robert Paehlke and Cameron Wright, "Niagara: A Wonder Besieged," *Alternatives: Perspectives on Society and Environment* 10 (Fall-Winter 1982): 27–32.

15. David Ehrenfeld, *The Arrogance of Humanism* (New York: Oxford University Press, 1978), 58, 269. Donald Worster, *Nature's Economy: A History of Ecological Ideas* (Cambridge: Cambridge University Press, 1985), observed an expression of humility very similar to this in the work of Rachel Carson and contrasted its militant political tone to the quieter humility of Gilbert White, who wrote some two hundred years earlier.

16. Several articles in the running and jogging magazines, including *Runner's World*, have recently discussed this.

17. This has been a particularly significant concern in the 1980s. See, for example, William U. Chandler, "Banishing Tobacco," in Lester R. Brown, et al., eds., *State of the World 1986* (New York: W. W. Norton, 1986) esp. pp. 148–49, 239–40.

18. See, for example, Linda R. Pim, *Additive Alert* (Toronto: Doubleday Canada), and *The Invisible Additive: Environmental Contaminants in Our Food* (Garden City, N.Y.: Doubleday, 1982). Note also the recent concern about toxic and oxidant air pollutants. See also Margaret Mellon, et al., *The Regulation of Toxic and Oxidant Air Pollution in North America* (Toronto: CCH Canadian, 1986).

19. Hays, *Conservation and Efficiency*, 21.

20. Frances Moore Lappé, *Diet for a Small Planet*, rev. ed. (New York: Ballantine Books, 1975

21. Some leading examples are Jean Hewitt, *The New York Times Natural Foods Cookbook* (New York: Avon, 1972); Elise Boulding, *From a Monastary Kitchen* (New York: Harper and Row, 1976); and Ellen B. Ewald, *Recipes for a Small Planet* (New York: Ballantine Books, 1975).

22. David Weir and Mark Schapiro, *Circle of Poison* (San Francisco: Institute for Food and Development Policy, 1981).

23. Cautious scientific opinion has not confirmed that ingested asbestos is a health hazard. See the conclusions of *Report of The Royal Commission on Matters Arising from the Use of Asbestos in Ontario*, 3 vols. (Toronto: Ontario Ministry of the Attorney General, 1984). However, the findings of I. J. Selikoff, J. Chung, E. C. Hammond, "Asbestos Exposure and Neoplasia," *Journal of the American Medical Association* 188 (1964): 22–26, and other studies indicate a higher incidence of cancers of the digestive tract among asbestos workers. Here is an opportunity to err on the side of caution.

24. On European diplomacy and cooperation on environmental standards in the European community see, for example, "Toning Down the Mediterranean Blues," *The Economist* (June 11, 1983): 97–100; J. Smeets, "The Labeling and Classification of Chemical Substances and Preparations in the European Community," *Regulatory Toxicology and Pharmacology* 3 (1983): 101–09; "Europe Must Soon Make Choices on Cleaning Up Cars," *The Economist* (April 7, 1984): 85–88; L. D. Guruswamy, et al., "The Development and Impact of an EEC Directive: The Control of Discharges of Mercury to the Aquatic Environment," *Journal of Common Market Studies* 22 (September 1983): 71–100; and especially Lynton Caldwell, *International Environmental Policy: Emergence and Dimensions* (Durham, N.C.: Duke University Press, 1984); and the special issue on International Environmental Politics and Policies, *The Journal of Public and International Affairs* 5 (Winter 1984).

25. In particular, Russia felt enough pressure from downwind European countries to provide information and discussion opportunities regarding releases. They also brought in external medical expertise and months afterward were asked to supply uncontaminated reindeer meat to the Laplanders to compensate for Chernobyl's effects—at a distance of well over a thousand kilometers. Regarding Chernobyl's impacts see, for example, John F. Ahearne, "Implications of the Chernobyl Nuclear Accident," *Resources* 86 (1987): 10–12, and Christopher Hohennemser, et al., "Chernobyl: An Early Report," *Environment* 28 (June 1986): 6–13, 30–43.

26. E.g., Barbara Ward and Rene Dubos, *Only One Earth* (New York: W. W. Norton, 1972).

27. James Gustave Speth, "Environment, Economy, Security: A New Agenda for OECD Countries," paper presented at the Colloquium on the

Environment, Toronto, Ontario, December 9–10, 1985, available from the Economic Council of Canada, Ottawa.

28. See Larry Solomon, *Energy Shock* (Toronto: Doubleday Canada, 1980); and Paul McKay, *Electric Empire: The Inside Story of Ontario Hydro* (Toronto: Between the Lines, 1983).

29. One might also note the environmental sensitivity of such anarchists as Peter Kropotkin and William Morris. See also Murray Bookchin, *Post-Scarcity Anarchism* (Berkeley: Ramparts Press, 1971); and John Wadland's comments in *Ernest Thompson Seton: Man and Nature in the Progressive Era, 1880–1915* (New York: Arno Press, 1978).

30. On a possible effect of this literature see Robert G. Healy and James L. Short, "The Changing Rural Landscape," *Environment* 23 (December 1981): 6–11, 30–34.

31. Recycling must reach down to the state and municipal level, where refuse collection is generally organized. But scrap markets, which must be stabilized, are national and international. Regarding a particularly successful municipal energy conservation effort (in Davis, California) see Reg Lang and Audrey Armour, *New Directions in Municipal Energy Conservation: The California Experience* (Toronto: Ontario Ministry of Energy, 1986).

32. Alvin Toffler, *The Third Wave* (New York: Bantam Books, 1981).

33. This is not new. As Max Weber wrote, "Every bureaucracy seeks to increase the superiority of the professionally informed by keeping their knowledge and intentions secret." H. H. Gerth and C. Wright Mills, *From Max Weber* (New York: Oxford University Press, 1946), 233.

34. If necessary (I doubt it really is), government agencies could review the generic contents of anonymous chemicals without revealing most ingredients to purchasers, workers, or the public.

35. Several communities have sought to replace declining heavy (polluting) industry by expanding educational institutions, retail outlets, handicraft production, and new high-tech and light industries. See, for example, the magazine *Changing Work* (Department of Sociology, Boston College).

36. Ernest Partridge, ed., *Responsibilities to Future Generations* (Buffalo: Prometheus Books, 1981). See also Marvin S. Soroos, "Ecology and the Time Dimension in Human Relationships," in David W. Orr and Marvin S. Soroos, eds., *The Global Predicament: Ecological Perspectives on World Order* (Chapel Hill: University of North Carolina Press, 1979).

37. Lynton K. Caldwell, "Environment: A New Focus for Public Policy?" *Public Administration Review* 23 (September 1963): 132–39.

38. Fairfield Osborn, *Our Plundered Plant* (Boston: Little, Brown, 1948).

39. Livingston, *One Cosmic Instant*, 23.

40. William Ophuls, *Ecology and the Politics of Scarcity* (San Francisco: W. H. Freeman, 1977), 222, 224.

41. Ibid., 224.

42. John Helliwell and Alan Cox, "Wood Wastes as an Energy Source for the B.C. Pulp and Paper Industry," in Peter N. Nemetz, ed., *Energy Policy: The Global Challenge* (Montreal: Institute for Research in Public Policy, 1982). Monica E. Campbell and William M. Glenn, *Profit from Pollution Prevention* (Scarborough, Ontario: Firefly Books, 1982).

43. See Lester R. Brown, *Building a Sustainable Society* (New York: W. W. Norton, 1981), 52–54, 40–45.

44. But fish is a high-quality, low-fat source of protein; the trend to lower-fat diets might increase the demand for fish.

45. See Sandra Postel, "Protecting Forests," in Lester R. Brown, ed., *State of the World 1984* (New York: W. W. Norton, 1984); and Jamie Swift, *Cut and Run: The Assault on Canada's Forests* (Toronto: Between the Lines, 1983). Acid rain damage has been most severe in West Germany, Eastern Europe, and the sugar maple bush of Quebec, Ontario, and New England. On clearcutting of rainforests, see Postel, "Protecting Forests"; Norman Myers, *The Primary Source: Tropical Forests and Our Future* (New York: W. W. Norton, 1984); and T. C. Whitmore, *Tropical Rain Forests of the Far East* (Oxford: Clarendon Press, 1984).

46. The SEP analysts estimate that in the many countries studied a five and even tenfold increase in use of wood is possible. This clearly involves massive transformation of our economy, social organization, and the physical artifacts of our civilization. See also Erik Eckholm, *The Other Energy Crisis: Firewood* (Washington, D.C.: Worldwatch Institute, 1975).

47. Ironically, Canadian foresters have helped reforestation efforts in many other nations. Mismanagement of forests in Canada is not a question of a lack of skill or committed professionals.

48. This tendency was particularly pronounced in the 1970s. If only domestic food demand is considered, of course, North Americans could afford to pave much more of our farmland. Omitted from these calculations are the needs of the rest of the world and the possibility that near-urban prime farmland will become increasingly important as energy prices accelerate in the decades to come.

49. The terminology comes from Larry M. Geno, "Ecological Agriculture: The Environmentally Appropriate Alternative," *Alternatives: Perspectives on Society and Environment* 5 (1976): 53–63.

50. Farmers tend to resist any policy that reduces their land speculation prospects.

51. The value of development rights can approach the actual market value of the land; thus in some places the program might be very expensive. But only a small proportion of prime farmland is at risk—precisely that which we most want to protect.

52. For popular discussions of organic farming see Ray Wolf, ed., *Organic Farming: Yesterday's and Tomorrow's Agriculture* (Emmaus, Penn.: Rodale Press, 1977); and Masanobu Fukuoka, *The One-Straw Revolution* (Emmaus,

Penn.: Rodale Press, 1978). See also Prince Edward Island Conference on Ecological Agriculture, *Proceedings* (Charlottetown, P.E.I., 1978).

53. Kenneth Boulding, "The Economics of the Coming Spaceship Earth," in Herman E. Daly, ed., *Toward a Steady-State Economy* (San Francisco: W. H. Freeman, 1973), 129.

54. Vance Packard, *The Waste Makers* (New York: D. McKay Co., 1960).

55. Stuart Chase and F. J. Schlink, *Your Money's Worth* (New York: Macmillan, 1927), 3.

56. James Whorton, *Before Silent Spring: Pesticides and Public Health in Pre-DDT America* (Princeton: Princeton University Press, 1974), 77.

57. Chase and Schlink, *Your Money's Worth*, 23, 83.

58. Brooks and McMullen, "Trade-Off," 36.

59. See, e.g., Elgin, *Voluntary Simplicity*.

60. Paul McKay, "Survival or Suicide: The Choice Is Ours to Make," *Alternatives: Perspectives on Society and Environment* 10 (Fall-Winter 1982): 10.

61. Ronald Inglehart, "Post-Materialism in an Environment of Insecurity," *American Political Science Review* 75 (1981): 880. This article is a classic within political science. Studies since 1981 suggest that if anything post-materialist attitudes continue to deepen and spread. See also Ronald Inglehart and Scott Flanigan, "Value Change in Industrial Societies," *American Political Science Review* 81 (December 1987): 1289–319.

62. Nineteen studies are cited ibid., 880, 898–900. See also Stephen Cotgrove and Andrew Duff, "Environmentalism, Values, and Social Change," *British Journal of Sociology* 32 (March 1981): 92–109. Cotgrove and Duff observe that environmentalists share with the political left a critical view of industrial capitalism, but that those on the left do not necessarily share environmentalists' post-materialist rejection of the primacy of economics and economic values.

63. See Helen and Scott Nearing, *Living the Good Life* (New York: Schocken Books, 1970). Stephen Cotgrove and Andrew Duff, "Environmentalism, Middle-Class Radicalism and Politics," *Sociological Review* 28 (1980): 333–51, link this to hatred of waste, observing empirically that environmentalists want above all a society in which "production is selective rather than aiming to satisfy the demand for consumer goods" (337).

64. Again one need only mention William Morris and Peter Kropotkin.

65. Ophuls, *Ecology and the Politics of Scarcity*, 224.

66. See Lovins, *Soft Energy Paths*, chap. 2, esp. 34; and his "Electric Utility Investments: Excelsior or Confetti?" *Journal of Business Administration* 12 (Spring 1981). Lovins at times expresses concern about unions. But especially in the case of pipelines, the source of what he sees as unwarranted union power may rest in regulatory regimes that set rates as a function of return on investment. If that rate of return is high enough and the market captive enough it is in the interest of management to pay the highest possible wages regardless of union pressure.

67. Nuclear regulatory agencies clearly have maximized their power on the basis of the widespread political perception of public ignorance. See the discussion in Charles Perrow, *Normal Accidents: Living with High-Risk Technologies* (New York: Basic Books, 1984).

68. See Christopher Flavin, *The Future of Synthetic Materials: The Petroleum Connection* (Washington, D.C.: Worldwatch Institute, 1980).

69. Ehrlich raises this point in the *Environment* 14 (April 1972) debate with Commoner. Cotton requires more pesticides than other crops by a considerable margin.

70. I take it that the defense of baby seals is so vehement in part because seals are cute. The campaign against billboards seemed innocuous but was not successful.

71. However, nuclear plants must be cooled either by a large body of water or by a large, usually ugly, cooling tower.

72. Calvinism, however, grants admission to heaven for high productivity, as evidenced by wealth.

73. E. F. Schumacher, *Small is Beautiful* (New York: Harper and Row, 1973), 55.

74. See, for example, Charles A. McCoy and John Playford, eds., *Apolitical Politics: A Critique of Behavioralism* (New York: Thomas Y. Crowell, 1967), for a series of articulate responses to the 1950s and 1960s attempts at empiricist revision of democracy.

75. See Lynton K. Caldwell, *Science and the National Environmental Policy Act: Redirecting Policy Through Procedural Reform* (Birmingham: University of Alabama Press, 1982).

76. See Craig W. Allin, *The Politics of Wilderness Preservation* (Westport, Conn.: Greenwood Press, 1982); and Robert Paehlke and Douglas Torgerson, "Environmental Problems and the Administrative State: The Case of Toxic Waste Management," in O. P. Dwivedi and R. Brian Woodrow, eds., *Public Policy and Administrative Studies* (Guelph, Ontario: Guelph University Political Studies Department, 1985).

77. See especially Allan Schnaiberg, *The Environment from Surplus to Scarcity* (New York: Oxford University Press, 1980); and Richard N. L. Andrews, "Class Politics or Democratic Reform: Environmentalism and American Political Institutions," *Natural Resources Journal* 20 (April 1980).

78. Especially, both federal and provincial Royal Commissions and task forces have been used—there have been dozens on environmental subjects in the 1970s and 1980s.

79. See Robert Paehlke, "Some Impressions of Three Environmental Enquiries," *Alternatives: Perspectives on Society and Environment* 7 (Winter 1978): 46–51.

80. Thomas R. Berger, *Northern Frontier/Northern Homeland* (Ottawa: Supply and Services Canada, 1977).

81. See Robert Paehlke, "Much to be Done: Exploring the Interface Be-

tween Occupational and Environmental Health," *Alternatives* 10 (Spring-Summer 1981): 13–20; G. B. Reschenthaler, *Occupational Health and Safety in Canada* (Montreal: Institute for Research on Public Policy, 1979); and Katherine Swinton, "Enforcement of Occupational Health and Safety Legislation: The Role of the Internal Responsibility System," in K. Swan and K. Swinton, eds., *Studies in Labour Law* (Scarborough, Ontario: Butterworths, 1982). Charles Noble, *Liberalism at Work* (Philadelphia: Temple University Press, 1986), in reviewing occupational health policy in the United States, strongly advocates greater mobilization of workers and their greater participation in their own protection.

82. Andrews, "Class Politics or Democratic Reform," 238.

83. T. F. Schrecker, *Political Economy of Environmental Hazards* (Ottawa: Law Reform Commission of Canada, 1984).

chapter seven

1. The word *inherently* is used here to make clear that environmentalism can be blended with almost any left or right ideology; in fact, it has most often been linked with the moderate left.

2. H. H. Gerth and C. Wright Mills, *From Max Weber: Essays in Sociology* (New York: Oxford University Press, 1946), 78–79.

3. Thomas Hobbes, *Leviathan* (Cleveland: World Publishing, 1963), 143.

4. John Lilburne quoted in George H. Sabine, *A History of Political Theory* (New York: Holt, Rinehart and Winston, 1961), 483.

5. Winstanley quoted ibid., 492.

6. Winstanley quoted in George H. Sabine, ed., *The Works of Gerrard Winstanley* (New York: Russell and Russell, 1965), 580–81.

7. William Shakespeare quoted in Samuel H. Beer, *British Politics in the Collectivist Age* (New York: Random House, 1965), 3–4.

8. The central importance of property rights and economic opportunities to liberal thinking is carefully set out in C. B. Macpherson, *The Political Theory of Possessive Individualism: Hobbes to Locke* (Oxford: Oxford University Press, 1962).

9. John Locke, *Of Civil Government, Second Treatise* (Chicago: Henry Regnery, 1955), 187–90.

10. Charles A. Beard, *An Economic Interpretation of the Constitution of the United States* (New York: Macmillan, 1935).

11. On the rise of socialism I have found particularly enlightening Edmund Wilson, *To the Finland Station* (Garden City: Doubleday, 1953); E. H. Carr, *Studies in Revolution* (New York: Grosset and Dunlap, 1964); Peter Gay, *The Dilemma of Democratic Socialism* (New York: Collier Books, 1962); and David McLellan, *Marx Before Marxism* (New York: Harper and Row, 1970).

12. This has been particularly true in Canada, especially Ontario, where

Conservative governments established the Canadian Broadcasting Corporation, the Canadian National Railroad, Ontario Hydro, and numerous other
public corporations. See Allan Tupper and G. Bruce Doern, *Public Corporations and Public Policy in Canada* (Montreal: Institute for Research on Public
Policy, 1981).

13. I take the very center of the left-right spectrum to be disposed to
moderate progressive intervention. Since 1980 the balance of forces has
shifted to the right, but for more than a century the norm, in terms of
advocacy if not action, has been on behalf of aid to those disadvantaged
within the marketplace.

14. Karl Polanyi, *The Great Transformation* (Boston: Beacon Press, 1957),
57.

15. S. M. Lipset in Chaim I. Waxman, ed., *The End of Ideology Debate* (New
York: Simon and Schuster, 1969), 72, 73.

16. This term was originally coined by E. E. Schattshneider and is discussed and developed in Peter Bachrach and Morton S. Baratz, "Two Faces
of Power," *American Political Science Review* 56 (December 1962): 947–52.

17. These costs involve both extractions and additions. For the way in
which economic expansion is rooted in unsustainable costs, especially in
the poor nations, see J. Leonard, *Divesting Nature's Capital* (New York:
Holmes and Meier, 1985).

18. The costs of compliance with 1970s environmental legislation have
been wildly overestimated by business in the 1980s. For various viewpoints
see Barry Mitnick, *The Political Economy of Regulation* (New York: Columbia
University Press, 1980); David Vogel, *National Styles of Regulation* (Ithaca:
Cornell University Press, 1986); S. J. Tolchin and M. Tolchin, *Dismantling
America* (Boston: Houghton Mifflin, 1983); Samuel P. Hays, *Beauty, Health,
and Permanence: Environmental Politics in the United States, 1955–1985* (New
York: Cambridge University Press, 1987); and Richard Kazis and Richard
L. Grossman, *Fear at Work* (New York: Pilgrim Press, 1982).

19. After completing several drafts of this chapter I came upon a similar
figure in Stephen Cotgrove's superb *Catastrophe or Cornucopia: The Environment, Politics and the Future* (Chichester, Eng.: John Wiley and Sons, 1982),
112.

20. John Stuart Mill, quoted in Herman E. Daly, ed., *Economics, Ecology,
Ethics* (San Francisco: W. H. Freeman, 1980), 14.

21. Karl Marx, quoted in Peter Victor, "Economics and the Challenge of
Environmental Issues," ibid., 208. For two clear and thoughtful views of
Marx and ecology see Val Routley, "On Karl Marx as an Environmental
Hero," *Environmental Ethics* 3 (1981): 237–44; and Donald C. Lee, "Towards
a Marxian Ecological Ethic: A Response to Two Critics," *Environmental Ethics*
4 (1982): 339–43.

22. Victor, "Economics and Environmental Issues," 209.

23. Marx quoted ibid. Recall Engels' concern about pollution (cited in
chapter 2).

24. This has been noted by Richard N. L. Andrews, "Class Politics or Democratic Reform: Environmentalism and American Political Institutions," *Natural Resources Journal* 20 (April 1980).

25. Or perhaps he has listened to the comments of his critics and peers. Recently Ehrlich has involved himself in such issues as the extinction of species and the environmental effects of nuclear war.

26. A private economy can be directed by government in a variety of ways; what must be accounted for is the political power of private capital.

27. For a Maoist perspective (formulated when Mao was still in power), see Barry Weisberg, *Beyond Repair: The Ecology of Capitalism* (Boston: Beacon Press, 1971), esp. chap. 6. Moderate social democrats include David B. Brooks, myself, and many others who have not explicitly identified themselves as such in their writings. Gorz is an unorthodox Marxist (see below) and the anticapitalist anarchist par excellence is Murray Bookchin.

28. The late U.S. Communist leader Gus Hall favored subsuming environmentalism. See his *Ecology: Can We Survive Under Capitalism?* (New York: International Publishers, 1974); and Richard J. Neuhauss, *In Defense of People: Ecology and the Seduction of Radicalism* (New York: Macmillan, 1971). Hans Magnus Enzenberger, "A Critique of Political Ecology," *New Left Review* 84 (March/April 1974): 3–31 to some extent downplays the importance of environmental issues.

29. For survey data on this point see the article by Robert Cameron Mitchell in *Natural Resources Journal* 20 (April 1980), esp. 354. See also Lester W. Milbrath, *Environmentalists: Vanguard for a New Society* (Albany: SUNY Press, 1984).

30. Amory B. Lovins, in *Renewable Energy News* (April 1983). See also "Reagan on Energy: Reactionary or Radical?" *Not Man Apart* (January 1981): 15.

31. Amory B. Lovins, *Soft Energy Paths* (Cambridge, Mass.: Ballinger, 1977), 164.

32. See Clifford S. Russell, "Discounting Human Life," *Resources* 82 (Winter 1986): 8–10.

33. I hope to undertake an extended series of comparative studies of environmental policies on completion of this work. For an early comparative study see Cynthia H. Enloe, *The Politics of Pollution in a Comparative Perspective* (New York: David McKay, 1975).

34. See note 28 above.

35. In the 1960s James Weinstein (editor of the "new left" journal *Studies on the Left*) made this case, which set him apart from the more orthodox Marxists of his day.

36. See the superb analysis of Volkmar Lauber, in "Ecology Politics and Liberal Democracy," *Government and Opposition* 13 (Spring 1978): 200–17.

37. On nationalization, see Barry Commoner, *The Poverty of Power* (New York: Bantam Books, 1977). For a moderate view on economic planning see David B. Brooks, *Zero Energy Growth for Canada* (Toronto: McClelland and

Stewart, 1981), esp. 238–53. For a more radical planning solution see Francis Sandbach, *Environment, Ideology and Policy* (Oxford: Basil Blackwell, 1980). On redistribution the pamphlet "Sharing Smaller Pies" (mimeo.) by Thomas Bender, a well-known U.S. West Coast environmentalist.

38. William Leiss, *The Limits to Satisfaction* (Toronto: University of Toronto Press, 1976), 108.

39. Andre Gorz, *Farewell to the Working Class* (London: Pluto Press, 1982), 72.

40. Ibid., 80.

41. Gorz, 135–36.

42. David Dickson, *Alternative Technology* (Glasgow: William Collins Sons, 1974), 204.

43. Of course, many of these jobs are vulnerable anyway, and industrial workers can be involved in industrial reorganization. In one aberrant case the union representing uranium miners opposed expansion of the industry into British Columbia on the grounds of health risk to workers.

44. Andre Gorz, *Ecology as Politics* (Montreal: Black Rose Books, 1980), 102.

45. In *Farewell to the Working Class* (123), Gorz suggests that "post-industrial socialism" will involve a conscious decision to shrink total production and to live better with less. The contrast to traditional Marxism could not be more complete.

46. Langdon Winner, *Autonomous Technology* (Cambridge, Mass.: M.I.T. Press, 1977), 39–40.

47. Gorz, *Ecology as Politics*, 28.

48. Leiss, *Limits to Satisfaction*, 105.

49. See, for example, Bayard Rustin, "No Growth Has to Mean Less and Less," *New York Times Magazine* (May 2, 1976).

50. Leiss, *Limits to Satisfaction*, 92.

51. Ibid., 38–43.

52. Leiss, 67, 77.

53. Marshall I. Goldman, *The Spoils of Progress: Environmental Pollution in the Soviet Union* (Cambridge: M.I.T. Press, 1972). See also Philip R. Pryde, *Conservation in the Soviet Union* (Cambridge: Cambridge University Press, 1972).

54. See *Final Report, Cluff Lake Board of Inquiry* (Regina, Saskatchewan: Ministry of the Environment, May 1978).

55. On several occasions mine tailings ponds have burst their containment and have been distributed into the wider environment. Occupational exposures to radiation have sometimes been higher than was suggested in the original hearings.

56. There has been some resistance to the Reagan administration's huge increases in military spending, but many progressives have not been firm in their opposition.

57. On the positive side, market economics helped energy conservation to be achieved rapidly when energy prices rose sharply. To achieve pollution abatement, however, political intervention seems essential.

58. Charles E. Lindblom, *Politics and Markets* (New York: Basic Books, 1977), 8.

59. For basic data and competent interpretation see Sidney Verba and Norman H. Nie, *Participation in America: Political Democracy and Social Equality* (New York: Harper and Row, 1972). For the flavor of the debate over the meaning of this fact see Graeme Duncan and Steven Lukes, "The New Democracy," *Political Studies* 11 (1963): 156–77.

60. Theodore J. Lowi, *The End of Liberalism* (New York: W. W. Norton, 1969), 71.

61. Walter Truett Anderson, ed., *Rethinking Liberalism* (New York: Avon Books, 1983), 246–47.

62. See Sam H. Schurr, "Energy Conservation and Productivity Growth: Can We Have Both?" *Energy Policy* (April 1985): 126–32; and William Walker, "Information Technology and the Use of Energy," *Energy Policy* (October 1985): 458–76.

63. Samuel P. Hays, *Conservation and the Gospel of Efficiency: The Progressive Conservation Movement, 1890–1920* (Cambridge: Harvard University Press, 1959), 2.

chapter eight

1. See Samuel P. Hays, "From Conservation to Environment: Environmental Politics in the United States Since World War Two," *Environmental Review* 6 (Fall 1982): 32, regarding environmentalists and deficits; and Robert B. Reich, "Why the U.S. Needs an Industrial Policy," *Harvard Business Review* 60 (January-February 1982): 74–81, regarding neoconservatives and consumer spending.

2. See, for example, Arthur J. Cordell, *The Uneasy Eighties: The Transition to an Information Society* (Ottawa: Science Council of Canada, 1985).

3. See, for example, Michael Barker, "The End of the Reagan Boom," *The New Republic* 193 (July 1, 1985): 19–21.

4. Two sources of interest here are Lester Thurow, *The Zero-Sum Society* (New York: Basic Books, 1977); and M. J. Daly and P. S. Rao, "Some Myths and Realities Concerning Canada's Recent Productivity Slowdown and Their Policy Implications," *Canadian Public Policy* 11 (June 1985): 206–17.

5. See G. Warren Nutter, *Growth of Government in the West* (Washington, D.C.: American Enterprise Institute, 1978). In Australia, for example, government expenditures as a percentage of national income grew from 28.59% in 1960 to 38.92% in 1974; in Norway from 30.19% in 1951 to 62.88% in 1974.

6. Thurow, *Zero-Sum Society*, 7.

7. See Heather Menzies, *Women and the Chip* (Montreal: Institute for Research on Public Policy, 1981). Some recent studies suggest that technological impacts on office employment may be less dramatic than it first appeared.

8. Alan Wolfe, *America's Impasse* (New York: Pantheon Books, 1981).

9. This is the phrase used by Marx and Engels to describe governments, including democratic governments, in the capitalist era.

10. See Reich, "Why the U.S. Needs an Industrial Policy," 74.

11. Thomas Ferguson and Joel Rogers, "The Myth of America's Turn to the Right," *The Atlantic* 257 (May 1986): 45.

12. Ibid., 44–45.

13. Ibid., 45.

14. Ironically, the environmental savings sought by neoconservatives are not very large—it is as if reduced protection, rather than reduced deficits, were the higher objective. See particularly the chapters by Bartlett, Caldwell, and Clark in an excellent volume edited by Norman J. Vig and Michael E. Kraft, *Environmental Policy in the 1980s: Reagan's New Agenda* (Washington, D.C.: Congressional Quarterly, 1984). On the other hand, deep across-the-board spending cuts such as those envisaged by the Gramm-Rudman-Hollings deficit reduction law could have serious consequences for environmental protection. See Robert Livernash, "Squaring up to Gramm-Rudman-Hollings: The 1986 Environmental Legislative Agenda," *Environment* 28 (March 1986): 16–20, 36–39; and Robert Livernash, "The Shrinking Environmental Dollar: A Congressional Wrap-up," *Environment* 30 (January/February 1988): 6–9, 38–43. This is not to say that superior environmental protection could not be achieved at equal or lower cost overall.

15. The late David Lewis pointed out the extent of that support system in his *Louder Voices: The Corporate Welfare Bums* (Toronto: James Lewis and Samuel, 1972).

16. See Thurow, *Zero-Sum Society*; and Roger Gibbins, *Conflict and Unity* (Toronto: Methuen, 1985), 131–76.

17. Robert Malcolm Campbell, "From Keynesianism to Monetarism," *Queen's Quarterly* 88 (Winter 1981): 637. See also Robert Malcolm Campbell, *Grand Illusions: The Politics of the Keynesian Experience in Canada, 1945–1975* (Peterborough, Ont.: Broadview Press, 1987).

18. See William DiFazio, *Longshoremen: Community and Resistance on the Brooklyn Waterfront* (South Hadley, Mass.: Bergin and Garvey, 1985).

19. There is considerable caution on military spending in the otherwise very encouraging work by representatives of several major U.S. conservation and environmentalist organizations. See *America's Economic Future: Environmentalists Broaden the Industrial Policy Debate* (Washington, D.C.: Natural Resources Defense Council, 1984). Lester R. Brown takes a stronger position in "Redefining National Security," in Lester R. Brown, ed., *State of the World 1986* (New York: W. W. Norton, 1986).

20. See Brown, "Redefining National Security."

21. Regarding the environmental advantages of some forms of economic deregulation see Pietro S. Nivola, *The Politics of Energy Conservation* (Washington, D.C.: Brookings Institute, 1986). But see also Don E. Kash and Robert W. Rycroft, *U.S. Energy Policy: Crisis and Complacency* (Norman: University of Oklahoma Press, 1984) and Richard H. K. Vietor, *Energy Policy in America since 1945* (New York: Cambridge University Press, 1987).

22. The Soviet logic is that SDI will never be more than 90–95 percent effective. But a U.S. first strike against Russian land-based missiles, if the United States has some unknown anti-submarine weapons, might reduce the Russian capability to a "tolerable" level. Any agreement to cut the number of U.S. and Russian missiles makes a U.S. first strike more likely if the United States alone has a strategic defense system. If both countries have it, either might strike first. The SDI is only a force for peace if all offensive weapons on both sides are eliminated. Needless to say, it would then be unnecessary except as "insurance" against cheating.

23. Perhaps the best and most relevant of Melman's many works are *The Permanent War Economy* (New York: Simon and Schuster, 1985); *Profits Without Production* (New York: A. A. Knopf, 1983); "Inflation and Unemployment as Products of War Economy: The Trade Union Stake in Economic Conversion and Industrial Reconstruction," *Bulletin of Peace Proposals* 9 (1978): 359–74; and "Beating Swords into Subways," *The New York Times Magazine* (November 19, 1978).

24. These markets include electronic technologies like VCRs and compact discs, clothing, and automobiles, as well as such underlying products as steel and computer chips. Recovery is still possible, but American nonmilitary industrial capability has lost much ground since the 1950s and 1960s. For some other important factors related to the decline see Robert B. Reich, *The Next American Frontier* (New York: Penguin Books, 1984).

25. Robert Lekachman, *Greed is Not Enough: Reaganomics* (New York: Random House, 1982), 151.

26. Amory B. Lovins and L. Hunter Lovins, *Brittle Power: Energy Strategy for National Security* (Andover, Mass.: Brick House Publishing, 1982), chap. 4.

27. In Canada, oil sands and Arctic and Eastern offshore projects are all on hold. Provincial and federal supports for energy conservation have all but ended. In the United States, oil shale development has been deferred and federal support for conservation and alternate energy virtually eliminated. (Nonetheless there has not been a dramatic resurgence of growth in energy demand.)

28. A similar result could be achieved by using a system of comparable oil import or excise taxes in the nonexporting states.

29. On the strategic potential of oil see David G. Haglund, "Canada and the International Politics of Oil," *Canadian Journal of Political Science* 15 (June 1982): 259–98 and sources cited therein. For an interesting discussion of

other minerals see W. Keith Buck, *Intergovernmental Mineral Commodity Arrangements* (Kingston, Ont.: Centre for Resource Studies, 1986).

chapter nine

1. See, for example, Frank J. Sorauf, *Political Parties in the American System* (Boston: Little, Brown, 1964), chap. 2.

2. See Walter D. Young, *The Anatomy of a Party: The National CCF* (Toronto: University of Toronto Press, 1971); and W. Christian and C. Campbell, *Political Parties and Ideologies in Canada* (Toronto: McGraw-Hill Ryerson, 1983).

3. For a history of the pastoral ideal in American culture see Wesley Marx, *The Machine in the Garden* (New York: Oxford University Press, 1964).

4. Soleri has not published extensively, but he has often been interviewed or written about. See, for example, R. F. Register, *Another Beginning* (Berkeley: Treehouse Books, 1978).

5. Theodore Roszak, *Where the Wasteland Ends* (Garden City, N.Y.: Doubleday, 1973), 382.

6. Howard T. and Elizabeth C. Odum, *Energy Basis for Man and Nature* (New York: McGraw-Hill, 1976), 247.

7. Soleri envisions housing a hundred thousand people in pillared vertical cities that use little land, while allowing all inhabitants instant access to nearby wilderness or near-wilderness areas that otherwise might be occupied by housing, schools, stores, and factories. Nash's article "Trouble in Paradise" is the only environmental argument against renewable energy with which I am familiar. It is based on the need for wilderness.

8. *A Study of the Relative Merits of Bulk and Individual Electrical Metering for Apartment Buildings in Ontario* (Toronto: Ministry of Energy, 1977).

9. U.S. Department of Commerce, *Statistical Abstract of the United States 1985, 105th Edition* (Washington, D.C.: 1984), 558.

10. This is suggested by a variation of energy consumption relative to family income in the source cited immediately above.

11. Many large North American cities are located near to prime agricultural land, which is particularly vulnerable to use for transportation because its flatness lowers construction costs.

12. Bott, et al., *Life After Oil* (Edmonton: Hurtig, 1983), 59, assumes that both the total number of autos and the total number of kilometers driven will "increase substantially."

13. See Andre Gorz, *Ecology as Politics* (Montreal: Black Rose Books, 1980), 69–77; and E. J. Mishan, *The Costs of Economic Growth* (London: Staples Press, 1967), 87–99. It is interesting that Gorz is a Marxist while Mishan is in many ways a conservative traditionalist. Mumford's 1958 article was included in his *The Highway and the City* (London: Secker and Warburg, 1964).

14. See several sources cited in James P. Lester and Ann O'M. Bowman,

eds., *The Politics of Hazardous Waste Management* (Durham, N.C.: Duke University Press, 1983) regarding the hazards associated with both incineration and landfills. See also Thomas Rahn, *Garbage Incineration: Lessons from Europe and the United States* (Toronto: Pollution Probe Foundation, 1987); and New Jersey First Incorporated, *Solid Waste Management in New Jersey* (Trenton: New Jersey County and Municipal Government Study Commission, 1987).

15. See, for example, Samuel S. Epstein, et al., *Hazardous Waste in America* (San Francisco: Sierra Club Books, 1982), chap. 2.

16. See Moni Campbell, "Industrial Waste Reduction and Recovery," *Alternatives* 10 (Fall-Winter 1982): 59–64.

17. For a discussion of the overuse of wilderness areas see Roderick Nash, ed., *The American Environment* (Reading, Mass.: Addison-Wesley, 1976), 265–75.

18. Jane Jacobs, *The Life and Death of the Great American Cities* (New York: Random House, 1961), 18.

19. Mumford, *Highway and City*, 186–87.

20. Coal can be liquified and alcohol produced on a renewable basis to serve as fuel. But these fuels probably cannot be produced in sufficient quantity without significantly depleting valuable resources including soil or producing a great deal of pollution. Irregular automobile use, however, is plausible; electric automobiles could help serve that need.

21. See here Lester R. Brown, *Building a Sustainable Society* (New York: W. W. Norton, 1981); and Paul Hawken, *The Next Economy* (New York: Ballantine Books, 1983).

22. One might make, for example, fewer trips to work, to the bank, or to the movies. A family might thus find they do not need so many automobiles, or they might need to replace their automobile less often. If people could call up the music or videos of their choice from a central library, fewer would maintain large personal record or tape collections. Researchers could summon and store data electronically and would not need large personal libraries. Electronic equipment is usually more compact than the mechanical equipment it replaces.

23. Progressives' traditional constituencies, particularly U.S. blue collar workers, seem restless with traditional progressive approaches anyway. Progressives' difficult task is to develop coherent new approaches that will appeal to some individuals within the ethnic, regional, and class categories of traditional progressivism.

24. There is a big difference between opposing economic growth and accepting full employment, for example, or reducing government deficits, as a higher priority.

25. See Andre Gorz, *Farewell to the Working Class* (London: Pluto Press, 1982), 1–13.

26. See Thomas J. Kneisner, "The Full-Time Workweek in the United States, 1900–1970," *Industrial and Labor Relations Review* 30 (October 1976):

3–15; and Richard B. Duboff, "Full Employment: The History of a Receding Target," *Politics and Society* 7 (1977): 1–25.

27. Gorz, *Farewell to the Working Class,* 135–36, 67.

28. This does not include human services—public sector jobs vulnerable to automation are mostly clerical. As for unnecessary jobs, we might seek to pay people to complete tasks well rather than to fill a desk or lean on a rake for a number of hours.

29. The cost of money is not in my view sufficiently taken into account as a component of consumer price index.

30. See Robert Paehlke, "Environementalisme et syndicalisme au Canada anglais et aux États-Unis," chap. 2.

31. Claus Offe, "Reaching for the Brake: The Greens in Germany," *New Political Science* 11 (Spring 1983): 50–51.

32. Medical costs have risen continuously as a proportion of GNP for several decades now, while not accompanied by a great improvement in, for example, life expectancy. (Gains in life expectancy are as much a result of improved diet and exercise as of improved or increased medical interventions.)

33. For an early consideration see Warren A. Johnson, "The Guaranteed Income as an Environmental Measure," in Herman E. Daly, *Toward a Steady-State Economy* (San Francisco: W. H. Freeman, 1973), 175–89.

34. Many such inducements lead to increased capital investment, improved productivity, and *reduced* employment per unit of output. The "gain" is only that a new facility opens in a given locality (while an old one closes elsewhere) or that an old facility is upgraded and thus does not close outright.

35. The assumption here is not that either older or younger teachers are better, but that the best teaching will occur when educational institutions employ teachers of all ages at any given time. And a smaller workload per teacher can only improve the quality of teaching.

36. For recent material on environmentally appropriate development see the special issue of *Energy Policy* 13 (August 1985); and the special issue of *Ambio* 14 (1985). An environmental opportunity within the third world debt crisis is discussed by Diana Page in "Cutting the Debt, Saving the Forest," *Environment* (September 1987): 4–5.

37. See articles by J. Horberry and B. Rich in *Ecology Law Quarterly* 12 (1985): 817–69, 681–747. See also Cheryl Payer, *The World Bank: A Critical Analysis* (New York: Monthly Review Press, 1982); and Robert Clarke and Richard Swift, eds., *Ties that Bind: Canada and the Third World* (Toronto: Between the Lines, 1982).

38. See Carolyn Merchant, *The Death of Nature: Women, Ecology and the Scientific Revolution* (San Francisco: Harper and Row, 1980); Carolyn Merchant, "Earth Care: Women and the Environmental Movement," *Environment* 23 (June 1981): 6–13, 38–40; Marti Kheel, "The Liberation of Nature:

A Circular Affair," *Environmental Ethics* 7 (Summer 1985): 135–49; Karen J. Warren, "Feminism and Ecology: Making Connections," *Environmental Ethics* 9 (Spring 1987): 3–20; Michael E. Zimmerman, "Feminism, Deep Ecology, and Environmental Ethics," *Environmental Ethics* 9 (Spring 1987): 21–44; Dorothy Nelkin, "Nuclear Power as a Feminist Issue," *Environment* 23 (January/February 1981): 14–20, 38–39; Elizabeth Dodson Gray, *Why the Green Nigger* (Wellesey, Mass.: Roundtable Press, 1979); Rosemary Radford Ruether, *New Woman, New Earth* (New York: Seabury Press, 1975). On women and occupational health, see Jeanne Mager Stellman, *Women's Work, Women's Health* (New York: Random House, 1977); Robert Clarke, *Ellen Swallow: The Woman Who Founded Ecology* (Chicago: Follett, 1973). On women and urban environments, "Women and the American City," special issue of *Signs* 5 (Spring 1980); and the journal *Women and Environments*, now in its ninth volume, available from the Centre for Urban and Community Studies, University of Toronto. Much superb academic work is now being done in this area; it is to be hoped that it will eventually contribute to stronger political links between the women's movement and the environmental movement. (Also increasingly visible in recent years in North America are connections between the women's movement and the peace movement.)

39. The health of mothers and infants is protected considerably by confining childbearing to a brief period from the early twenties to the early or mid-thirties.

40. Feminists disagree among themselves about wages for housework—see Susan Wheeler, "Liberation Feminism and Marxism," *Our Generation* 11/3 (1977).

41. Reported in Walter A. Rosenbaum, *Environmental Politics and Policy* (Washington, D.C.: Congressional Quarterly, 1985).

42. This pattern (particularly visible in recent U.S. elections) sharply contrasts with the typical electoral conservatism of women in an earlier period. See S. M. Lipset, *Political Man* (Garden City, N.Y.: Doubleday, 1963), chap. 7.

43. People on low and fixed incomes spend a larger portion of their incomes on energy. Efficiency standards for appliances have been highly successful in Denmark. See also *Environmental Action* 18 (January/February 1987): 22, for a brief discussion of Reagan's pocket veto of such standards. After the 1986 Congressional elections this bill was passed again and signed into law in the Spring of 1987.

44. See Bruce Stokes, "Recycled Housing," *Environment* 21 (January/February 1979): 5–14; M. A. P. Taylor and P. W. Newton, "Urban Design and Revitalization—An Australian Perspective," *Urban Ecology* 9 (1985): 1–23. On the decline of public transportation, which underlies many urban problems, see J. Allen Whitt and Glenn Yago, "Corporate Strategies and the Decline of Transit in U.S. Cities," *Urban Affairs Quarterly* 21 (September 1985): 37–65.

chapter ten

1. See Robert Cameron Mitchell, "Public Opinion and Environmental Politics in the 1970s and 1980s," in Norman J. Vig and Michael E. Kraft, *Environmental Policy in the 1980s: Reagan's New Agenda* (Washington, D.C.: Congressional Quarterly, 1984), 51–74. Early studies suggested an inverse relationship between social class and environmental concern, but Buttel and Flinn convincingly argued that the relationship was only significant as regards education. See Frederick H. Buttel and William L. Flinn, "Social Class and Mass Environmental Beliefs: A Reconsideration," *Environment and Behavior* 10 (September 1978): 433–50. This conclusion is also supported in the excellent recent study by Lester W. Milbrath, *Environmentalists: Vanguard for a New Society* (Albany: State University of New York Press, 1984). Milbrath also reports a 1983 *New York Times*/CBS poll that showed blacks and whites equally concerned to maintain high standards of environmental protection. Earlier studies had concluded that blacks were disinclined to environmentalism even when class variables were controlled. See M. R. Hershey and D. B. Hill, "Is Pollution 'A White Thing?' Racial Differences in Preadults' Attitudes," *Public Opinion Quarterly* 41 (1977–78): 439–58.

2. These are the Social Democratic-Liberal Alliance and (especially on disarmament) Labour in Britain and the Liberals and the NDP in Canada. But none of these parties is purely or consistently environmentalist. In Canada, for example, the Liberal Party in Quebec has had a poor environmental record, the Ontario party a good one, the federal party a mixed record at best.

3. See the lead story in Toronto's *The Globe and Mail* (January 21, 1987).

4. See *Environmental Action* 18 (January/February 1987): 6, 17–19.

5. John H. Adams, et al., *An Environmental Agenda for the Future* (Washington, D.C.: Island Press, 1985). Perhaps even more promising are the recent successes of one particular organization in the U.S., the Citizen's Clearinghouse for Hazardous Wastes, a group that developed out of the Love Canal controversy. It is now based in the U.S. South, has a large permanent staff, and is deliberately developing extensive links with low-income and minority communities and women. See Will Collette, "Institutions: Citizen's Clearinghouse for Hazardous Wastes," *Environment* 29 (November 1987): 44–45.

6. The World Commission on Environment and Development, *Our Common Future* (New York: Oxford University Press, 1987), 297.

Index

Agriculture, 67–70, 163, 193, 250, 261, 272
Akarea, T., 106
Ames, Bruce: Ames test, 33
Anderson, Walter Truett, 210
Andrews, Richard N. L., 175
Appropriate development, 266
Arctic oil and gas pipelines, 239
Armstrong, Reverend Benjamin, 23
Arsenic/lead arsenate, 25–27
Asbestos, 25–26, 32, 153
Asceticism, 145, 164–71, 251
Audubon, John James, 14
Automation, 107–08, 199–201, 258–59
Automobiles, 47, 101–02, 128, 136, 161, 202, 219, 248, 253
Ayres, Russell W., 87

Bacon, Sir Francis, 148, 205
Bahro, Rudolph, 9–10n, 194
Barnet, Richard J., 75, 175, 194
Bennett, Tiny, 84
Berger inquiry, 175
Besecker, Janet, 65–66, 72
Bezdek, Roger, 106
Bioaccumulation, 30–31
Biomass, 162
Biotechnology, 108–09, 139, 199, 255
Birthrates. See Population stabilization
Blueprint for Survival, 129, 131
Bookchin, Murray, 194, 199, 245
Borgstrom, George, 121

Boulding, Kenneth, 129, 164, 204
Brazil, 197
Brooks, David, 52, 54–55, 96, 105, 146, 167, 194, 211
Brown, Harrison, 46, 48–50
Brown, Lester, 67–69, 140–41, 195
Buddhist economics, 173
Burden of proof, 32, 119, 125, 146
Bureaucratic capitalism, 225
Burke, Edmund, 9, 181, 259

Caldwell, Lynton, 159
Cancer and carcinogens, 24–25, 28, 30, 32–33, 37–38, 151
Carrying capacity, 52–53, 57, 66–69, 71, 120
Carson, Rachel, 21, 26, 28–30, 54, 115
Carter, President Jimmy, 227
Catton, Jr., William R., 120–23
Chase, Stuart, 166–67
Collins, Joseph, 67–71
Commoner, Barry, 34–37, 39, 58–61, 70, 86, 131, 194, 251
Computers, 136, 139, 156, 199, 255
Condorcet, Marquis de, 41, 43
Conservation movement, 14–20, 23, 145–46, 212
Conservatism: classic, 183–84, 191, 212; neoconservatism, 4, 193, 217–44, 261
Conserver society, 137–40
Cost-benefit analysis, 118–25
Cousteau, Jacques, 86

Daly, Herman, 130–31, 251, 266
DDT, 26–29, 31
Decentralism, 156–57, 194, 199, 206, 217, 226, 232, 235, 244–46
Deficits. See Governmental deficits
Delaney Clause, 28
Democratic Party (U.S.), 231–32
Dickson, David, 194, 201–03
Diet, 151–53
Diggers. See Levellers
Disraeli, Benjamin, 23–24, 191
Distributive issues, 127, 273; and food 70; and natural resources, 72
Distributive politics, 7, 188, 193, 198, 202
Donora (Pennsylvania), 29
Drucker, Peter, 140

Ecofeminism, 268
Ecology: origin of term, 29
Economic growth: harmless forms, 7, 54, 124–29, 133; pursuit of, 206–07, 212, 234–36, 260
Economic power and elitism, 208–09
Edsall, J. T., 85
Ehrenfeld, David, 150
Ehrlich, Paul, 55–56, 58–62, 75, 194–95
Elder, Phil, 65–66, 72
Ellul, Jacques, 202
Emerson, Ralph Waldo, 16, 26
Employment. See Jobs and the environment
Energy: conservation, 90, 100–01, 103–06, 109; fossil fuel scarcity, 43–44, 48–49, 68, 72, 77, 97–98, 121–23, 130; OPEC and energy prices, 2, 53–54, 84, 90–91, 103–04, 109, 129, 153, 161, 187, 196, 208–09, 240–41, 270; renewable sources, 77–79, 97–99, 100–01, 204; soft energy paths (SEPs), 76–110, 122–23, 134, 136, 155, 159–60, 171, 239–40, 246; SEP (Canada), 92–94, 96; SEP (West Germany), 95–96, 101; solar energy, 82–84
Energy Probe, 155
Engels, Frederick, 23, 114
Environmentalism and the socially and economically disadvantaged, 38, 230–33, 270
Environmentalism and urban issues, 245–51, 271

Environmental movement: defined, 21–22
Environmental politics: defined, 189
Environmental regulation, 208
Epidemiology, 25, 28, 32–33
Epstein, Samuel, 40
Evelyn, John, 24

Feminism and environmentalism, 63, 266–69, 271
Ferguson, Thomas, 228
Food: additives, 152; aid, 56, 65; luxury crop exports, 70–71
Ford, Charlotte, 106
Foreign aid, 266, 271
Forests and reforestation, 14, 19, 162–63, 260–61, 272
Fossil fuels. See Energy

Gaskell, Elizabeth, 23
German Green Party, 3, 107, 177, 236, 263
Germany, West, 197; SEP study, 95–96, 101
GNP, 100–01, 124–28, 130–35, 204, 251–52, 260
Godwin, William, 41
Goldman, Marshall I., 206
Gorz, André, 194, 199–204, 248, 258–59
Gospel of efficiency (conservation movement), 14–15
Governmental deficits, 4, 126, 262, 271
Graham, Frank, 28
Groncki, P. J., 106

Haeckel, Ernst, 29
Hamilton, Alice, 27
Hamrin, Robert, 140–41
Hannon, Bruce, 106
Hardin, Garrett, 56–60, 62–66, 68, 73, 75, 120
Harkin, J. B., 19
Hawken, Paul, 135–36
Hays, Samuel, 143, 151, 212
Heilbroner, Robert, 74–75, 132, 134–36, 194–95

Helliwell, John, 162
Henderson, Hazel, 195
Hobbes, Thomas, 1, 178–79, 205
Hottel, H. C., 83
Howard, Ebenezer, 250
Hubbert, M. King, 49

Ideological left, 196, 206, 230
Ideological right, 196, 207–08
Ideological spectrum, 3, 7, 184–86, 190, 220, 236
Ideology: defined, 5, 211
Inflation, 4, 54, 261–62
Informative economy, 135–36
Inglehart, Ronald, 169, 173
Interest group liberalism, 210, 232

Jacobs, Jane, 245, 248–50
James, Bernard, 48
James, William, 205
Jevons, W. Stanley, 43–44
Jobs and the environment, 104–10, 162, 224. See also Work reduction/full employment

Kallett, Arthur, 166
Kennedy, Senator Edward, 106
Keynesianism, 213, 223–24, 227–28, 232–34; military Keynesianism, 228
Klein, Louis, 24
Kneese, Alan, 141
Kondratiev, Nikolai, 139
Kuhn, Thomas, 118

Lappé, F. M., 67–71, 152, 194
Lead, 35
Left. See Ideological left; Socialism
Leiss, William, 148, 194, 198–99, 205
Leisure time, 132, 200, 204–05, 236, 255
Leopold, Aldo, 18, 28–29
Levellers, 179
Liberalism, 8–9, 180–83, 191, 210–12
Liberal Party (Canada), 231
Lilburne, John, 179
Limits to Growth, 50–54, 132
Lindblom, Charles E., 207–09
Lipset, S. M., 186–87

Livingston, John A., 147–49, 159
Locke, John, 181
Lof, George, 83
Love Canal, 32, 39
Lovins, Amory B., 76–110, 138, 171, 195, 199, 235, 239, 245–46, 251–53, 261
Lovins, L. Hunter, 86, 239, 245–46
Lowi, Theodore J., 210

McMullen, Doris, 146, 167, 211
Malthus, Reverend T. R., 41–43, 68, 73
Malthusian thought, 41–75, 113, 120; neo-Mathusianism, 46, 50, 74
Market intervention, 7, 89–90, 185, 198, 211
Marsh, George Perkins, 15–16, 18, 29, 162
Marx, Karl, 8, 43, 114, 192, 201–03, 205, 241
Marxism, 197–98
May, Jacques, 32–33
Melman, Seymour, 237
Military spending, 207, 213, 226–42
Mill, J. S., 191
Mishan, E. J., 124–28, 199, 248, 251
Mitchell, Robert, 268
Moderate progressivism, 4, 6, 230, 232–33, 235
Morrison, Denton, 109
Muir, John, 16–18, 22, 212
Mulroney, Prime Minister Brian, 229–30

Nash, Roderick, 17–18, 99, 246
National parks, 14, 19
Natural dispersion, 31
Natural resistance, 31
Nelles, H. V., 19, 149
Neoconservatism. See Conservatism
New Democratic Party of Canada, 206, 244
Nichol, J. I., 19
Norman, Alma, 54–55
Nuclear power, 77, 84–89, 98–99, 168, 200, 239; accidents, 85, 87, 100; commercial viability, 81, 89, 91
Nuclear weapons proliferation, 86–89, 236–37
Nutter, G. Warren, 223

Occupational health, 24–25, 27, 33, 36–40, 85, 175, 271
Odum, Elizabeth C., 246
Odum, Howard T., 246
Offe, Claus, 194, 263
Oil. See Energy: fossil fuel scarcity
OPEC. See Energy
Ophuls, William, 74–75, 132, 160, 171, 194–95, 246
Ordway, Jr., Samuel, 46–48
Osborn, Fairfield, 46, 159
Overshoot, 120, 123, 160

Partridge, Ernest, 158
PCBs, 31, 36
Peace movement, 9, 213, 234–35
Pesticides, 26, 152
Pim, Linda R., 152
Planned obsolescence/product durability, 132, 135–36, 258, 270
Plutonium, 87–88
Polanyi, Karl, 185
Pollution: defined, 22
Pollution Probe, 152
Population stabilization, 41–75, esp. 55–57, 59, 69, 72–73, 121, 248, 267
Postindustrialism, 3, 219–22
Postmaterialist values, 169, 173
Pott, Percivall, 24–25
Progressivism. See Moderate progressivism
Public participation, 174–75
Public transportation, 101–02, 107, 128, 132, 168, 209, 248, 260, 271

Ramazzini, Bernardino, 24
Reagan, President Ronald, 217, 229
Recycling, 99, 102, 106–07, 132, 141, 165, 249, 261, 270
Refillable containers, 6, 260, 263, 270
Reforestation. See Forests and reforestation
Resources for the Future, 82
Right. See Conservatism; Ideological right
Rogers, Joel, 228
Rosenbluth, Gideon, 133–34
Roszak, Theodore, 246
Rowland, Wade, 84

Science: role in environmental movement, 115–20
Schapiro, Mark, 152
Schlink, F. J., 166–67
Schnaiberg, Allan, 1, 22
Schrecker, Ted, 175
Schumacher, E. F., 173, 195, 199, 245
Selikoff, Irving, 38
Sierra Club, 40. See also Muir, John
Snow, C. P., 115–17
Socialism, 8–9, 193, 197–207
Soft Energy Path (SEP). See Energy
Soleri, Paolo, 199, 245–46
Spaceship earth, 154
Steady-state economy (SSE): defined, 130; 118, 124, 129, 131, 136, 191
Stillman, Peter, 57
Sustainable growth/sustainability, 140–41, 161–64
Swallow, Ellen, 29
Synergism, 31–32

Taylor, Charles, 128–29
Technological choices, 58–61, 118–19, 201–04, 206, 212, 245, 251–55, 270
Technology: appropriate, 108, 132, 228
Telkes, Maria, 83
Thatcher, Prime Minister Margaret, 218, 227, 229
Thoreau, Henry David, 14, 22
Thurow, Lester, 223–24
Transportation. See Automobiles; Public transportation
Trudeau, Prime Minister Pierre E., 227

Union of Soviet Socialist Republics, 197, 206
United States, 197, 244
Uranium, 25, 27, 100, 206–07
Urban issues. See Environmentalism and urban issues

Van Leeuwenhoek, Antonie, 29
Vegetarianism, 65–70
Victor, Peter, 192
Vogel, Karl, 26

Wadland, John, 13, 20–21
Wagoner, Joseph K., 25–34
Weber, Max, 115, 178
Weinberg, Alvin, 86
Weir, David, 152
Weisberg, Barry, 194
White, Jr., Lynn, 147
Whorton, James, 26

Wilderness preservation, 14, 16–18, 246
Winner, Langdon, 202–03
Winstanley, Gerrard, 179–80
Work reduction/full employment, 133,
    199–201, 255–60, 262, 264, 267, 270.
    See also Jobs and the environment

Yeats, W. B., 1, 10